THE STUDY

OF

THE PARABLES

THE STUDY

OF

THE PARABLES

BY

ADA R. HABERSHON

WITH A PREFACE BY

SIR ROBERT ANDERSON

KREGEL PUBLICATIONS

Grand Rapids, Michigan 49501

Library of Congress Catalog Card Number 62-19175
ISBN 0-8254-2802-5 Clothbound
ISBN-0-8254-2852-1 Paperback

First American Reprint Edition 1957
Second Printing 1963
Third Printing 1967
Fourth Printing 1973
Fifth Printing 1975
Sixth Printing 1978

Printed in the United States of America

CONTENTS

CHAP.   PAGE

   I. INTRODUCTION 1

  II. METHODS OF INTERPRETATION 8

 III. THE LORD'S PORTRAIT OF HIMSELF IN THE

        PARABLES 22

 IV. PICTURES OF MEN IN THE PARABLES . . 29

  V. THE SETTING OF THE PARABLES . . . 34

 VI. THE TRINITY IN THE PARABLES . . . 55

VII. THE LORD'S INCARNATION AND DEATH . . 64

VIII. HIS ABSENCE 70

 IX. HIS COMING AGAIN 77

  X. THE KINGDOM 98

 XI. THE PARABLES OF MATTHEW XIII . . . 118

XII. ISRAEL'S HISTORY IN THE PARABLES . . 148

XIII. OLD TESTAMENT SYMBOLISM 170

XIV. THE MIRACLES AND THE PARABLES . . . 222

XV. THE PARABLES AND THE EPISTLES . . . 233

XVI. THE PARABLES AND THE APOCALYPSE . . 254

v

CONTENTS

CHAP.   PAGE

XVII. PRACTICAL TEACHING 269

XVIII. DOUBLE PARABLES 294

XIX. DOUBLE PARABLES (*continued*) . . . 311

CONCLUSION 332

APPENDIX 337

INDEX TO PARABLES 357

INDEX 362

ANALYSIS OF CONTENTS

CHAPTER I

INTRODUCTION

Symbolic teaching in different forms—Grouping of parables with types, miracles, similes, &c.—Acted parables and visions—The audience—Purpose of the parables—The outer circle and the inner—Simplicity or depth—The conduct of the disciples —Asking—Alone—The same Spirit   .   .   .   pp. 1–7

CHAPTER II

METHODS OF INTERPRETATION

According to belief in inspiration, and estimate of Author— Interpretation of details—Those explained for us — Several meanings given—The thorns — Patristic exposition — Only one interpretation allowed by "Higher critics" and "ultra-dispensationalists" — A threefold interpretation, historical typical, and prophetic—The double purpose of the parable of the unjust judge—The prophetic also typical—Matthew and Romans—The sower successive ones—The parable of the husbandmen illustrating manifold interpretations—Progressive teaching .   .   .   .   pp. 8–21

CHAPTER III

THE PORTRAIT OF THE LORD HIMSELF

A complete picture—Divinity and humanity—The Man of Sorrows, but the King's Son—The Judge—"As one having authority " — His sayings — The Jehovah of the Old Testament, the parable of the husbandmen—The Judge and the Justifier, the Pharisee and the publican—His attributes—List of figures .   .   .   .   pp. 22–28

CHAPTER IV

PICTURES OF MEN IN THE PARABLES

List of figures — Other similes — As houses — Two or more *classes* — Three sorts of acceptance — Two kinds of seed — Two groups of watchers—Two sorts of fish—Two *individuals* —Two builders—Two suppliants—A rich man and a poor man— Two sons (twice)—Two debtors (twice)   pp. 29–33

CHAPTER V

THE SETTING OF THE PARABLES

The Historical Setting.—I. Parables spoken in answer to *questions.* —1. "Why eateth your Master with publicans and sinners?" (Matt. ix. 11) — The physician. 2. "Why do . . . Thy disciples fast not?" (Matt. ix. 14)—The bridegroom. 3. "Why do Thy disciples transgress? . . . for they wash not their hands" (Matt. xv. 2)—Defilement of the body. 4. "Knowest Thou that the Pharisees were offended?" (Matt. xv. 12)— Plants and blind leaders. 5. "What shall I do? . . . Who is my neighbour?" (Luke x. 25, 29)—The good Samaritan. 6. "By what authority doest Thou these things?" (Matt. xxi. 23)—The husbandmen. 7. "How oft shall my brother sin against me, and I forgive him?" (Matt. xviii. 21)—The debtors. 8. "What good thing shall I do that I may have eternal life? . . . What shall we have therefore?" (Matt. xix. 16, 27)—The labourers in the vineyard. 9. "Lord, are there few that be saved?" (Luke xiii. 23) — The strait gate and the shut door.

II. Parables spoken in answer to *requests.*—1. "Lord, teach us to pray" (Luke xi. 1)—The three friends. 2. "Master, speak to my brother that he divide the inheritance with me" (Luke xii. 13)—The rich man and his barns. 3. "Sir, we would see Jesus" (John xii. 21)—The corn of wheat.

III. An *accusation* by the Pharisees was answered by the parable of the strong man armed (Matt. xii. 24).

IV. Their *action* towards the blind man (John ix.) led to the discourse about the good Shepherd.

V. Their *murmuring* was answered by Luke xv.—The key to the chapter.

VI. Their *derision* (Luke xvi. 14) followed by the parable of Dives and Lazarus.

VII. Two of the parables spoken at feasts—the great supper and the two debtors—The latter answered a *thought* (Luke vii. 39).

The *purpose* for which the parable is given mentioned in that of the unjust judge (Luke xviii. 1) — The Pharisee and the publican (verse 9)—A double reason for that of the pounds (Luke xix. 11).

The inspired setting of the parables.—Matthew's Gospel —Mark— Luke, the Gospel of prayer and praise—The opening and closing scenes—The great example—The model prayer—The threefold precept — Appropriate setting of the parables on prayer.

An illustration of parables, miracles, and incidents, together forming a *chain*—" Far off " and " near " in Luke.

Characteristic touches.—The budding fig-tree, Luke adds, " and all the trees "—The evil spirit, Matthew adds, " So shall it be unto this wicked generation "—The city and the candle in Matthew, not in Luke—Two parables of the debtors, legal aspect in Matthew, free grace in Luke—The interpretations of the seed in the parable of the sower suit the character of the Gospels —The old garment only in Matthew, the new garment also in Luke.

The progressive order of the parables . . . . pp. 34–54

CHAPTER VI

THE TRINITY IN THE PARABLES

The Three Persons.—All three interested in the giving and preserving of the parables—In Luke xv.—In the feasts, as the King, the King's Son, and the Servant.

The Father and the Son.—The wicked husbandmen—The barren fig-tree—The true vine—The Father represented as looking for fruit in each—Three aspects of the Lord Jesus—Loyalty to His Son the test in the parable of the husbandmen—Conversations between the Father and the Son—Genesis iii. a broken sentence—The owner and the dresser of the fig-tree— Harmony between them—Both concerned in the safety of the sheep.

The Father.—His love to the wanderer, in the prodigal—His love to His Son—His plan for the honour of His Son in the marriage feast.

The Son and the Spirit.—The cloud and the wind pp. 55–63

CHAPTER VII

THE LORD'S INCARNATION AND DEATH

His Incarnation.—Implied in the parable of the wicked husband-
men, the sent One of John's Gospel—In the hidden treasure—
The pearl—the good Samaritan.
His Life and Ministry.—Three years in the parable of the fig-tree
—The children in the market-place.
His Rejection and Death.—In the parable of the husbandmen—
The corn of wheat—The good Shepherd.
His Resurrection implied in the parables which speak of His
return.
His Ascension in the figure of travelling into a far country and of
leaving His household . . . . . . pp. 64–69

CHAPTER VIII

HIS ABSENCE

Some parables cover the whole time of His absence—"On a far
journey"—Absent "a long time"—The talents and the
pounds—Till time of harvest, the growing seed—The absent
host—The good Samaritan—The absent master—The night
season—The virgins—The bridegroom—The attitude of His
people—Growing and bearing fruit—Accepting and giving
His invitation—Tending wounded ones—Watching for His
return—Caring for fellow-servants—Having lamps trimmed
and burning—Sins of omission noted—Trading with His
money . . . . pp. 70–76

CHAPTER IX

HIS COMING AGAIN

A certain fact—An era not an isolated event—His first "coming"
thirty-three years—The "parousia"—Isaiah lxi.—The coming for the Church a special revelation to Paul—The coming
viewed as a whole in the parables—Applications to both
stages of the coming—Its announcement—The awakening of
the virgins—Not teaching a divided rapture—The house and
the household—"A thief in the night"—Three kinds of judgment—(1) *Discriminative*—Separation between righteous and
wicked—A sevenfold picture in Matthew—Between wheat

and tares—Good and bad fish—Guests with and without wedding garments—Wise and foolish virgins—Faithful and unfaithful servants—Sheep and goats. (2) *Distributive* judgment for reward—Faithful servants—Traders—Sheep—The three judgments. (3) *Retributive* judgment—Stone which the builders rejected, grinding to powder. A time of *Harvest*—The seed (Mark iv.)—The tares—The first-fruits—The feast of ingathering — A time of *Rest* from earthly toil — The labourers in the field and vineyard — A time of *Joy*—The bridegroom's return . . . . pp. 77–97

CHAPTER X

THE KINGDOM

The rejection of the King in the Old Testament—The kingdom in Isaiah xl.—The dialogue in Isaiah xlix. compared with Matthew xi.—The kingdom of heaven—Various explanations —The kingdom of heaven and the kingdom of God—-The God of heaven and the Lord of all the earth — Other expressions—Hid from the foundation of the world—The mysteries of the kingdom—The mysteries—" Learn to think imperially " . . . . pp. 98–117

CHAPTER XI

THE THIRTEENTH OF MATTHEW

Methods of interpretation—Consecutive panorama—Break at close of fourth parable—All four true in time of apostles— True now—A future fulfilment—Only lead to the threshold of the kingdom—The two groups—The eighth picture—Its importance—The octave in the scale—" Things new and old " included in the mysteries of the kingdom—1+3, 3+1— The parable of the sower—The key to the change of dispensation—The tares—The field—The children of the wicked one—The enemy's work—Scattering the good seed—The "much fruit" borne by the corn of wheat—The harvest— The mustard-seed and the leaven—Two opposite views— Kingdoms compared to trees—Good or bad?—Faith as a grain of mustard-seed—Jotham's parable—Leaven a symbol of evil—Three measures—The meal-offering — Typical of Christ, of His Word, of the Church—Oil needed with the meal-offering—Progress of evil depicted in the four parables

—The treasures and the pearl—Opposite views—Varied interpretation—What is the treasure?—What went before?—What follows?—What is the pearl?—A collective aspect—Various estimates of the kingdom in the chapter—The net—The householder—The first and the eighth, the sower and the householder—The second and the seventh, the tares and the net—The third and the sixth, the mustard-seed and the pearl—The fourth and the fifth, the leaven and the treasure—The first four show mistakes which may be made—Three speak of the presence of evil, the tares, the leaven, and the bad fish—The fifth and the eighth, the treasure and the treasury—Four were spoken on the seashore, and two, the pearl and the net, speak of another sea—A great conflict—The first and second describe directly the enemy's work—The second and seventh tell of the angels . . . . pp. 118–147

CHAPTER XII

ISRAEL'S HISTORY IN THE PARABLES

Their past history—1. God's presence withdrawn—The husbandmen—The call of the prophets—The husbandmen and the marriage supper.

2. Reformation under the preaching of John—The unclean spirit.

3. Great profession—The two sons (Matt. xxi. 28–32).

4. Blindness of their leaders—Blind leaders of the blind (Matt. xv. 14)—The cloud and the shower (Matt. xvi. 1–4).

5. Their rejection of Himself—The invitation despised—The nobleman hated—The Son slain—The corner-stone refused.

6. Their opportunity of agreeing with the adversary (Matt. v. 25, 26).

7. Unfruitfulness during Christ's ministry—The fig-tree (Luke xiii. 6–9).

8. His intercession for them—The fig-tree.

9. The second offer—The fig-tree, "this year also"—The marriage feast, "again"—The great supper, the city.

10. The enmity to His messengers — Old Testament prophets, the husbandmen—Old Testament and New, the wedding feast.

11. The destruction of Jerusalem—The wedding feast—Forty years.

12. The setting aside of Israel—The feasts.

13. The message sent after Him—The pounds (Luke xix. 14).
14. Leading out from Judaism—John x.
15. Their jealousy at grace being bestowed upon the Gentiles —The debtors (Matt. xviii. 23-35)—The elder brother (Luke xv.).
16. The covenant of works contrasted with grace—The labourers in the vineyard (Matt. xx. 1-16).
17. Their reception of Antichrist accounted for—The unclean spirit (Matt. xii. 43-45).
18. Judgments—Cast into prison, the debtors (Matt. xviii. 34)— The adversary (Luke xii. 58, 59)—Broken by falling on the corner-stone (Matt. xxi. 44)—Their city destroyed (Matt. xxii. 7)—The rebels slain (Matt. xxii. 7 ; Luke xix. 27)—The tree cut down (Luke xiii. 9 ; Matt. iii. 10)— Their final doom, the rich man and Lazarus (Luke xvi.).
19. Fresh signs of life before final troubles—Budding of fig-tree (Matt. xxiv. 32, 33; Mark xiii. 28, 29 ; Luke xxi. 29-31).
20. Their sorrows to be avenged—The unjust judge (Luke xviii. 7, 8).
Fruit and no fruit—Fruit to themselves, the wicked husband-men—No fruit, the fig-tree—Axe laid to root—In symbol, tree cursed and withered—Budding again.
The city—A city lighted and shining (Matt. v. 14)—A city invited (Luke xiv. 21)—A city rebelling (Luke xix. 14)—A city destroyed (Matt. xxii. 7)—"A widow of that city" (Luke xviii. 2, 3).
Lessons for us from Israel's history—Understanding God's purposes—Typical teaching for unsaved as well as saved, as brazen serpent in John iii. 14—Individual and collective lessons, e.g., the parables of the evil spirit, the fig-tree, and the husbandmen . . . . . . pp. 148-169

CHAPTER XIII

OLD TESTAMENT SYMBOLISM

Types and Symbols—Illustrate the parables—A suggestion in Deut. viii. that the children of Israel understood something of typical teaching—The rock in Deut. xxxii.—The vineyard —The vine, fig, and olive.
I. *Typical Substances.*—Oil—Wine—Salt.
II. *Typical Ordinances.*—Lev. xxiii.—The feast of unleavened bread—The first-fruits—The harvest—Clean and unclean animals—The leprous house—The guilty city—Mixed seed

—Weights and measures—The lost sheep and fallen animal—
The rebellious son.

III. *Old Testament Illustrations.*—Joseph—We will not have this
man to reign over us—The well-beloved Son sent by the
Father—Conspired against—Explanation of double symbolism
—Six dreams—Sheaves and shining—Bring these men home.
Joash, a kingdom in mystery.

Naboth's vineyard, the wicked husbandmen—Jezebel's plot,
two false witnesses.

The widow's cry—The Shunamite and Ruth.

The purchase of a field (Jer. xxxii.)—The evidence sealed,
witnessed, in an earthen vessel—" Until the redemption
of the purchased possession."

The man with the inkhorn (Ezek. ix.)—" It is done as Thou
hast commanded " (Luke xiv.).

The calling of him that was bidden (Esther vi. 14).

The wall daubed with untempered mortar (Ezek. xiii.).

The clothing of Joshua (Zech. iii.)—Zechariah's vision of the
ephah (chap. v.)—The parable of the leaven.

IV. *Old Testament Characters.*—Shepherds—Moses, the leading
of the shepherd (John x.)—David, the deliverance by the shepherd—Zech. xi. 16, 17, the hireling—Jacob, the responsibility
and care of the shepherd—The suffering of the shepherd
(Luke xv.)—David, the reigning shepherd (Matt. xxv.)—Two
kinds of shepherds (Ezek. xxxiv.).

V. The *Psalms.*—A prophecy of the parables (Ps. lxxviii.)—
The two classes of servants (Ps. i.)—The wicked husbandmen
and the adversary (Ps. ii.)—The shepherd (Psalms xxiii.,
lxxx., cxix.)—The marriage (Ps. xlv.)—The sunrise and the
bridegroom (Ps. xix.)—Waiting for the morning (Ps. cxxx.)—
The Lord our rock.

VI. *Solomon's parables and proverbs.*—The little city (Eccl. ix.
13-17)—The poor wise youth (chap. iv. 13-16)—A good
appetite (chap. v. 18-20)—A bad appetite (chap. vi. 1, 2).

Proverbs which remind of the parables.—The house builded (Prov.
xxiv. 3 ; xii. 7 ; xiv. 11)—The Lord the builder (chap. xxiv. 27)
—Wisdom's banqueting-house (chap. ix. 1)—The invitation
refused (chap. i. 24-27)—A low place (chap. xxv. 6, 7)—The
King's eye (chap. xx. 8)—The King's favour (chap. xiv. 35)—
Watching at His gates (chap. viii. 34)—The mouth and the
heart (chap. iv. 20-29)—Sowing and reaping—Riches (chap.
xi. 4, 28)—Branch and root (chap. xi. 28 ; xii. 12)—The
prodigal (chap. xxviii. 19)—Poor but rich (chap. xiii. 7)

pp. 170-221

CHAPTER XIV

THE MIRACLES AND THE PARABLES

The miracles and parables do not cover the same ground ; no miraculous event in the parables.

I. Miracles which were evidently *acted* parables.—The miracles of healing—Their spiritual significance proved by Matt. ix. 12 ; Mark ii. 5 ; and Luke v. 24—Each disease a picture of the effects of sin—The two draughts of fishes, with the parable of the net—The cursing of the fig-tree and the two parables of the fig-tree.

II. Miracles *followed* by parables.—The casting out of the devil followed by the parable of the strong man—The healing of the man with a withered hand followed by the parable of the sheep in a pit.

III. Miracles *linked* to the parables by some word, expression, or character.—The crumb which the Syrophœnician woman craved, Lazarus at the rich man's gate, Lazarus of Bethany— " Far off," the lepers and the publican, healed and justified— The law of leprosy—The publican Zacchæus. Spiritual bankruptcy in miracle and parables, the woman with the issue of blood, the prodigal, the debtors.

IV. The *night* season parables and miracles.—The disciples in the storm (Matt. xiv.).

V. Miracles linked with *types* proving them to have been acted parables.—The feeding of the five thousand.

VI. Miracles like the parables which have a *dispensational meaning.*—The cursing of the fig-tree—The crumb to the Gentile woman—The storm on the lake—The turning of the water into wine—The miraculous draught of fishes—Mary Magdalene—The demoniac . . . . . . pp. 222–232

CHAPTER XV

THE PARABLES AND THE EPISTLES

I. The parables explain the epistles—The bridge between the dispensations—The Acts of the Apostles, " this year also," the second offer—Final turning to the Gentiles, leading to the writing of the epistles to Gentile churches.

II. The epistles as sequels to the parables.—Progressive revelation

III. The parables explained by the epistles.—A little leaven
(1 Cor. v. 6, Gal. v. 9) explaining the parable of the leaven.

IV. The epistles prove that Israel's history is typical.—A warrant
for taking the Jewish parables typically.

V. The epistles explain that Old Testament symbolism has largely
changed its meaning—The olive (Rom. xi.)—The vineyard
(1 Cor. ix. 7).

VI. Much that the Lord stated concerning Himself proved by the
epistles to be true of the Church.—The Husbandman, the
husbandmen—The Shepherd, under shepherds—The Sower,
sowers—Isaiah lii. 7 as quoted in Romans x. 15—Isaiah
xlix. 6 as quoted in Acts xiii. 47.

The symbolism of the epistles of two kinds.—That which links
itself with the parables—The sower (2 Cor. ix. 6, 10 ; Gal.
vi. 7–9; 1 Cor. xv. 35–38; Gal. v. 22) — The husbandman
(2 Tim. ii. 6; Heb. vi. 7, 8 ; James v. 7, 8)—Parts and building (Col. ii. 7 ; Eph. iii. 17 ; 1 Cor. iii. 9) — The same similes
linked together in the parables—Two classes of builders in
1 Cor. iii., as in the parable of houses on rock and sand—The
foundation (2 Tim. ii. 19 ; Eph. ii. 20)—A collective aspect in
the epistle—The temple, individual believers (1 Cor. vi. 19),
the whole Church (2 Cor. vi. 16; Eph. ii. 21 ; 1 Pet. ii. 4, 8)
—Contrast with Satan's dwelling-places—The great house
(2 Tim. ii. 20, 21)—Watching in the night (1 Thess. v. 5–10)
—Paul's parable of the night (Rom. xiii. 11–14)—Ambassadors
for Christ (2 Cor. v. 20)—Stewards (1 Cor. iv. 1)—The ox
(1 Cor. ix. 9, 10), Paul's conversion, "kicking against the
pricks."

II. New similes.—Two leaders of Israel, Moses and Joshua ; two
Apostles, Peter and Paul—Peter the shepherd (1 Pet. v. 4 ;
ii. 25)—Paul the warrior—The soldier's armour (Eph. vi.)—The
soldier (2 Tim. ii. 3, 4 ; iv. 7)—The captain (Heb. ii. 10)—
Races and games, familiar scenes to Romans and Greeks
(1 Cor. ix. 24–27 ; 2 Tim. ii. 5 ; iv. 7 ; Heb. xii. 1–3).

Words which suggest parables.—Pedagogue (Gal. iii. 24)—Adoption (Gal. iv. 5 ; Rom. viii. 15, 23 ; Eph. i. 5)   pp. 233–253

CHAPTER XVI

THE PARABLES AND THE APOCALYPSE

' The Revelation of Jesus Christ which God gave unto Him "—The
same authorship—" He that hath ears to hear"—" The hearing ear" in the parable, " the seeing eye" in the visions.

Rev. ii. and iii.—The epistles to the seven churches—Many interpretations—(1) Literal churches in Asia Minor—(2) A chronological panorama—(3) Present interpretations—(4) Individual
lessons—(5) Future fulfilment—(6) The promises to the over-
comers and the dispensations—(7) A parallel between the
epistles and the parables in Matthew xiii.
Rev. v.—The opening of the title-deeds and the treasure hid in the
field.
Rev. vii.—The key to the separation between sheep and goats.
Rev. xii.—The adversary of the widow.
Rev. xiv.—The first-fruits, the harvest and the vintage.
Satan's counterfeits.
Rev. xviii.—Mystery Babylon and Matt. xiii.
Rev. xix., xxi., xxii.—The marriage supper and the bride
                                                    pp. 254-268

CHAPTER XVII

PRACTICAL TEACHING

Prayer.—Importunate prayer for herself, the widow—for others,
the friends—A prayer that was no prayer, the Pharisee's
prayer of pride—A justifying prayer, the publican's prayer of
humility—A wrong sort of prayer, the prodigal's prayer of
discontent—A prayer that was never uttered, the prodigal's
planned prayer—No prayer, the elder brother—Prayers that
were too late, the rich man's (Luke xvi.), the servants' (Luke
xiii. 25, 26), the virgins' (Matt. xxv.)—Intercessory prayer, the
vine-dresser.

Service.—In all places—the sower—the marriage supper—and the
great feast.   To all sorts of people—the feasts—the faithful
steward.   At all times—the watching servants.   Late as well
as earlier—the labourers.   With all kinds of gifts and opportunities—the talents.   Individual work—"to every man his
work."   To the right master—the husbandmen.   The diversity
of service—the work of sowers — messengers — stewards—
porters—husbandmen — traders—reapers—field labourers—
farm servants—indoor servants.   The rewards of service—
Telling the Master—the tares—the debtors—Yokes and
ploughs.

The Word of God.—Hearing and doing, the house on rock and
sand—Hearing and understanding, hearing and receiving,
hearing and keeping, the sower—Three things which prevent
fruitfulness ; the birds, the rock, and the thorns—Fourfold

interpretation of the thorns; cares, riches, lusts (or desires)
and pleasures—Three things which scorch; tribulation, persecution, and temptation—In the rocky soil, no depth, no
moisture, no root—Three standards of fruit-bearing, thirty-fold,
sixty-fold, and hundred-fold—On, and in, and down, and up—
It is not said that only a quarter of the seed was fruitful—
How is the sower to judge of the soil?—The supernatural
power of the seed of the Word, able to kill the thorns and
soften the rock — "Take heed what ye hear," "Take heed
how ye hear." Food of the right sort, "Things new and old"
(Matt. xiii.) — At the right time "meat in due season"
(Matt. xxiv.) — Refusing to hear the Word, the wicked
husbandmen and the bidden guests—Two ways of hearing,
the two sons—A seeming reception, the rocky ground hearers,
the marriage feast, the great supper, the two sons—The effect
of believing the Word, the watching servants—Putting out
the Word to interest, the pounds—Outward conformance to
the Word, the Pharisee — Doing without the Word, blind
leaders of the blind—Hearing the Shepherd's voice, John x.—
Clean through the Word, and fruitful, John xv.—Similes of
the Word, a rock, seed, provision, a light, money—Contains
commands, claims, invitations, messages, warnings, testimony,
directions, and calls—The heart which receives it, good soil, a
lamp or candle, a storehouse, a bank, a branch—The voice of
a Father, a Master, a King, a Bridegroom, and a Shepherd—
Judgment upon rejecting, disobeying, neglecting, and making
light of the Word.

Joy.—The Lord's joy—Over the treasure discovered (Matt. xiii.)
—Over lost ones found in Luke xv.—Over the fruit borne
(John xv.)—Over the harvest reaped (John iv.)—Shared joy
(Luke xv.)—Joy at the Bridegroom's voice, joy in His presence
—"The joy of the Lord."

The use of earthly and heavenly riches.—Treasuring all for self,
the rich man and his barns—Spending all for self, the rich
man and Lazarus—Using it for others, the householder, the
good man—Wasting the Master's goods, the unjust steward—
Trading, the talent and pounds—A change of dispensation,
the rich man and Lazarus.

Over-anxiety unnecessary. — Springing seed — Our service — The
lilies of the field—Our needs.

Consistency.—Two sons, between promises and performances—
Two debtors, between forgiveness received and forgiveness
given —Two houses, between our hearing and doing—Sower,
between our root and our fruit   .   .   .   . pp. 269–293

CHAPTER XVIII

DOUBLE PARABLES

I. Parables which have *two parts*.

1. Luke xiv. 7–11, addressed to the guests ; 12–14, to the host.
2. Matt. xxi. 33–41, the husbandmen reject the messenger ; 42, the builders refuse the stone.
3. Luke xix. 14, 27, the citizens ; 13, 15–26, the servants.
4. Matt. xxii. 1–8, those which were bidden ; 9, 10, those which were brought. Luke xiv. 16–20, 24, those which were bidden ; 21–23, those which were brought.

II. *Double symbolism in the same parable.*

Concerning the Lord—
1. In the parable of the husbandmen.
2. The Sower.
3. In Matt. xvi. 18.
4. In John x.

Concerning men—
5. The Sower.
6. The marriage feast.
7. The tares.
8. The good Samaritan.

III. *Parables immediately following one another.*

1. The sower and the tares (Matt. xiii. 3–23, and 24–30).
2. The mustard seed and the leaven (Matt. xiii. 31, 32, and 33).
3. The treasure and the pearl (Matt. xiii. 44, and 45, 46).
4. The tares (interpretation) and the treasure (Matt. xiii. 36–43, and 44).
5. The strong man armed, and the unclean spirit (Matt. xii. 29, and 43–45).
6. The tower and the kings (Luke xiv. 28–30, and 31, 32).
7. The prodigal son and the unjust steward (Luke xv. 11–32, and xvi. 1–8).
8. The unjust steward and the rich man and Lazarus (Luke xvi. 1–8 and 19–31).
9. The unjust judge, and the Pharisee and the publican (Luke xviii. 1–8, and 9–14).
10. The bridegroom and the thief in the night (Luke xii. 35–38, and 39, 40).
11. The ten virgins and the talents (Matt. xxv. 1–13, and 14–30)
12. The salt and the light (Matt. v. 13, and 14–16).

13. The ravens and the lilies (Luke xii. 24, and 27, 28).

14. Signs from heaven—The cloud and the wind (Luke xii. 54 and 55).

15. Signs from heaven—The red sunset and the red sunrise (Matt. xvi. 2 and 3).

16. New cloth and new wine (Luke v. 36, and 37–39).

IV. *Parables which are differently paired in the different Gospels.*

1. The sower and the tares, in Matt. xiii.

2. The sower and the candle, in Mark iv. 3–20 and 21, and Luke viii. 11–15 and 16.

3. The sower and the growing seed, in Mark iv. 3–25, and 26–29.

4. The city and the candle, in Matt. v. 14 and 15.

5. The candle and the eye, in Luke xi. 33 and 34.

6. The strait gate and the wide gate, in Matt. vii. 13 and 14.

7. The strait gate and the shut door, in Luke xiii. 24, and 25, 26.

V. Parables in which the *story* is very *similar*, but in which there is some different teaching.

1. The marriage feast and the great supper.

2. The talents and the pounds   .   .   .   .   pp. 294–310

CHAPTER XIX

DOUBLE PARABLES (*continued*)

VI. Parables which *link* themselves together *by their symbolism.*

1. Two debtors (Matt. xviii. 23–35, and Luke vii. 40–50).

2. Rich men who left all behind them (Luke xii. 16–21, and xvi. 19–31).

3. Travellers in difficulties—The good Samaritan and blind leaders of the blind (Luke x. 30–37, and Matt. xv. 14).

4. A woman's household work—The lost piece of silver, the leaven (Luke xv. 8–10, and Matt. xiii. 33).

5. Two classes of builders—The houses on rock and sand, and Paul's parable (Matt. vii. 24–29, and 1 Cor. iii. 10–17).

6. The rock foundation (Matt. vii. 24–29, and xvi. 18).

7. Christ the foundation-stone and the head-stone (see 6, and Matt. xxi. 42).

8. The good Shepherd (John x. and Luke xv.).

9. The wandering sheep lost on the mountains, fallen into the pit (Matt. xviii. 11–14, and xii. 11, 12).

10. The fig-tree, fruitless and budding again (Luke xiii. 6–9, and Matt. xxiv. 32, 33).

11. Food for the household—"Things new and old," "in due season" (Matt. xiii. 52, and xxiv. 45).

12. Things new and old, to be used in turn, and to be kept distinct (Matt. xiii. 52, and ix. 16, 17).

13. Festal garments—The wedding garment and the best robe (Matt. xxii. 11, 12, and Luke xv. 22).

14. An adversary (Matt. v. 25, 26, and Luke xviii. 3).

15. Payment to the uttermost—The adversary and the debtors (Matt. v. 25, 26, and xviii. 34).

16. A shut door, the Master claiming admittance, and refusing admittance (Luke xii. 36, and xiii. 25 ; Matt. xxv.).

17. A woman's earnestness, seeking the lost and pleading for help (Luke xv. 8, and xviii. 4, 5).

18. The Master's reckoning (Matt. xviii. 24, and xxv. 19).

19. Two journeys—Incarnation and ascension (Luke x. 33, and xix. 12 ; Mark xiii. 34).

20. Blind men who were led—Led astray or to a feast (Matt. xv. 14, and Luke xiv.).

VII. *Parables linked by the use of the same expression.*

1. "The last shall be first, and the first last" (Matt. xix. 30, and xx. 16 ; Luke xii. 30 ; xiii. 1).

2. "Whosoever exalteth himself shall be abased" (Luke xiv. 11, and xviii. 14).

3. "Lord, Lord, open to us. . . . I never knew you" (Matt. xxv. 11, 12 ; viii. 21-23, and Luke xiii. 25).

4. "A great way off" (Luke xiv. 32, and xv. 20).

5. "With what measure ye mete it shall be measured to you" (Mark iv. 24 and Luke vi. 38).

6. "He that hath to him shall be given" (Mark iv. 25, &c. ; Matt. xxv. 29; Luke xix. 26).

9. "Many are called but few are chosen" (Matt. xxii. 14, and xx. 16).

VIII. Parables which give *different aspects* of teaching on the same subject, but with different symbolism.

1. Importunate prayer—The unjust judge and the three friends (Luke xviii. 1-8, and xi. 5-8).

2. What men do with useless things—The savourless salt and the fruitless branches (Matt. v. 13, and John xv. 6).

3. Reconciliation before it is too late—The adversary and the kings (Luke xii. 58, 59, and xiv. 31, 32).

IX. Parables giving *collective* and *individual* aspects
of the same subject.

1. Buildings (see part vi. 6).
2. Builders (see part vi. 5).
3. Harvests (see part iii. 1).
4. Satan's dwelling (see part iii. 5).
5. Light-givers (see part iv. 4).
6. Importunate petitioners (see part viii. 1).

X. Parables which give *present* and *future* aspects.

1. Harvests (see part iii. 1).
2. Striving to enter (see part iv. 7).
3. The Master's reckoning (see part vi. 18) .   . pp. 311-331

CONCLUSION

The Author of the Parables still alive—Subjects for Prayer and
Praise—" That I may know Him "—" Even so, come, Lord
Jesus "   .   .   .   . pp. 332-336

APPENDIX

I. The Parable of Day and Night.
II. Division.
III. Isaiah liii. illustrated by the Parables.
IV. Peter and the Parables.
V. The Seven Churches in Asia.
VI. The Disciples' Prayer Illustrated by the Parables.
VII. Double Parables Tabulated.
VIII. Things Noted and Quoted   .   .   . pp. 337-355

PREFACE

IN the note which follows the Bishop of Durham's Preface to my "Bible and Modern Criticism," I acknowledged my indebtedness for valuable help received from two other friends in the preparation of that work. Of these I named the Rev. Robert Sinker, D.D., of Trinity College, Cambridge. The other to whom I referred was the writer of the present volume.

This fact expresses more forcibly than words my sense of Miss Habershon's fitness for the task she has here undertaken.

In our study of either the Word of God, or the works of God, no two of us ever see exactly alike. And every Bible student will possibly question many a detail in the exegesis here offered of the Parables. But this consideration in no way lessens my appreciation of the book.

For when both the aim and the spirit of a book are right, the true student of Scripture values it, not according as it contains what he already believes and knows, but according as it suggests thought and stimulates inquiry. And the present volume will be found to be eminently stimulating and suggestive. To some readers, indeed, the perusal of it may prove an education in Bible study, by reason of the proof it gives of what Pusey aptly terms the "hidden harmony" of Holy Writ.

ROBERT ANDERSON

PREFATORY NOTE

IF I were to attempt to mention the names of all the friends to whom I am indebted for help in the preparation of this Bible study, the list would have to be a long one. I am very grateful to all, whatever their share has been.

From some I have received thoughts upon the Parables; others have given me much encouragement in my happy but laborious task; and others again have devoted valuable time to the manuscript or the proofs.

Of those who most kindly read through the chapters in their earlier form, I would specially mention Dr. Anderson-Berry and Mr. George Soltau, from whom I received many helpful suggestions.

My indebtedness to Sir Robert Anderson is very great, not only for what he has said, but for what he has done in patiently reading through the proofs, and giving very many valuable criticisms and corrections, of which I have most gratefully availed myself.

A. R. H.

THE
STUDY OF THE PARABLES

CHAPTER I

INTRODUCTION

A VERY large portion of the teaching of the Word of God, both in the Old and New Testament, is conveyed to us in symbolic guise, and though the forms under which it is presented may differ considerably, the underlying teaching is always consistent. In studying the parables it is very important to bear this in mind, for by attempting to separate the passages which may be correctly called parables from others which are like them in teaching, we may lose a good deal. The form in which the meaning is conveyed is not so important as the lessons themselves.

The volumes which have been published on the parables are countless, and it seems almost presumptuous to attempt to add another to the list, but in most cases the sermons preached, the addresses given, and the books written, have treated them one by one, or at least in succession. In the present volume the plan is rather to suggest the importance of studying them together; grouping them in various ways; comparing them with other portions of Scripture, and tracing separate lines of teaching throughout the series.   Something similar was attempted in a former volume in connection with the types.[1]

Types, parables, miracles, and similes are all interlaced together like links in a chain.   So inseparably are they united that they can only be severed at the expense of some of the links.   The chain of truth needs them all, and though very different in form and pattern, and enriched and beautified with varying gems and ornaments, they combine to make one perfect whole.   Viewed in its completeness this shows a unity of design running throughout the entire Word of God, proving that He Himself inspired it.

The parables join the types on the one side, and the miracles on the other.   They expand, and explain, or are themselves made clear by what has gone before. In our study, therefore, we shall do well not to separate them, but to try and trace the pattern as it is carried from link to link, and worked out in the jewels that add beauty to these links.   Thus we shall find that the study of the parables involves the study of the whole Bible, both Old and New Testaments.

The teaching of our Lord was so largely made up of parables that if we would at all enter into His meaning we must of necessity make them our study. It was no new thing in Israel for God-sent prophets to make use of some such method to convey their message.   Sometimes indeed in Old Testament times they were commanded to represent an acted parable before the eyes of their audience, at others they in vision saw one for themselves.

We know that to this day the language of Eastern nations is much more figurative in character than that of the more matter-of-fact Western nations.   There was, however, a deeper meaning in our Lord's constant use of this method of teaching, for after His

---

[1] " The Study of the Types,"   **Kregel Publications**

public rejection by Israel, we are told that "without a parable spake He not unto them."

In the early part of His ministry He spoke more plainly to the people, but when the chief priests and Pharisees, as representatives of the nation, refused His teaching and rejected His Person, He veiled His meaning in the parables. They were addressed to various audiences. Some were spoken to the disciples in private, others were addressed to them, in the hearing of the Pharisees and scribes. Several were spoken to individuals, as when the woman who was a sinner anointed His feet in the house of Simon, and He said, " Simon, I have somewhat to say unto thee," and told the story of the two debtors ; or as when in answer to the question of the lawyer in Luke x., He replied by the parable of the good Samaritan.

The greater number, however, were uttered in the hearing of the multitude. They could not understand the deep teaching underlying them, though they were astonished at His doctrine, for " He taught them as one having authority," and they could perceive that He was a prophet.

Our Lord in Mark iv. 11 divides His hearers into two classes, those who "are without," and " you," My disciples ; and the purpose of the parable was very different in the case of these two sorts of hearers. They were intended to teach the disciples the things that had hitherto been kept secret, but they were uttered in order that those who refused Christ's teaching might not understand.

In the giving of the parables the terrible prophecy of Isaiah vi. was beginning to be fulfilled. "This style of speaking was one kind of judgment upon Israel. It was as the raising of the pillar between Israel and the Egyptians, only Israel was now put on the dark side of it."[1] They had wilfully refused the light, and

[1] J. G. Bellett.

turned a deaf ear to His teaching, and from this time His meaning was purposely hidden from them.

"Why do ye not understand My speech?" He asked, "even because ye cannot hear My Word" (John viii. 43). As they listened to the parables they could see the meaning that lay, as it were, on the very surface, but there was much more than this which the Lord meant only for His own. When they heard the parable about the wicked husbandmen, they could not fail, from their knowledge of the Old Testament Scriptures, to perceive that He spake of them; but had they fully understood the meaning, they would have seen what awful judgment they were bringing upon themselves.

Those who read the parables now, even while professing to be disciples of the Lord, seem to be divided into these two classes. They are not like scribes and Pharisees in their hatred of Him, yet some appear quite satisfied to be like them in seeing very little in the parables.

They admire the beauty of the story, they see the moral teaching that lies on the surface, but if a deeper meaning is suggested, or the parables are shown to bear a prophetic interpretation, they at once cry out that it is fanciful.

Those who know something of the fulness of meaning that is to be found in the inspired Word of God, will not, however, be satisfied with merely seeing the first lessons of the parables, which were plain to all the multitude, but will, like the disciples, long to be instructed in all the meaning which they contain. If there had been nothing beyond what the scribes and Pharisees could understand, the disciples would not have needed to be privately taught. Again and again we read that when the multitudes were dispersed, and He was alone with

His disciples, they asked Him to explain His meaning, and He expounded all things to them.

It has been lately affirmed that "in studying the exposition of the parables by some well-known authors we are in positive danger of being beguiled through subtilty of reasoning from 'the simplicity that is in Christ.' Of that simplicity we have no such enduring memorial as the parables." It is true that there is a beautiful simplicity which even the Pharisees could see, and which moved the multitude to say with admiration, "Never man spake like this man." But if this had been all, the disciples would not have needed the private interpretation.

Like children on the shore, there are many who seem to prefer to paddle in the shallows ; but let not such find fault with those who attempt to swim out into deeper waters, very soon beyond their depth probably, yet finding out something of the ocean's fulness. The little ones on the shore are not so ignorant as to imagine that all the sea is ankle-deep ; but to think that there are no unfathomed depths in the parables would be just as foolish.

A well-known writer said of the parable of the good Samaritan : "I find in it a reproving and guiding example of a true and effective compassion, but I find *nothing more.*" [1] What a confession to make ! and yet there are many who resolutely set their faces against seeing anything "more," lest they should be considered fanciful. Shall they who profess to be spiritual boast that they see "nothing more" in our Lord's words than can be discerned by the natural man ? The latter can admire the compassion of the good Samaritan, and strive to copy the example of philanthropy ; but surely the spiritually minded will delight in recognising that it is a picture of the

[1] "The Parables of Our Lord," by Rev. W. Arnot. The italics are mine.

Lord Himself, who had with scorn and hatred been called a Samaritan by the Jews (John viii. 48).

The conduct of the inner circle of hearers when He first uttered these wonderful discourses will teach us how we too may be let into His secrets. We are told that "when He was alone they that were about Him with the twelve asked of Him the parable" (Mark iv. 10), and we may learn two things from this. First, that we too must ask. He still says to us, as He said to Jeremiah, "Call unto Me, and I will answer thee, and show thee great and mighty things (or hidden, *mar.,* or difficult, R.V.) which thou knowest not" (chap. xxxiii. 3); and second, that we must be alone with Him. Does not this afford a clue as to our inability to understand? In these days of hurry and rush, of busy work and many meetings, we often have but little time for sitting at the Master's feet and hearing His Word. "The words of the wise are spoken (or heard, A.V.) in quiet" (Eccl. ix. 17, R.V.), but we are restless and do not care to be quiet. The little city is too full of turmoil to listen to the words of the poor wise man.

When He would open the ears of the *deaf* man we read in the same gospel that "He took him aside from the multitude" (Mark vii. 33), and in opening the eyes of the *blind* He first "took the blind man by the hand and led him out of the town" (chap. viii. 23). "The hearing ear and the seeing eye" are gifts from Himself, and we too need quiet times alone with Him, aside from the multitude, that He may open our ears to hear, and our eyes to see the "many things" that He would teach us. "Who hath *ears* to hear let him hear," said He, when speaking in parables; and again, "Blessed are your *eyes*, for they see; and your *ears*, for they hear. For verily I say unto you, That many prophets and righteous men have desired to see those things which ye see, and have not seen them;

and to hear those things which ye hear, and have not heard them " (Matt. xiii. 9, 16, 17).

We have often wished, perhaps, as we have read the gospel narrative, that we too could have heard the gracious words that fell from His lips. We have longed that we also might ask Him what His Word meant, and we have almost envied the disciples as they walked by His side and listened to the explanation which He gave to them. But since the day when the cloud received Him out of their sight and the Holy Spirit descended from heaven to take up His abode in the Church as the indwelling Spirit of truth, a clearer unveiling of God's purposes has been given than the disciples could have borne when our Lord was with them. The revelation received by the Apostle Paul of the mystery of the Church (Eph. iii.) was unknown before. It had been a secret hid from prophets and even from angels, but since that wonderful unveiling many things in the Lord's teaching are clearer than they could have been made during His lifetime. "I have yet many things to say unto you, but ye cannot bear them now."

By His Spirit He is as ready to teach us now as He was of old, and the reason we do not better understand His teaching is probably because we are content with the little we have already understood, and we do not spend enough time alone with Him, like Mary sitting at His feet and hearing His word.

CHAPTER II

IN our study of the parables the methods of interpretation which we adopt will, in the first place, vary
according to the measure and kind of inspiration
which we accord to them. Those who do not believe
in the inspiration of Scripture will see but very little.
They will regard them perhaps with just a trifle more
reverence than Æsop's fables, but will look at them
very much in the same manner. They say, "Treat
the Bible like any ordinary book," but the Bible is
not like an ordinary book, and the parables are *not*
like human parables. Such readers will of course
deny the prophetic character, and see nothing in the
details. Their view will be something like the definition given by the little girl in Sunday School, who
having learnt that a parable was "an earthly story
with a heavenly meaning," became somewhat mixed,
and announced that a parable was "a heavenly story
with no earthly meaning."

Then there are those who do not believe in verbal
inspiration. Many of them profess to believe in the
Deity of the One who spake the parables, but even on
this point their opinions vary very much, and their
limited view of inspiration practically denies it :
neither will they allow that those who gave the
record of His sayings were guided by the Spirit as
to the very words which they should write.

We who believe that the Speaker of the Gospel
parables was the Son of God, and that the Evangelists

who related them were inspired as to the words used, the parables recorded, and the details given, shall see a great deal more in them than those who believe in a lesser form of inspiration, or none at all. We shall be confident that there is a meaning or reason for every word, and shall delight in comparing the records.

The differences in the various gospel narratives will not cause us difficulty. We shall not call them contradictions, but shall know that the varying accounts are intentional evidences of the inspiration of selection or omission, each Evangelist giving, under the guidance of the Holy Spirit, the portions of the spoken parable which are best suited to the purpose of his gospel.

These and other similar things become difficulties to many, because they are approached from the wrong direction. Men find something which they cannot understand, and say that therefore they cannot believe in inspiration, whereas if they first accepted inspiration, the "difficulties" would either disappear or change their character.

The writer of the epistle to the Hebrews says, "Through faith we understand;" but now men would reverse it, as though it must be "By understanding we believe." The Psalmist said, "I had fainted unless I had *believed* to *see*," but to-day men want to see in order to believe. We should not hear nearly so much about the difficulties of believing in the inspiration of Scripture if only the Bible were treated as we treat a front door. Most front doors can present many difficulties from the outside. They were not made to be opened from without. Only the owner possesses a latch-key, and those to whom he may have entrusted one. But gain admission to the house in the accustomed way, and when you are within look at the door, and you will probably find that a little child could turn the handle. The latch is on the *inside*.

What we find in the parables will also depend very much on our estimate of their Author. If we know Him to be God we shall expect them to be much more than mere human productions. "Thy thoughts are very deep." If I am shown a box, and told that it contains the last invention of an Edison or a Marconi, I shall, according to my conception of their wonderful scientific discoveries in the past, expect something very marvellous. The case from the outside may look like an ordinary box, but my knowledge of the maker will determine my expectations. Will it not be so in our study of the parables?

With reference to the details, we may be quite sure that every one had meaning in it. This is very clearly proved by the two parables to which the Lord gave full interpretations, viz., those of the sower and the tares. From these we may judge how very full of teaching are all the parables. Almost every detail is explained, showing that they are pictures drawn by a Master hand, where no touch is useless. In that of the tares, He gives an explanation of the sower, the wheat, the tares, the field, the enemy, the reapers, and the harvest, nothing is omitted. If this interpretation had not been given, and a Bible student in the present day had suggested a spiritual meaning for all these particulars, he would at once have been pronounced very fanciful by those who resemble the outer circle of hearers.

In explaining the parable of the sower, there was one important detail which the Lord did not mention. He did not define whom the sower was intended to represent, though in the parable of the tares He says, "He that soweth the good seed is the Son of Man." This omission in the previous parable is very suggestive, and probably has a twofold significance. First, it implies that the sower has several meanings. When the Lord was on earth, He Himself scattered

the grain, and also sent forth His disciples. Now
the Word is sown by His people, so that Paul prays,
"Now He that ministereth seed to the sower, both
minister bread for your food, and multiply your seed
sown." By-and-by the Church will be taken away,
and then the believing remnant of Israel will be the
sowers. It is probable that the Psalmist refers to
them when he says, "They that sow in tears shall
reap in joy. He that goeth forth and weepeth, bearing precious seed, shall doubtless come again with
rejoicing, bringing his sheaves with him." Thus the
sower may be taken to represent all who sow the
Word, from the time of the Lord's rejection to the
time when He comes in glory. But there is probably
a second reason why the interpretation is not given,
viz., to emphasise the importance of the seed, rather
than of the hand that scatters it.

It is not surprising that where no interpretation
is given, different meanings are suggested for the
details, as in the instance just mentioned. It is
very important to acknowledge that there may be
truth in more than one. If we had been left to define
the meaning of thorns in the same parable, some
might say that they signified poverty, others might
think that they referred to riches, but both would
be correct, for our Lord gave no less than four
meanings, showing that the circumstances must determine the explanation. "The cares of this world," "the
deceitfulness of riches," "the pleasures of this life,"
and "the lusts of other things" may all choke the
Word.

Thus we may be quite certain that each detail had
a meaning, and may be quite prepared to find
that some of them had several.

It has often been said that the extravagances of
Patristic literature prove that it is wrong to spiritualise the details of the parables. We know that the

writings of the early fathers became more and more unlike those of the apostles, and would not bear comparison with Scripture ; for in some of their attempts at allegorising both Old and New Testament passages, they went to great extremes. But this does not at all prove that we are wrong in thinking that there was a meaning in all these things. We have the Lord's own warrant for that method of interpretation which gives a value to each word. But, as in a picture, if the details are made unduly prominent, there is a danger of losing the broad lights and shades, and spoiling the effect, so the details of the parables must not be pressed so as to obscure the general teaching.

Like all other things which have come from the hand of God, they will bear the closest examination under the most powerful microscope, but we must not confine ourselves to this method, for otherwise we shall not obtain the more general view of the whole. In botany we must study many things in order to learn all we can about a plant, yet it would be very absurd if we found fault with those who looked at the petals of the flower or the pollen of the stamens under the microscope because these do not give any idea of the nature of the root or the mode of growth.

The differences of opinion concerning the details are of less importance than those which exist about the scope of the parables, but the more we study them, singly, collectively, and with reference to the whole Bible, the more do we become convinced of the manifold meanings hidden in each one. Much controversy would be avoided if this important principle were acknowledged.

One object of this volume is, if possible, to promote harmony in this respect, rather than controversy ; and to show how it is quite possible for some of the varying views which men so tenaciously hold to be equally correct. There are many Christians who are almost afraid to study the parables because of the way in which they have been claimed by various schools of prophetic interpretation as arguments in favour of their own line of teaching. But there would be far less discussion if it were allowed that the parables contain several meanings. It is quite certain that there would be less denunciation of the views of others if each student tried to see how his opponent's interpretation might be true as well as his own.

No single explanation will exhaust the meaning of the simplest parable which our divine Lord spoke, and if we recognise this, we shall also be prepared to gather from them "great spoil" of every kind.

Long ago those who disbelieved in the inspiration of the Bible stated that it must only be allowed one interpretation,[1] and we are not surprised at their attitude; but there are others who profess to believe in inspiration who say the same thing from their point of view. Seeing a prophetic aspect in the parables, a Jewish application, they endeavour to confine the teaching to this one view. On this point the "higher critics" and the "ultra-dispensationalists" unite, and both alike would rob us of much that we are intended to find in them.[2]

He who is the incarnate Word speaks of Himself as "Alpha and Omega, which is, and which was, and which is to come," and this threefold description is also true of the written Word, and, in a very marked manner, of the parables. Of course all will agree that some parts of Scripture refer to the past, that

[1] Prof. Jowett in " Essays and Reviews," answered by Dean Burgon.

[2] With reference to the former class, it is curious to notice that the very men who would deny the spiritual teaching of types, miracles, parables, &c., are themselves anxious to allegorise the earlier chapters of Genesis, for it suits their purpose to get rid of the inspired account of the fall of man, and other facts.

some look forward to the future, and that some are ever in the present; but there is something beyond this. There are passages which evidently have a threefold interpretation, applying at the same time to the past, present, and future; and Bible readers and students seem naturally to divide themselves into five classes, according to how much they see of the "was," "is," and "is to come" meanings of Scripture.

(1) There are, alas! some who are not even sure of the "was," such as "higher critics" who deny Old Testament facts.

(2) There are others who believe in the "was," but cannot see the "is." They believe, for example, that certain events happened to the children of Israel in olden days, but do not see any spiritual typical teaching for us now. They have never seen the "is."

(3) There are some who are convinced of the "was," and enjoy the "is," but do not recognise the "is to come,"—such as those who do not look for the Lord's personal return, who only spiritualise the prophecies to Israel, and see nothing of dispensational truth. They fail to recognise the dispensational character of the parables.

(4) There are a few who seem to believe in the "is to come," almost to the exclusion of the "is." These are the "ultra-dispensationalists" who tell us that there is only one interpretation, the literal, for Israel, and pronounce all others to be wrong. They see nothing but the Jewish aspect of many of the parables.

(5) Shall we not aim at belonging to the fifth class, those who equally recognise the truth of the "was," "is," and "is to come" interpretations? We shall then find a threefold line of teaching in many of the parables.

It is not merely that there may be many *applications* which were not originally intended, for we believe that these several interpretations were often purposely enfolded by the Holy Spirit in the one passage. Not only are all true, but all are intentionally given to us by the Holy Spirit, and it is not for us therefore to say which is the primary teaching, nor must we put more weight upon one than upon another. To ignore the "is to come" is wrong, but so would it be to deny the "is." The "one interpretation" theory treats the Bible too much like a book of merely human origin, instead of divinely inspired Scripture.

We must not ignore one meaning in order to give weight to another, even though that other may have been much neglected and overlooked ; for we lose the balance of truth quite as much by putting too much weight on one side of the scale, as by putting nothing into the other. Sometimes we see different schools of Biblical interpretation clustering round past, present, or future fulfilments, each party maintaining its own view, but losing sight of that of others. We are in less danger of doing this if we see the truth of all three. The Word of God is like a prism—for it breaks up the white light of His truth into many beautiful colours—yet prisms are three-sided, and all three sides are needed if we are to see the varied tints.[1]

Bishop Butler well explains interpretation by saying that "the meaning of a book is the meaning of the author."[2] There was a literal meaning intended by the great Author at the time when the parables were delivered—a spiritual meaning, true then and now, and in many, a prophetic one also. All therefore, whether referring to past, present, or future, are interpretations. The spiritual lessons for us are the same as for the disciples, and yet in some respects different, for the

---

[1] The last few paragraphs are largely quoted from an article in the *Morning Star*—"Fulfilled in the Kingdom"—which has been reprinted as a booklet.

[2] Quoted by Dean Burgon in " Inspiration and Interpretation."

Lord who was with them when they listened to the parables has now left the scene, and the dispensation has changed.

We have a striking proof and example of the double intention of a parable in that of the unjust judge. We are told at the beginning that the purpose for which it was spoken was to teach a spiritual lesson, "that men ought always to pray, and not to faint," but the comment at the end shows very clearly that the illustration by which the Lord enforced the lesson had a dispensational application also. "And shall not God avenge His own elect which cry day and night unto Him, though He bear long with them? I tell you that He will avenge them speedily. Nevertheless, when the Son of Man cometh shall He find faith on the earth?"

Like dissolving views the two imperceptibly pass into one another, and both were equally intended by the Lord, the spiritual and the prophetic; the time of His absence as well as the time of His return. This one example is a conclusive proof that the Lord's parables were intended to teach more lessons than one.

As to the prophetic aspect it sometimes covers all dispensations, as in the parable of the sower. It describes the days when the Lord was here, and when He is absent; while the Church is on earth, and after the Church has been removed—when Israel is rejecting and rejected, and when the remnant is again taken up by God. The disciples were representatives of a two-fold company, and because they were Jews must not be taken to represent only the Jewish remnant of later days. For as believers they were also to become members of the Church which is His body. Some parables, although referring to the Jewish remnant, evidently have a first interpretation for believers living in this dispensation, such as the parables about watching. The command is to all, "What I say unto you, I say unto all, Watch." Therefore these parables belong to the whole time of His absence, although many of the events depicted in them, in connection with His return, are those which are to take place when He comes in glory to the earth after the Great Tribulation. The saying, " One interpretation, many applications," is an entirely unwarranted distinction, for if the application is designed by the Holy Spirit, surely it *is* an interpretation.

Many applications are made which can scarcely be called interpretations ! For instance, a learned professor, fifty years ago, having disposed of the inspiration of Scripture to his own satisfaction, and proved, as he thought, that it was to be treated like any other book, triumphantly claimed to have "found the pearl of great price after sweeping the house ! "[1] thus mixing the parables of Matt. xiii. and Luke xv., and making the pearl to mean his own very partial belief in the Bible.

To see only moral and practical teaching in the parables is to miss much of their meaning. To see only the dispensational and prophetic is also to have but a limited view.[2]

It is of the utmost importance that we should understand the distinction between the Jews, the Gentiles, and the Church of God. This is indeed the key to what has been termed " dispensational teaching." The Bible becomes a new book to us, as thus we learn to understand something of God's purposes for the future.

[1] Professor Jowett.

[2] In Chap. V., on " The Setting of the Parables," we study them in their first aspect, noting the incidents that, taking place at the time, first called them forth, and the results which followed their reception. The moral and spiritual lessons are chiefly taken up in Chap. XVII. on " Practical Teaching," but it needs many volumes to exhaust their fulness. The dispensational view is touched upon principally in Chaps. VIII. to XII. and XV.

The prophetic Scriptures of the New Testament include, and are largely made up of, the parables, and it is impossible to understand their deeper meaning without acknowledging this. Yet whilst recognising the fact that many of them relate to Israel's history, we may at the same time be quite sure that each one is also intended to teach spiritual lessons to the children of God at all times, and that the parables which are clearly Jewish in one aspect, are as much intended for us as were the events in the history of Israel, which "happened unto them for ensamples" or types.

The apostle Paul, writing to the Corinthians, said, " Having therefore these promises, dearly beloved, let us cleanse ourselves." The promises to which he referred were words which he had just quoted from the Old Testament, promises to Israel, interpreted for the Church.

In the same manner we may say of the most Jewish of the parables, those which clearly contain prophecies of future events, " Having therefore these parables ; " and thus claiming them for ourselves, we may gather from them practical lessons and solemn warnings, and see that they were intended for the present time as well as for the future.

It is not possible to exclude entirely the events of the present dispensation even from the dispensational aspect of the parables, as some would do. To state that because Matthew is Jewish and Messianic in character, therefore the parables in it have only to do with the nation of the Jewish remnant, would be like saying that because the Epistle to the Romans is Gentile in character, therefore all the people spoken of must be Gentiles. We know that, Paul has much to say about Israel. It is indeed a Gentile epistle, addressed to Gentiles, but in order to explain the favours shown to them, the former blessings and the subsequent cutting off of Israel must be described.

In the same way Matthew is a Jewish Gospel, but the bringing in of the Gentiles must be described in order to show how during the times of Israel's rejection the kingdom in power is postponed, and the kingdom in mystery is substituted.

The parable of the husbandmen is a striking example of a parable relating to Israel which has typical teaching for the days in which we live. The Lord describes Israel's history from the days of the prophets to the time when they were rejected as a nation. It was at the same time history and prophecy, and as He uttered it referred to their past, present, and future. But is there nothing in it for us ? Did He not intend us to learn something from Israel's failure ? The apostle Paul tells us that the events of the Exodus, and the wanderings " happened unto them for ensamples (for us) : and they are written for our admonition upon whom the ends of the world are come." We may be quite sure therefore that the record of their subsequent history in parable form is equally intended for our admonition, and was indeed preserved for this very purpose.

If the warnings had been heeded, Israel's history would not have had its counterpart as, in fact, it has had in the annals of the Church. The circumstances indeed have been different, but in how many respects have there been the same unfaithfulness and lack of understanding, the same failures springing from similar heart-wanderings from God ? Intermingling with those around, imitating their ways, keeping to themselves privileges which were intended for all, allowing the place of God to be assumed by men, refusing to give to God what was His due, all these things led in olden days to Israel's fall, and the very same causes have produced the weakness of the Church.

The parable is full of warning to the professing

Church of to-day. Is there not a tendency amongst the husbandmen to keep the fruit for themselves instead of giving it to God ?

But not only is this parable full of typical teaching for us now, it also implies a change of dispensation.

Just as the apostle shows us that Gentile branches have been grafted into the *olive* tree, so the vineyard has been given to them. The witness-bearing and the fruit-bearing are now entrusted to both Jew and Gentile, some of the natural branches still remaining. (See page 237.)   By-and-by the vineyard will once more be entrusted to Israel, and this is probably also foretold in the parable, for the giving to others may include the double meaning.   (See page 165.)

The parable of the husbandmen, therefore, may be taken as an example of manifold interpretations, the historical, typical, and dispensational.   That of the sower is a striking instance of successive interpretations.

One important point is often forgotten. The parables were spoken to the disciples as they were able to bear it. Before the Lord Jesus Christ was raised from the dead, His disciples were not ready for much that He would teach them.   He said, " I have yet many things to say unto you, but ye cannot bear them now." Even in His lifetime there was progressive revelation. After His resurrection He could tell them more, but still He could not reveal His purposes fully. There was much that was only to be made plain after His ascension, and after the descent of the Holy Spirit. " He will guide you into all truth . . . He will show you things to come." We must, therefore, look for the fuller explanation of the parables in the epistles (see Chap. xv.), when the apostle Paul had received of the Lord the further teaching promised. Because many things concerning this dispensation are not revealed in the parables, we must not dismiss them as having nothing to do with us.

This principle is especially applicable to the parables about the coming of the Lord. (See Chap. ix.) The two stages of His personal return were not clearly revealed till the taking up of the saints was made known to Paul. The parables speak of His coming to the earth in His glory, but read in the light of the further prophetic teaching of the epistles we need not hesitate to apply each to the present dispensation. We may be quite sure that the Lord never meant them to lie useless for nearly two thousand years, or to be taken as referring only to the period after the close of this dispensation.

CHAPTER III

OUR Lord and Saviour Jesus Christ gives a very complete picture of His own character and work in the parables, for almost all of them describe Him in one or another of His various relationships. As we place them side by side we see what a wonderful revelation they give of Himself. In the simple illustrations, gathered from everyday life, He describes His attitude to the world, His relationship to Israel, and to all His own. He shows how He meets the sinner's every need, and He leaves out nothing that could add beauty to the picture of His grace and of His goodness. And yet the parables depict very fully both sides of His person and character—His divinity and His humanity. He is not only the humble Sower, the patient Shepherd, the eager Seeker for goodly pearls or treasure, but He is the Master, the Judge, the King.

As He spake, His hearers saw before them a Man of Sorrows, and acquainted with grief, One who had not where to lay His head; but in the scenes He pictured He takes His rightful place. He is the rich nobleman, the royal prince, the King's Son, yea, the King Himself. The people knew Him as one born in a stable, but He revealed His noble birth; they knew His poverty, He told of His wealth; they saw His sorrow, He looked forward to the joy; they despised and rejected Him, but He showed that He was to be their Judge. We need to ponder prayerfully these marvellous unfoldings of Himself, and the more we do so the more shall we be able to discern the ever fresh beauties that lie hidden in these seemingly simple stories.

They present a very different view of our Lord Jesus Christ from that which is given in much of the hymnology and the theology of the present day, and worse than all, in the irreverent religious stories which have become so popular. If we gathered our conception of Him from such sources, we should be inclined to think of the One who executes judgment upon His foes as a very different being from the One who said, " I am meek and lowly in heart." But the parables very clearly represent Him in all His majesty and power, and show that the same One who as the Good Shepherd " giveth His life for the sheep " and seeks the lost, also says, " Depart from Me, all ye workers of iniquity," and executes vengeance on His enemies, saying, " Those Mine enemies which would not that I should reign over them, bring hither and slay before Me." The One on whose bosom the beloved disciple leaned at supper was the same as He whom he saw in the glory on Patmos, at whose feet he fell as dead.

A reverent study of the parables from this point of view, is a sure antidote to the poison of the " Higher Criticism." By the so-called " Kenosis [1] theory " the " critics blasphemously assert that our Lord so ' emptied ' Himself of His deity that He was only human and on a level with His hearers and liable to mistakes." It is not possible to listen for a moment to such antichristian suggestions if we study His parables, for the more we examine the picture He gives the more are we assured of His divinity. He

[1] A Greek word, the noun of the verb used in Phil. ii. 7, " He emptied Himself."

actually claimed to be God Himself. No wonder
then that the people marvelled at the authority
with which He spake, for we read, "They were
astonished at His doctrine, for He taught them as
one having authority." This was their comment
immediately after listening to the parable of the
builders on the rock and on the sand. It was a high
claim that He there made. The two builders whom
He described were judged not by the care which
they took in erecting the houses, but by the foundations on which these stood. He left the people in
no doubt as to what the right foundation must be.
"These sayings of Mine," and the way in which
they were treated, this was to be the test. No wonder
that the multitudes were astonished at the authority
He claimed for His words, which He put on an
equality with His Father's will (see page 279). It
was the same as though He had said that they were the
Word of God. We who have been taught by the Holy
Spirit to acknowledge His deity know that He was
indeed what He claimed to be, for "the Word was
with God, and the Word was God."

Then, too, in other passages He claimed to be the
Jehovah of the Old Testament. In His parables of
the wicked husbandmen and of the feasts, He
described how messengers had been sent to demand
the fruit, or to invite to the banquet. So plain was
the picture that they could not fail to understand that
He was describing the treatment bestowed upon the
prophets by their fathers and themselves. But in
Matt. xxiii. 34, He claims to be Himself the
sender of those messengers. "Behold *I* send unto
you prophets." Divinely inspired prophets, like
those who had before appeared in Israel, might
have foretold events that would happen to the
nation, but He not only did this, predicting such
things as the destruction of their city, but He proved

Himself greater than the prophets by claiming to be the King's Son, and even the King Himself.

In the parable of the Pharisee and the publican we have a proof of His omniscience. He could read the heart of the Pharisee. He knew his thoughts as he prayed within himself, but more wonderful still He could follow the two prayers, and tell the result of each. The first was a prayer only in name, and it never reached the throne. That of the publican was heard, accepted, and answered by the One to whom it was addressed. He could assert, therefore, that the publican was justified. Who but the Judge Himself could give this verdict? He prefaces it by the words of authority, "*I* tell you," and He alone can tell.

The parable of the two debtors was spoken in answer to the unexpressed thought of Simon. It was, therefore, also a proof of His deity, for "The Lord searches all hearts, and understandeth all imaginations of the thoughts." Simon was saying to himself that if the Lord Jesus had been a prophet, He would have known the character of the woman who touched Him; but by this parable He showed that He knew not only all about the woman's life but about Simon's heart as well.

Our Lord also claims divinity in connection with the parable of the strong man who is overcome by the stronger than he. He had cast out a devil, and they murmured that it was by the power of the devil, but He said, "If I with the finger of God cast out devils, no doubt the kingdom of God is come upon you." It was the hand of God Himself that worked by means of His finger, and He gave the parable to show that He was stronger than Satan.

In the parable of the tares He showed that as Son of Man He not only sowed the field, but commanded the angels to reap it. And in the various revelations of the power which He will exhibit at His return, in judgment and reward, He again and again gave proofs that He was indeed one with the Father, Son of God as well as Son of Man.

Many other of the divine attributes are illustrated in the parables, such as :—

His grace and mercy in the parable of the debtors.

His patience in the parables of the lost sheep and the growing seed.

His compassion in the parables of the good Samaritan and the debtors.

His power and majesty in the parables of the pounds and the two kings.

His greatness and liberality in the parable of the marriage supper.

His love in the parables of the treasure, the pearl, and the prodigal.

His care in the parables of the true vine and the good Shepherd.

His tenderness and pity in the parable of the lost sheep.

His longsuffering in the parables of the husband-men and the fig-tree.

His sovereignty in the parable of the labourers in the vineyard.

His strength in the parable of the strong man.

His faithfulness in the parable of the good Shepherd.

The following is a list of the various relationships under which the Lord describes Himself and His Father [1] :—

---

[1] In making a list of the parables it is impossible to separate those generally recognised as such from some of the shorter utterances of our Lord which contain figurative language; these have therefore been included.

The Figure.	The Parable.	References.
A king . . .	The King and his Servants	Matt. xviii. 23–35.
,, . . .	The Marriage Feast .	Matt. xxii. 1–14.
,, . . .	The Two Kings . .	Luke xiv. 31, 32.
A nobleman . .	The Pounds . . .	Luke xix. 12–27.
A bridegroom .	The Marriage Feast .	Matt. xxii. 1–14.
,, .	The Ten Virgins . .	Matt. xxv. 1–13.
,, .	The Returning Bridegroom	Luke xii. 35–48.
,, .	The Present Bridegroom	Matt. ix. 15 ; Mark ii. 19, 20; Luke v. 34, 35.
A creditor . .	The Two Debtors . .	Luke vii. 40–50.
,, .	The King and his Servants	Matt. xviii. 23–35.
A judge . .	The Unjust Steward .	Luke xvi. 1–13.
,, .	The Adversary . .	Matt. v. 25, 26 ; Luke xii. 58, 59.
,, .	The Unjust Judge . .	Luke xviii. 1–8.
A master . .	The Talents . . .	Matt. xxv. 14–30.
,, .	The Pounds . . .	Luke xix. 12–27.
,, .	The Absent Lord . .	Luke xii. 35–48.
,, .	The King and his Servants	Matt. xviii. 23–35.
,, .	The Marriage Feast .	Matt. xxii. 1–14.
,, .	The Man on a Journey .	Mark xiii. 32–37.
,, .	The Unjust Steward .	Luke xvi. 1–13.
,, .	The Field Labourers .	Luke xvii. 7–10.
A host . . .	The Marriage Feast .	Matt. xxii. 1–14.
,,	The Great Supper . .	Luke xiv. 16–24.
A sower . . .	The Sower . . .	Matt. xiii. 3 – 23 ; Mark iv. 1 – 20 ; Luke viii. 5–15.
,, .	The Tares . . .	Matt. xiii. 24–30, 36–43.
,, .	The Mustard-seed . .	Matt. xiii. 31, 32.
,, .	The Growing Seed . .	Mark iv. 26–29.
An owner of a vineyard	The Labourers . .	Matt. xx. 1–16.
,, ,,	The Father and his Sons	Matt. xxi. 28–31.
,, ,,	The Wicked Husbandmen	Matt. xxi. 33–46; Mark xii. 1–12 ; Luke xx. 9–19.
,, ,,	The Fig-tree . . .	Luke xiii. 6–9.
A husbandman .	,, . . .	,,
,, .	The True Vine . .	John xv. 1–8.
A planter of trees .	The Plants . . .	Matt. xv. 13.
A shepherd . .	The Lost Sheep . .	Luke xv. 3–7 ; Matt. xviii. 11–14.
,, .	The Sheep in a Pit . .	Matt. xii. 11, 12.
,, .	The Good Shepherd .	John x. 1–30.
A father . .	The Prodigal Son . .	Luke xv. 11–32.
,, .	The Father and his Sons	Matt. xxi. 28–31.
A Samaritan . .	The Good Samaritan .	Luke x. 30–37.
A finder of treasure	The Hidden Treasure .	Matt. xiii. 44.
A merchantman .	The Pearl of Great Price	Matt. xiii. 45, 46.
A physician . .	The Physician . .	Matt. ix. 12, 13; Mark ii. 17; Luke v. 31, 32.
A conqueror . .	The Strong Man . .	Matt. xii. 25–29; Mark iii. 27; Luke xi. 17–22.

The Figure.	The Parable.	References.
A builder . .	" On this Rock " . .	Matt. xvi. 18.
A rock . . .	,, ,, . .	,,
,, . . .	The House on the Rock .	Matt. vii. 24–29 ; Luke vi. 46–49.
A corner stone .	The Husbandmen . .	Matt. xxi. 42–44 ; Mark xii. 10, 11 ; Luke xx. 17, 18.
A cloud and shower	The Cloud . . .	Matt. xvi. 1–4 ; Luke xii. 54–56.
A corn of wheat .	The Corn of Wheat .	John xii. 24.

A glance at this list immediately suggests one way in which the parables naturally group themselves. Where two or three represent the Lord in the same character it is helpful to compare them, and to notice how as a rule each one emphasises a different lesson. Many are thus coupled together in the chapters on " Double Parables."

CHAPTER IV

PICTURES OF MEN IN THE PARABLES

THE parables which represent the Lord's Person and work under so many different aspects, depict men in a corresponding variety of ways, sometimes referring to His own people, sometimes to men of the world, sometimes speaking of His friends, sometimes of His enemies.

We find that men are represented as follows:—

THE FIGURE.	THE PARABLE.	REFERENCES.
As debtors . . .	The Two Debtors . .	Luke vii. 40–50.
,, . .	The King and his Servants	Matt. xviii. 23–35.
,, . .	The Adversary . .	Matt. v. 25, 26 ; Luke xii. 58, 59.
As sons . . .	The Two Sons . .	Matt. xxi. 28–31.
,, . . .	The Prodigal . . .	Luke xv. 11–32.
As guests . .	The Marriage Feast .	Matt. xxii. 2–14.
,, . .	The Great Supper . .	Luke xiv. 16–24.
As travellers . .	The Good Samaritan .	Luke x. 30–37.
,, . .	The Blind Leaders of the Blind	Matt. xv. 14.
,, . .	The Strait Gate . .	Matt. vii. 13, 14 ; Luke xiii. 24.
As virgins . .	The Ten Virgins . .	Matt. xxv. 1–13.
As keepers of a vineyard	The Husbandmen . .	Matt. xxi. 33–46; Mark xii. 1–12; Luke xx. 9–16.
As servants . .	The Talents . . .	Matt. xxv. 14–30.
,, . .	The Pounds . . .	Luke xix. 12–27.
,, . .	The Absent Lord . .	Mark xiii. 34–37.
,, . . .	,, ,, . .	Luke xii. 35–48.
,, . .	The Marriage Feast .	Matt. xxii. 1–14.
,, . .	The Labourers in the Vineyard	Matt. xx. 1–16.
,, . .	The Field Labourers .	Luke xvii. 7–10.
,, . .	The Faithful Steward .	Luke xii. 42.
,, . .	The Unjust Steward .	Luke xvi. 1–13.
As a householder .	The Householder . .	Matt. xiii. 52.

The Figure.	The Parable.	References.
As a rich man .	The Rich Man and his Barns	Luke xii. 16–21.
As a rich man and a beggar	The Rich Man and Lazarus	Luke xvi. 19–31.
As a king . .	The Two Kings . .	Luke xiv. 31, 32.
As worshippers .	The Pharisee and Publican	Luke xviii. 9–14.
As builders . .	The Corner Stone . .	Matt. xxii. 42–44; Mark xii. 10, 11; Luke xx. 17, 18.
,, . .	Houses on Rock and Sand	Matt. vii. 24–29; Luke vi. 46–49.
,, . .	The Tower . . .	Luke xiv. 28–30.
As dwelling-places .	The Strong Man . .	Matt. xii. 29; Mark iii. 27; Luke xi. 21, 22.
,,	The Unclean Spirit . .	Matt. xii. 43–45; Luke xi. 24–26.
As good and bad soil	The Sower . . .	Matt. xiii. 3–23; Mark iv. 3–20; Luke viii. 5–15.
As good seed . .	The Growing Seed . .	Mark iv. 26–29.
As wheat . .	The Corn of Wheat .	John xii. 24.
As wheat and tares .	The Tares . .	Matt. xiii. 24–30, 36–43.
As wheat and chaff	(By John the Baptist) .	Matt. iii. 12; Luke iii. 17.
As plants . .	......	Matt. xv. 13.
As trees . .	......	Matt. vii. 16–20; Luke vi. 43, 44; Matt. xii. 33.
As branches . .	The True Vine . .	John xv. 1–8.
As a fig-tree . .	The Fig-tree . . .	Luke xiii. 6–9.
As sheep . .	The Good Shepherd .	John x. 1–30.
,, . .	The Lost Sheep . .	Luke xv. 4–7; Matt. xviii. 12, 13.
,, . .	The Sheep in a Pit . .	Matt. xii. 11, 12.
,, . .	The Sheep and the Goats	Matt. xxv. 31–46.
As fish . . .	The Drag Net . .	Matt. xiii. 47–50.
As a piece of silver .	The Lost Silver . .	Luke xv. 8-10.
As a treasure . .	The Hidden Treasure .	Matt. xiii. 44.
As a pearl . .	The Pearl of Great Price	Matt. xiii. 45, 46.
As lights . .	The City set on a Hill .	Matt. v. 14.
,, . .	The Candle . . .	Matt. v. 15; Mark iv. 21; Luke viii. 16.
As salt . . .	......	Matt. v. 13.

To this list we might add other similes used by the Lord. He referred to the ox patiently labouring in the yoke, to sparrows insignificant but numbered and noticed, to ravens unclean but cared for, to harmless doves and wise serpents, linking these two to show that the double characteristics must go together;

there must not be the wisdom of the serpent without the harmlessness of the dove. Then too, when mourning over Jerusalem, He used the beautiful figure of the hen gathering her chickens under her wing, and it is noteworthy that it is immediately preceded by the reference to Herod as the fox.

All these illustrations were from the animal kingdom ; others He took from the vegetable world, such as the flower of the grass fading and quickly destroyed, the lilies which without toil are beautifully apparelled, the thorns which cannot produce grapes, and the thistles which never bring forth figs.

As in the former case, this list suggests to us many ways of grouping the parables. By comparing those which represent men under the same simile we find out many points of teaching which otherwise might be missed.

To take one example, we notice that there is a great deal said about houses, sometimes representing the heart of an individual, at other times giving a picture of the nation. This figure runs through both Old and New Testaments, and by placing them together we gather the following details and descriptions. We read of two foundations, rock and sand ; of two sorts of building material, viz., wood, hay, and stubble, or gold, silver, and precious stones ; of two reasons for emptying, reformation and judgment (see page 183) ; of two kinds of besiegers and conquerors, the enemy and the deliverer, who represent two kinds of occupants. There are also two ways of storing the house, for self and for others, and there is lastly a house that is lighted.

The contrast between the last and the first on the list is striking. One shows the importance of having something which no one can see—the foundation ; while the other teaches there must be something which all men can see—the light.

Three of the earliest parables speak of houses. The first tells about the foundation, the second about the owner, the third about the tenant. In the first the house is built, in the next it is fortified, besieged, and taken, in the last it is emptied, swept, and garnished, and again occupied.

In the same way we may link together the teaching about servants, sheep, sons, debtors, &c.

In many parables two or even more *classes* of people are presented in the picture. There are wise and foolish, good and bad, faithful and unfaithful, profitable and unprofitable, fruitful and unfruitful.

We have the latter, for example, in the parable of the sower, where the hearers of the Word are represented under the figure of *four* kinds of soil; but these may again be grouped into *two*, prepared or unprepared, ploughed or unploughed land, for none of the unfruitful soil had been ploughed. Who would plough the wayside? Who could plough the rock? It would be useless to do the one and impossible to do the other; and the weeds were a sure sign that the thorny ground had not been ploughed. As we read in Jer. iv. 3, "Break up your fallow ground, and sow not among thorns."

The two pictures which represent the great feasts tell of *three* sorts of invited guests, who in various degrees accepted the King's invitation, or professed to do so. Those that were "bidden" had doubtless meant to come when first invited; just as they had said at Sinai, "All that the Lord hath spoken, we will do." They seemed to accept the invitation, but when finally told that the feast was ready made excuse. They accepted, but did not come. The man that had not on a wedding garment is a sample of another class. He accepted the invitation, came to the feast, but thought his own clothing sufficiently good, and so was not ready to accept the garment provided.

The others accepted the invitation, and also the King's provision by which they were made fit for His palace. They knew that the dust of streets, lanes, and highways had made their own dress quite unfit for His presence. From these three classes we learn that it is not enough to say we accept, we must come; it is not enough to come, we must come in God's way.

We have two varieties of seed in the parable of the tares; two kinds of plants in Matt. xv. 13; two groups of watchers in the parable of the virgins; two sorts of fish gathered in the net; and two classes of servants in several parables.

In many of the parables the character, behaviour, or experience of two *individuals* is contrasted. There are two builders in that of the houses on the rock and on the sand; there are two suppliants in the story of the Pharisee and the publican; there are two experiences contrasted in the history of Dives and Lazarus. Twice over we have a parable about two sons, and there is a good deal of resemblance between the two sets of brothers. The elder brother in Luke xv. reminds us somewhat, in character, of the one who said "I go, and went not;" while the prodigal had indeed rebelled against his father, and had said, "I will not," but afterward repented. Twice over, also, there are brought before us two debtors.

CHAPTER V

THE SETTING OF THE PARABLES

To study the parables apart from the setting would be to miss very much of their meaning and their beauty, but in order to gather all we can from the position in which they are found in the Gospel narratives, we must take up this part of our study in several different ways. We must mark the events which preceded and followed the several parables, the conversations of which they formed a part, the questions and cavillings to which they were answers, and the actions of which they were the explanations. This might be called their *historic* setting. Then again we must carefully note their position in the inspired record. It is not by accident that some appear in one Gospel and are omitted from others, for on closer examination it will generally be seen that their record is in keeping with the character of the Gospel in which they appear. "A harmony of the Gospels" is very useful in comparing the records, but is never altogether satisfactory ; for the incidents must often be taken entirely out of their places in order to make them appear opposite the accounts of the same events in the other Gospels. The Evangelists were instructed by the Holy Spirit not only *what* to record, but *when* to record it, and all attempts to " harmonise," produce discords if we forget this. One Evangelist may be giving a chronological report, whilst another tells of the same conversation in connection with some other incident. We should have lost a great deal if the four Evangelists had combined and produced one book between them.

This aspect of the placing of the parables, which we may call the *inspired* setting, is full of interest.

With regard to the events which called forth the parables :—

I. Several of them were spoken in answer to *questions*.

1. The Pharisees questioned His conduct, "Why eateth your Master with publicans and sinners?" (Matt. ix. 11), but He showed that He chose His company according to those who needed Him most, and answered by the little parable, "They that be whole need not a physician, but they that are sick."

It is interesting to note that this is followed by the quotation from Hos. vi. 6, "I will have mercy, and not sacrifice." If we turn to the prophecy we find that these words are preceded by a reference to the sickness and wounds of Israel (Hos. v. 13), "When Ephraim saw his sickness, and Judah saw his wound, then went Ephraim to the Assyrian, and sent to king Jareb,[1] yet could he not heal you, nor cure you of your wound." In chap. vi. 1, the prophet continues, "Come, and let us return unto the Lord; for He hath torn, and He will heal us; He hath smitten, and He will bind us up." How appropriate then the quotation from the same passage after the words in the Gospel, "They that be whole need not a physician, but they that are sick."

2. The disciples of John questioned the demeanour of His disciples, "Why do we and the Pharisees fast oft, but Thy disciples fast not?" (Matt. ix. 14). He explained that there was no need of fasting when they

---

[1] Thought by some to be the name of Sargon before he usurped the crown of Shalmaneser. It was Sargon who captured Samaria, and on his seizing the throne of Assyria it was very likely that the besieged Samaria, and Judah also, would send an embassage.

had His presence, and He illustrated this by comparing Himself to the bridegroom. "Can the children of the bridechamber mourn, as long as the bridegroom is with them?" This was in reference also to John's own words. He had said, "He that hath the bride is the bridegroom, but the friend of the bridegroom, which standeth and heareth Him, rejoiceth greatly because of the bridegroom's voice: this my joy therefore is fulfilled."

Fasting and rejoicing could not go together, and He proved it to them by John's own words. Then he added the short parable about the folly of adding new cloth to an old garment, or putting new wine into old bottles. The fasts they were observing were part of the Jewish system, but the need of the old ceremonials and types had passed away when He to whom they pointed had come. To fast when there was cause for nothing but joy was equally foolish.

3. Then there was the third question about eating and drinking. The Pharisees found fault with the conduct of the disciples in eating with unwashen hands (Matt. xv. 2). He replied by the parable, which the disciples did not at first understand, about that which really defiles a man. In answer to Peter's question, He explained that it is not the food that is taken *into* the mouth, but the words that come *out* of the mouth which make a man unclean.

4. This greatly offended the Pharisees, and the disciples asked the Lord if He knew that it had done so. He replied by the two parables about plants which His Father had not planted, and the blind leaders of the blind, the first to be rooted up, the others to fall ignominiously with those they had misled.

5. A certain lawyer stood up and tempted him, saying, "Master, what shall I do to inherit eternal life?" Then followed the question from the Lord Jesus as to what was written in the law, and the

lawyer's comprehensive and true answer, to which He replied, "Thou hast answered right, this do, and thou shalt live." Convicted by the very words he had himself spoken, and by the Lord's answer, the lawyer wished to justify himself. In order to change the subject he asked a further question, "Who is my neighbour?" The parable of the good Samaritan taught him that a man's neighbour was the one who needed his help; and in another aspect it gave a reply to the other question, "What shall I do?" What could the man do who had fallen among thieves? He was dependent entirely upon the help of another.

"Who is my neighbour?" Not only is it the one who needs our help, but in Exod. xii. 4, there is another thought in connection with the keeping of the Passover. "If the household be too little for the lamb, let him and his neighbour next unto his house take it according to the number of the souls." Our neighbour is the one with whom we may share the Lamb. We have neighbours on both sides, those who are saved, those who are unsaved, those to whom we can offer succour, those with whom we can hold fellowship. In the fifteenth of Luke we have neighbours mentioned again, they were those who could rejoice over the lost one that had been found. We are called to be "a people near unto Him," His neighbours, and thus bidden to rejoice with the good Shepherd.

6. The parable of the wicked husbandmen immediately[1] followed the question of the chief priests and scribes and elders, "Tell us by what authority doest Thou these things? or who is He that gave Thee this authority?" First He silenced them by His question as to John's baptism, and when they said they could not tell whence it was, He replied, "Neither tell I you

---

[1] See Mark xi. and xii.; Luke xx. In Matt. xxi. the parable of the two :sons comes between.

by what authority I do these things." But though He would not answer them, He turned to the *people* (Luke xx. 9), and spoke that wonderful parable in which He clearly showed who it was that had given Him authority. He was the beloved Son of the Lord of the Vineyard, and He came to the husbandmen with the full authority of His Father. The previous day He had cursed the fig-tree on which He had found nothing but leaves, and that morning as they passed it again on the way from Bethany to Jerusalem the disciples marvelled to see that it had withered away. The fig-tree that bore no fruit for Him was henceforth to bear fruit for no man (Mark xi. 14) ; the husband-men who would not render the fruit of the vineyard to their lord would henceforth have the vineyard taken away from them. The miracle demonstrated what the parable foretold. There is deep significance in the fact that this parable was spoken just after the crowds had been crying, " Hosanna." Though they said, " Blessed is He that cometh in the name of the Lord," they were not willing to submit to His claims, and He knew and foretold that they would soon cry, " Crucify Him." Then again we read that they had greeted Him, and rightly so, as the son of David ; in the parable He claimed to be of far higher parentage than this.

In all three Gospels we gather that the chief priests and Pharisees were very angry, for they perceived that He had spoken the parable against them, and after taking counsel how they might entangle Him in His talk, they sent spies to ask Him about the tribute money.[1]

His answer, " Render to Cæsar the things that are Cæsar's, and to God the things that are God's," must be taken in connection with the parable. He had just been showing them that like the wicked husbandmen

---

[1] Here again Matthew interposes another parable also teaching the rejection of Israel.

they had refused to render to God the things that were God's.

7. There were two parables spoken in answer to Peter's questions.[1] When he asked, " How oft shall my brother sin against me, and I forgive him ? " the parable of the debtors showed that the free forgiveness he had himself received must be the incentive to his forgiveness of his brother. If he forgave him seventy times seven offences the amount would still be far less than he had himself been forgiven. The forgiveness must not be grudging but " from your hearts," for this is how God forgives us, and who can express the love in His heart making Him long to forgive.

8. The other question was asked by Peter after our Lord's conversation with the rich young man. The latter had made the same inquiry as the lawyer, but from very different motives. " What good thing shall I do that I may have eternal life ? " The one desired to tempt the Lord Jesus, the other was in real earnest, and came running eagerly with his question, but walked sorrowfully away with his answer.

In this case the Lord Himself enumerates the commandments, omitting the last, " Thou shalt not covet," which the young man could not truly say he had kept. The Lord soon showed him that he had not loved his neighbour as himself, for otherwise he would not have failed to meet the test commandment, " If thou wilt be perfect, go sell that thou hast." The young man was like the apostle Paul, " touching the righteousness which is in the law blameless," but convicted by the one commandment that touched the heart. It was the law, " Thou shalt not covet," which " slew " Paul. This is " the commandment " to which he refers so often in Rom. vii. 7–13. " When the commandment came, sin revived, and I died," and so it was with this rich young

[1] See Appendix IV.   " Peter and the Parables."

man. The disciples did not understand the Lord's
answer to him. They seem to have thought that
salvation was to be a reward for giving up all, and did
not see that the Lord had been showing the rich man
how impossible it was to earn it by law-keeping.
Peter thinks that as riches are not the way into the
kingdom, poverty may be, and asks the question,
" Behold, we have forsaken all and followed Thee,
what shall we have therefore ? " The sacrifice was
not despised, as was shown by the answer. The
apostles were to have great honour bestowed upon
them ; they were by-and-by to sit on twelve thrones
judging the twelve tribes of Israel.

But lest there should be any mistake as to whether
eternal life is by desert or by gift, the Lord gives the
parable of the labourers in the vineyard. The question asked by the rich young man and by the lawyer
was, " What shall I do to *inherit ?* " None but heirs
can inherit, and as the Lord Jesus Christ is Himself
heir of all things, none can become inheritors except
in Him. If it is to be a question of what we have
earned the apostle Paul makes it very clear what our
wages would be, " The wages of sin is death, but the
gift of God is eternal life, through Jesus Christ our
Lord ; " through Him we become heirs of God, joint-
heirs with Himself.

9. " Lord, are there few that be saved ? " was the
question put to the Lord by one of the multitude as
" He went through the cities and villages teaching
and journeying toward Jerusalem " (Luke xiii. 23).
His reply was the double parable about striving to
enter. The first half must not be taken as the answer
to the inquiry without the second.

" The Lord answers with a home thrust at the
questioner himself. ' Strive to enter in at the strait
gate,' to which He adds also that many would seek to
enter in and would not be able. But He bases this

upon something else than the straitness of the gate ; the difficulty, or rather the impossibility, of entrance is only found when once the Master of the house is risen up, and has shut to the door. It was a shut gate that was to be dreaded, not a strait one." [1]

It does not say that any who earnestly endeavour to enter at the strait gate will be unable to do so. The passage can only be made to read thus by stopping in the middle and leaving out the reference to the shut door. For want of seeing this it has been said that this passage ought not to be used as a warning now. The man probably made the inquiry, "Are there few that be saved ?" from mere curiosity, and, as may be seen from the context, the Lord replied not only to him but to the others who were rejecting His message. He was warning them that the question that concerned each one was their personal position, and that they must see to it that they themselves were not left outside. If they did not exchange their careless indifference for real earnestness there was very great fear that it would be so. It is quite true that the way of salvation is very simple and easy, but it is also true that there must be deep heart exercise. There is nothing contradictory in the two aspects. Converts from Judaism might have found the gate harder to enter than we who live in days of gospel privilege, the position in the kingdom may be different, but the principle is just the same.

II. Three parables were spoken after certain *requests* had been made.

1. The first was that of the disciples : "Lord, teach us to pray" (Luke xi. 1). After giving the model prayer He illustrated His lesson by the beautiful parable of the three friends. (See pp. 270, 271.)

2. The parable of the rich man and his barns was the outcome of a request from one of the company :

---

[1] " The Numerical Bible."   F. W. Grant.

" Master, speak to my brother, that he divide the inheritance with me." The Lord replied, " Man, who made Me a judge or a divider over you ? " (Luke xii. 13, 14). These words were almost the same as those used to Moses by one of the Hebrews whose quarrel he tried to settle. As Stephen tells us, Moses "supposed his brethren would have understood how that God by his hand would deliver them, but they understood not." If the Lord Jesus had tried to "set them at one again" as Moses did, He would have met with the same treatment. The people in both cases were not yet ready to receive their deliverer, who must consequently leave them for many days. The parable was to teach them to "beware of covetousness, for a man's life consisteth not in the abundance of the things which he possesseth." After telling of the foolish rich man who determined to build larger barns in which to bestow all his fruits and all his goods, the Lord went on to teach by contrast the better way. "Consider the ravens : for they neither sow nor reap ; which neither have storehouse nor barn. . . . Consider the lilies . . . they toil not, they spin not." The rich man thought to have in his barns "goods laid up for many years," how different from the ravens ! The rich man had toiled hard, now he thought to take his ease, but the lilies toil not at all, and yet the ravens are well fed and the lilies are well clad. " How much more are ye better than the fowls ? " and we may add, how much more are ye better than the lilies ? One day to be arrayed in more beautiful apparel than Solomon in all his glory, and meanwhile to be provided with necessary food and raiment. In verse 33 He shows that the only storehouse we have is "in the heavens."

3. The other parable which followed a request was His allusion to the corn of wheat, uttered immediately after certain Greeks came to Philip and

"desired him, saying, Sir, we would see Jesus." The first time Philip is mentioned in the Gospel, after having been found by the Lord, he is telling Nathaniel "Come and see," and here he is selected by these Gentile proselytes to bring them to the Master. Perhaps he had become known as one who loved to introduce others to Him; it may be that he often invited others to "Come and see."

When the Lord heard the request His thoughts passed at once to the harvest which His death would produce. These Greeks were the earnest of the "much fruit" that would be reaped not from Israel only, but from the whole world. When the men of Samaria believed on Him, His eyes saw the fields "white already to harvest," a present harvest, but here He is looking forward to the day of His glory. "The hour is come that the Son of Man should be glorified. Verily, verily, I say unto you, except a corn of wheat fall into the ground and die, it abideth alone, but if it die, it bringeth forth much fruit." Unless we see that this was His answer to the request of these foreigners, we shall miss much of its meaning. It has been well said that in these verses "all the materials of the kingdom in which He is to be glorified now pass before the Lord. The people are moved as with the joy of the feast of Tabernacles,[1] and take branches of palm trees and gladden their king. The nations, as it were, come up to keep the feast, glory shines for a moment on the land of the living. Here was Lazarus raised from the dead, the city receiving her king, and the nations worshipping."[2]

III. The parable of the strong man was spoken in answer to the *accusation* that the Lord cast out devils through the power of the devil (Matt. xii. 24), and as we have seen (page 25), it is one of those in which the Lord claims to be very God.

---

[1] See Zech. xiv. 16-21.   [2] J. G. Bellett.

IV. The *action* of the chief priests and Pharisees brought forth the teaching contained in the tenth of John, for the key is to be found in the story, in the preceding chapter, of the man born blind, whose eyes had been opened. We read at the close that the Jews " cast him out." This was taken up by the Lord, and the same word is used in John x., where, speaking of His own sheep, He said that the Shepherd goeth before them, and leadeth them out. The *casting out* from the fold of Judaism was the *leading* forth of the good Shepherd. (See pp. 157–159.)

V. The parable in Luke xv. was in answer to the *murmuring* of the Pharisees. " This man receiveth sinners, and eateth with them." [1] The last clause in Luke xiv. should not be separated from the following chapter. " He that hath ears to hear let him hear. Then drew near unto Him all the publicans and sinners for to hear Him." The Pharisees and scribes were not only blind, but deaf. They did not want to hear Him themselves, and yet they did not desire sinners to do so. We have seen how they asked a question on this same subject, but still they murmured, so the beautiful threefold parable was the answer.

The great importance of studying the parables with their setting is strikingly exemplified in this case. Many difficulties have been introduced into the fifteenth of Luke through omitting to use the very simple key which hangs at the door of the chapter. It has been said that the lost sheep and the lost son cannot represent unsaved ones, that we must not use these beautiful stories as gospel messages because

[1] Note the three things said of our Lord in connection with publicans and sinners : a beautiful progress, and a gracious increase of condescension, "A *friend* of publicans and sinners" (Luke vii. 34); "This man *receiveth* sinners, and *eateth* with them " (xv. 2); " Gone to be *guest* with a man that is a sinner " (and a publican) (Luke xix. 7). All gloriously true, His reproach is His glory.

of what is *not* in the story. One writer points out that there is no faith, no redemption, no atonement, no redeemer, no blood shedding, &c. This is very much like a person to whom is shown a sketch of a Swiss river, objecting that it cannot represent a place in Switzerland because it does not include Mont Blanc, the Wetterhorn, the Jungfrau, the Lake of Geneva, or Lucerne. There was no place for them in the picture, as it was not meant to be a map.

The object of the chapter is not so much to show *how* men are saved, but *why* they are saved. The scope of the fifteenth of Luke is exactly as large and comprehensive as the word *sinner*. The Pharisees murmured that He received sinners, He gloried in the fact, and showed that He did much more, and that the whole Godhead was interested in seeking them (see page 55). All may be included in the word sinners. Those to whom the parable had reference in the first instance were the most needy of Israel's sons and daughters. Their salvation could only be accomplished through the same means as ours is now. The finding of the lost sheep meant much more than bringing it to the fold of Judaism, but already they had begun to show the first sign that the work of the good Shepherd had commenced. They "drew near unto Him . . . for to hear Him," and they would never have done this if He had not been drawing near to them, and looking for them. Not only is the hearing ear a mark of His sheep, it is the opened ear that brings us into the flock.[1] "Other sheep I have which are not of this fold, them also I must bring, and they shall hear My voice." He counts them His sheep before they have been brought, and

---

[1] It is quite true that there is a prior relationship suggested in each of the three pictures, but when does the relationship commence? We date it, perhaps, from our passing from death unto life, but in God's sight it begins long before this.

thus He makes intercession, " Neither pray I for these alone, but for them also which shall believe on Me through their word." Hearing the Word, they are numbered amongst His own. So too with those who are sons, " As many as received Him, to them gave He power to become the sons of God, even to them that believe on His name." It is not their love to Him that brings them into the family, but His love to them.

It is quite true that the complete gospel is not contained in the fifteenth of Luke, but it is also true that the gospel would not be complete without it. It is only in the gospel that the Lord's heart of love is revealed. There was nothing like this under the law, which provided stripes and stones for the prodigal (see page 191), and never killed the fatted calf for him. To bring forth the best robe, the shoes for the feet, and the ring for the hand, this is "what the law could not do." It never clothes, but strips the sinner naked in God's sight ; it never feeds, but shows the sinner's hunger ; it never gives the kiss of reconciliation, but pronounces the curse of condemnation.

The setting of the parable, for it is one, not three, proves, therefore, that the object for which the Lord gave it was to illustrate, by the three pictures, the painful toil, the diligent search, and yearning desire with which He finds the lost.

We need not be afraid of applying the chapter to all sorts and conditions of sinners, but let us be very careful of asserting that it does *not* apply to any. Much of the unnecessary controversy on the parables arises from saying what the parables do *not* contain.

VI. Whilst the fifteenth of Luke was the response to the murmuring of the Pharisees, in the next chapter we see that they went a step further, and *derided* Him ; and as a result the terrible picture is given of the rich man in Hades. " Ye are they which justify yourselves before men, but God knoweth your hearts, for that which is highly esteemed among men is abomination in the sight of God."

Dives was highly esteemed among men, but his life was an abomination to God. This is a strong word, and we should not have wondered at it being used about the prodigal of the preceding chapter, but no, it applies to the wealthy man courted by all, gorgeously apparelled, and living in luxury.

Whatever dispensational aspect we may see in this parable it is a realistic picture of the disembodied state before the resurrection, for Dives prayed that one might rise. It does not depict the final hell fire of Gehenna into which are cast soul and body, reunited at the resurrection of condemnation (Matt. v. 29–30), but the condition of the departed immediately after death and burial.

VII. Two of our Lord's parables were spoken at *feasts*. That of the two debtors (Luke vii. 36–50) was in the house of Simon the Pharisee. The Lord had just been repeating the scornful epithet given by the Pharisees that He was "a friend of publicans and sinners," but when Simon the Pharisee desired Him that He would eat with him, He went into the Pharisee's house and sat down to meat, as much as to say, " I am willing to eat with you too if you need Me." Did He ever refuse the invitation of one who desired His company ? And there He was found by the woman who was a sinner.

Perhaps she had heard the taunt of the Pharisees as it was acknowledged and gloried in by the Saviour. It may be that she was encouraged by this to approach with her alabaster box of ointment. In the parable which followed, the Lord answered the unspoken thought in Simon's heart, and showed that He was the friend of sinners, because they needed His much forgiveness. We have noticed parables that were replies to questions, requests, remarks, but this one answered *a thought*. Simon said in his heart that if He had known what she was, He would not have allowed her to touch Him. The Lord replied by showing that He knew far more than this, for He read what was in Simon's heart as well.

The other which was spoken at a feast was that of the great supper. In Luke xiv. we read, " He put forth a parable to those which were bidden, when He marked how they chose out the chief rooms." He first instructed them as to the way to select places at a feast, and then as to the manner of choosing the guests. "And when one of them that sat at meat with Him heard these things, he said unto Him, Blessed is he that shall eat bread in the kingdom of God." Then follows the parable of the great supper, illustrating His own teaching as to the choice of guests, showing that God Himself brings to His table the very ones He has been telling them to invite, "When thou makest a feast, call the poor, the maimed, the lame, the blind ; " and secondly, answering the exclamation of the one who sat at meat with Him as to the blessedness of those called to the heavenly feast.

What the man said was indeed true, they are blessed, but men do not act as if they believed it. When the invitation is given they all with one consent began to make excuse.

VIII. We also find that the *purpose* for which parables were spoken is given in several cases. The last mentioned, the parable of the great supper, is one of these.

In Luke xviii. 1, we read, " He spake a parable (the unjust judge) unto them to this end, that men ought always to pray, and not to faint." Then again in verse 9, " He spake this parable (the Pharisee and the publican) unto certain which trusted in themselves that they were righteous, and despised others," and in chap. xix. a double reason is given for the parable of the pounds. " He added and spake a parable, because He was nigh to Jerusalem, and because they thought that the kingdom of God should immediately appear." Jerusalem, which was before them, was the guilty city which said, " We will not have this man to reign over us." [1]

The *second aspect* of the setting of the parables, that of their place in the different gospels, would require several volumes. Many such have been written dwelling on the characteristics of the Evangelists.[2]

There is only space to call attention to the importance of this aspect of the subject, which gives fresh proof of the inspiration of the Word. We may call it the *inspired setting* of the parables.

The parables in *Matthew* and the way in which they are recorded are suited to the Messianic character of the book, they are the parables of the King and the kingdom. Those in *Mark* are equally suited to the revelation which is there given to us of the Lord Jesus as Servant of Jehovah.

" In Mark the Lord is rather doing than teaching, for doing is the humbler work. We have few parables and no lengthened discourses. . . . There is one parable which is found only here, the seed that grew secretly, in chapter iv. It occupies the same place in Mark that the parable of the wheat and tares does in Matthew, viz., following the parable of the sower ; in this, small as it is, the characteristic of Mark's Gospel is still preserved.

" The parable of the wheat and the tares gives us a sight of the Lord in the place of authority, for He has

---

[1] There is an interesting fact of history which has often been pointed out in connection with this parable. (See Appendix VIII.)

[2] *e.g.* " The Evangelists," by J. G. Bellett ; " The Numerical Bible," by F. W. Grant ; " Israel my Glory," by Rev. John Wilkinson ; works on the separate Gospels, by C. E. Stuart ; and many others.

both servants and angels at command, and He orders the harvest as He pleases. The parable of the seed that grew secretly, on the contrary, exhibits Him in the place of service and not of authority, for it is He Himself who at first is the sower and at the end the reaper." [1]

The parables in *Luke* are much more general in character. Those in which the practical teaching seems most marked are principally to be found in that Gospel. This is specially noticeable in connection with the parables which teach lessons about prayer, for it is the Gospel of prayer and praise, and it is therefore appropriate that they should be found interwoven with many examples, the same line of teaching running through narrative and parable.

The opening scene represents the people praying without at the time of the evening sacrifice whilst the priest within is offering incense. The closing scene is that which the opening one typified, the disciples "continually in the temple praising and blessing God" (xxiv. 53), the great High Priest having gone within the vail.

Luke tells us much more than any of the other Evangelists about the life of prayer of our great Example, for He is represented not as the King but as the dependent Man. We read of Him praying (1) in the Jordan (iii. 21); (2) in the wilderness (v. 16); (3) on the mountains (vi. 12); (4) after the crowds had left Him (ix. 18); (5) on the Mount of Transfiguration (ix. 28); (6) teaching His disciples (xi. 1), and (7) in the garden (xxii. 41–44). The model prayer is given in Luke xi. 2–4, followed by the threefold precept. Then we have many instances of prayers which are also recorded by the other Evangelists; those which were answered by miracles of healing; the terrible prayer of the Gadarenes that He would

---

[1] "The Evangelists."   J. G. Bellett.

depart from them (viii. 37), and the other prayer offered at the same time by the healed demoniac that he might be with Him; the former answered by the Lord, and the latter, which seemed likely to be well-pleasing to Him, denied. The prayer of the dying robber is alone recorded in Luke, and the only instance of the Lord being thanked is to be found in this Gospel. The Samaritan was not merely the only one of the ten who thanked Him, but it is the solitary case where it is mentioned that any one *thanked* Him. We hear of others worshipping, and there must, we know, have been gratitude, but it is sadly suggestive of man's unthankfulness that once only in all the Gospels should it be recorded. As Christopher Ness (1678 A.D.) quaintly put it, "God hath but the tenth of praises, and it is ten to one whether you practise His praise."

It is thus appropriate that so many of the parables about prayer should be found in this Gospel (see pp. 269–274), forming with examples, exhortations, incidents, and illustrations one continuous chain of teaching.

In the same way we may follow throughout a Gospel some word, expression, or thought. As an example, take for instance in the Gospel of Luke the words "far off" or "near," or others which express the thought of distance. We have first a reference to a type in the mention of the Queen of Sheba who "came from the utmost parts of the earth" or "a far country" to hear the wisdom of Solomon (Luke xi. 31 ; 1 Kings viii. 41 ; x. 1). The rebel king when "yet a great way off" from the mighty king, sends an embassage (chap. xiv. 32); the publicans and sinners draw "near unto Him" (chap. xv. 1) ; the prodigal goes deliberately into the "far country" (verse 13); the father when he is "yet a great way off" runs to meet him (verse 20) ; the rich man, too late, finds himself "afar off" in Hades (chap. xvi. 23); the lepers stand "afar off" because of their leprosy (chap. xvii. 12); the publican stands "afar off" because of his sin (chap. xviii. 13). Then there follow two parables which speak of the Lord Himself being afar off. The nobleman goes "into a far country, to receive for himself a kingdom, and to return" (chap. xix. 12); the owner of the vineyard leaves it "for a long time" and goes "into a far country" (chap. xx. 9). Then there are two instances of actual distance from the Lord, in both cases the literal emblematic of the spiritual. "Peter followed afar off" because his faith and love had grown dim (chap. xxii. 54); and at the cross "all His acquaintance and the women . . . stood afar off" (chap. xxiii. 49) because they could not draw near (see Psa. xxxviii. 11; lxxxviii. 8, 18); and at the close of the Gospel we have the sweet words, "Jesus Himself drew *near* and went with them" (chap. xxiv. 15).

No more "afar off," reconciled ones, forgiven ones, healed ones, restored ones have His presence with them; and though to the natural man He seems in a far country, His own recognise that He is near. "The Lord is at hand."

This brief outline is but a suggestion to fellow-students of a method by which the parables may be viewed in connection with other portions of the Gospel in which they are recorded.

There are in the repeated parables several characteristic touches in which the special features of each Gospel are preserved—only a word or two of variation, but sufficient to add a stroke to the picture, always consistent with the Gospel in which it appears. For instance, in the reference to the budding fig-tree, Luke adds "and all the trees." Matthew is speaking of the fig-tree, Israel or Judah, but Luke with a larger scope refers to others also. Does it not suggest that when the fig-tree begins to bud the other trees will show signs of fresh life? The olive and the vine will also be more productive, there will be more witnessing for God and more fruit. While we see signs of revival in Israel is there not also increased fruitfulness in the branches of the vine (John xv.) and the olive (Romans xi.) in which Gentiles also are included? We do see signs of the budding of the fig-tree, but the Church has also been revived in many ways during the past century, both as to fruit-bearing to God and witness for Him. All this may point to the fact that His coming draweth nigh.

It is interesting to note the words in Matthew at the close of the parable of the unclean spirit, "So shall it be also unto this wicked generation," thus applying it to the apostate nation. These words do not appear in other accounts. Then in Matthew v. the light of the candle is linked with the light of the city. It is a city set on a hill which cannot be hid, and again there is an evident application to Israel which is omitted in Luke. There the light of the eye and the light of the candle are mentioned. But in speaking of the former, Luke adds a characteristic phrase not in Matthew. The candle is to give light not merely to " all that are in the house," as in Matthew v., but to all who *enter* in, all the strangers or friends who may come to the house, the visitors who may call. This was a truth which Israel never learnt, they would have preferred to have kept the light to themselves. Solomon understood that it was God's purpose for them to shine for the strangers that might come from a far country. He acted thus when the Queen of Sheba visited him. The candle shone for her when she entered the king's house. Hezekiah failed in this respect, for when the messengers came from Merodach Baladan, instead of witnessing for Jehovah, he boasted of his wealth, and as the Assyrian documents inform us, made an alliance with him to revolt against Sargon.

The two parables about debtors are appropriately recorded, the one in the Jewish gospel which speaks of the law of the kingdom requiring forgiveness of others before forgiveness can be enjoyed, and the other in Luke which speaks of grace.

This is never so clearly revealed in Matthew, and it is, therefore, not surprising that the account is to be found in Luke of the master who freely forgave his debtors when they had nothing to pay.

Then again in the interpretation of the parable of the sower, the explanation of the seed in each case suits the Gospel in which it is found. In Matthew it is the Word of the kingdom, in Mark the Word, and in Luke the Word of God.

There is a striking difference between the accounts of the Lord's reference to the uselessness of patching an old garment. In Matt. ix. 16, no mention is made of the new garment, "No man putteth a piece of new cloth unto an old garment," but in Luke v. 36, we read, "No man putteth a piece of a new garment upon an old." It is appropriate that in the former, prominence should be given to the impossibility of patching the old garment, the Jewish dispensation that was passing away ; while in the latter there is the additional thought that the new garment would be spoiled if a piece were taken from it.

It has often been pointed out that there is progression in the *order* of the parables. This is specially noticeable in the Matthew series. We cannot imagine the order being reversed, for those naturally come last which refer to last events, and the revelation is more clear as the Gospel nears its close.

CHAPTER VI

THE TRINITY IN THE PARABLES

ALL the three Persons of the Godhead were deeply interested in the giving of the parables, and their preservation for us. They were not merely the words of the Man, Christ Jesus, a great Teacher, and a God-sent Prophet. They were, like all that He said, the words of His Father given Him to speak, for He said, "Whatsoever I speak, therefore, even as the Father said unto Me, so I speak" (John xii. 50). He taught also "through the Holy Ghost," and it was the Spirit, who, as the Lord promised His disciples, brought all things to their remembrance so that they could record them in the Gospels.

The great mystery of the Trinity had been hinted at in the Old Testament in such passages as Isaiah xi. 1, 2 ; xlii. 1 ; xlviii. 16 ; lxi. 1, but it was not clearly revealed until in the upper room the Lord taught His disciples about the coming of the other Comforter, nor was it understood by them until the Spirit had descended upon them at Pentecost.

In the light of this fuller revelation we can see suggestions of the Trinity in the parables, for reference is made to all three Persons of the Godhead. Especially is this the case, as so often pointed out, in the fifteenth chapter of Luke. "This man," murmured the Pharisees in derision, "receiveth (or as it is in the R.V., waiteth for) sinners, and eateth with them." He shows that not only does He receive and wait for them, but that Father, Son, and Holy Spirit are all engaged in the work of seeking and welcoming the lost; the Son as the Good Shepherd, the Holy Spirit through the agency of the Church, and the Father Himself.

It is probable that in the two parables of the marriage-feast, and the great supper, we have again all the three Persons of the Trinity, represented by the king, the king's son, and the servant, who in the latter parable brings in the guests from the streets and lanes of the city, or compels them to come in from the highways and hedges. They are specially described in Luke as those who could not come alone, the maimed, the halt, and the blind, for the lame must be carried and the blind led. We do not find this in Matthew, where servants are sent out instead of the one servant. None but the Holy Spirit can really "compel" and "bring in," and none but He can say to the Master, "Lord, it is done as Thou hast commanded, and yet there is room." The parable in Luke, therefore, seems to refer specially to the Spirit's work; and the two pictures placed side by side supplement one another. In Matthew, where the plural is used, "the servants" are told to go into the highways, and *bid* as many as they shall find, and that is all that the servants can do. When the work of the one servant is described as in Luke, no sifting is required, for no one has slipped in without a wedding garment or banqueting robe, but the servants are not able to judge, they can only gather together both good and bad as they have been commanded.

The first group of parables in Luke xv. shows, therefore, the attitude of the three Persons of the Trinity towards that which is lost, while the two parables of the marriage-feast, and the great supper, represent their plan of filling the king's house with guests. The Father prepares the feast for the honour of Himself and His Son, and the Holy Spirit prepares the guests.

The Father and Son.—In the same way we may link together three passages where reference is made to the first two Persons of the Trinity.   It is easy to compare them, for the symbolism is the same in each; they all tell us about a vineyard, and a vine or fig-tree.   They are these, the parables of the wicked husbandmen, and the barren fig-tree, and the description of the true vine in John xv.   In the first the householder sends servants to the vineyard, but after they have failed in their mission, and have been shamefully handled and even killed, " having yet one son, his well-beloved, he sent him also last unto them, saying, They will reverence my son."

The Father and the Son are evidently also referred to in Luke xiii. as conversing about the fig-tree, when the owner of the vineyard says to the dresser, " Behold, these three years I come seeking fruit on this fig-tree and find none ; cut it down, why cumbereth it the ground ? "   And the dresser of the fig-tree pleads that another opportunity may be given to it.

In John xv. we again have the Father and the Son brought before us as interested in the fruit-bearing of a tree, for our Lord says, " I am the true vine, and My Father is the Husbandman."

There is one point common to these three pictures, viz., the Father is represented in each as looking for fruit.   In the parable of the husbandmen He sends His servants to the keepers of the vineyard that He may receive the fruit thereof, but it is true as of old, " Israel is an empty vine, he bringeth forth fruit unto himself," and therefore in God's sight there was no fruit at all.   The second parable reveals Him waiting patiently for three years for fruit from the fig-tree, and again He is disappointed.

In the third passage the Lord tells us that He is the Husbandman, and He says, " Herein is My Father glorified that ye bear much fruit."   Is He to be again disappointed by those over whom He watches with such patient care ?

We have in these three pictures different aspects of the attitude and work of our Lord Jesus Christ. In the first He is represented as bearing His Father's message to the keepers of the vineyard ; in the second He is Himself the keeper, and does all that is possible for the fig-tree in order to promote fruitfulness, and when it fails He pleads that it may have another opportunity ; but in the third He is Himself the vine, and the source of all fruit-bearing.

Prominence is given in the parable of the wicked husbandmen to this aspect of the sending of the Son. We know from other parts of Scripture that there were other reasons for His coming, but here the object was that the Father might demand the fruit from His vineyard. His appearance was a test of their loyalty. "They will reverence My Son." And the way in which He is treated is still the great test. The husbandmen were not judged by the amount of fruit that the vineyard yielded under their care, for what mattered it if the branches were laden with grapes if they refused to give the fruit to Him, and if His Son were murdered by them ? Have we not here an answer to the false theology which teaches that men will be judged by their lives, and not by their creeds ? Fruitful vines with nothing for Him are but empty vines in His sight. The Father, the Son, and the Holy Ghost are all represented as labouring to promote fruitfulness. The fruitful plants are plants " which My heavenly Father hath . . . planted." The Father Himself is the Husbandman in John xv. The Lord Jesus is the keeper of the fig-tree in Luke ; and in the Epistles we learn that any fruit we produce for God is the " fruit of the Spirit."

It is very beautiful to trace throughout the Bible the conversations between the Father and Son to which we are permitted to listen. Only a few sentences reach us, but they are full of teaching for the listening ear. This one in the parable of the barren fig-tree is an example.

In the very first chapter of Genesis we have a suggestion of a conversation, "Let us make man in our image." Then, after the Fall, there is a broken sentence, for we are only permitted to hear the beginning of it : " Behold the man is become as one of us, to know good and evil ; and now lest he put forth his hand, and take also of the tree of life and eat and live for ever . . ." Here the record breaks off abruptly, but the ear of faith can almost catch the wonderful conversation that must have followed. The Fall had made man "as one *of*" them, but the glorious remedy placed him in a far higher position, as unfolded in the seventeenth of John, where we are allowed to hear the outpouring of the heart of our Lord to His Father. "That they may be one *in* us" was now His prayer. To that interrupted sentence in Gen. iii. may we not add the great plan of salvation ? "Yet doth He devise means that His banished be not expelled from Him." But until this plan had been worked out man must be kept from the tree of life, for to live for ever in his sin would have been a curse instead of a blessing ; and so where the sentence breaks off we read that the cherubim were placed at the east of the garden. When the banished ones have been brought home they will be welcomed once more to the tree of life, as we see in Rev. xxii. 2.

In this short parable of the fig-tree, we are also permitted to hear part of a dialogue,[1] and the Lord reveals Himself in the character of Intercessor. We know that the owner of the vineyard was not unwilling to spare the tree, nor to give it another opportunity of fruit-

[1] Another beautiful dialogue is ecorded in Isaiah xlix., to which reference is made in Chap. X., pp. 100–102.

bearing. The heart of the Father is not less loving than that of the Son, for there is always perfect harmony of thought between them. The Son who is the express image of His Person, is also the expression of the Father's heart, the Word that voices His thoughts towards Israel, or towards the world, or towards His people now. There is a tendency in some theological teaching to represent the Lord Jesus as full of tenderness and pity, pleading with a God full of wrath, and at last winning Him over and turning away His anger. The Bible refutes this. Both are equally angry at sin, both are alike full of love to the sinner. Like Abraham and Isaac on the Mount of Moriah, " They went both of them together." " God so loved " that He sent ; the Son so loved that He came.

The Father and the Son are both concerned in the safety of the sheep. This we learn from two passages, not indeed in the parables themselves, but in our Lord's comment upon them. In Matt. xviii., after speaking of the man who having a hundred sheep goeth into the mountains and seeketh one which is lost, He says, " Even so it is not the will of your Father which is in heaven, that one of these little ones should perish." In John x. He says, " I give unto My sheep eternal life ; and they shall never perish, neither shall any pluck them out of My hand. My Father, which gave them Me, is greater than all ; and no man is able to pluck them out of My Father's hand. I and My Father are one." One in this as in everything else, and thus the sheep are perfectly safe. The Father who gives them also holds them, and they are doubly secure, because of the will of the Father, and the work of the Son.

It is most instructive to notice the place given to the Father in all these parables, and to study in them His character and purposes. In the story of the prodigal son we have a glimpse of His heart, His

yearning love over the wanderer. In the parable of
the wicked husbandmen, the Lord tells us something
of the great love which existed from all eternity
between the Father and Himself.

In the few words that describe the relationship how
much is expressed, "Having one son, His well-beloved,"
all His thoughts, hopes, affections centred in Him.
Then again we notice in the parable of the marriage-
supper that the plan of making the feast comes from
the Father's heart. His delight in His Son moves
Him to celebrate the occasion of His marriage on a
lavish scale, with great festivities, and many guests.
He spares no expense to make the occasion worthy
of such an event.   Again we have a glimpse of His
heart, and of His joy in His Son.

In preaching the gospel from the beautiful story
of this feast, attention is seldom called to this side
of the picture, yet it is very plain that the invitations are sent forth, and the tables spread, not merely
for the enjoyment and satisfying of the guests, but for
the honour of the King and His Son.   The refusal of
His invitation and the excuses made are accordingly
judged as insults to Himself. It is for His own
honour and glory that God hath devised a way of
salvation for sinners. It might be said as of Israel
of old, "Not for your sakes do I this, saith the Lord
God," but "for My Name's sake."   It is wondrous grace
that brings in such guests to the banquet, but it is
for His own Name's sake that His house must be
furnished with guests. By despising the invitation,
and refusing to come, men not only miss the feast but
insult Him who invited them.

At the close of Luke xii. there is a beautiful little
parable from Nature, in which reference is evidently
made to the Second and Third Persons of the Trinity.
The Lord Jesus " said also to the people, When ye see
a cloud rise out of the west, straightway ye say there

cometh a shower, and so it is. And when ye see the
south wind blow, ye say, there will be heat, and it
cometh to pass. Ye hypocrites·! ye can discern the
face of the sky, and of the earth, but how is it that ye
do not discern this time ? "

These things were meant to be much more than
mere weather signs, for "without a parable spake He
not unto them." Both cloud and wind bringing with
them refreshing showers and heat were Old Testament figures of the Lord Himself and the Spirit. The
soft south wind by which He quieteth the earth (Job
xxxvii. 17), and which blowing on the garden causeth
the spices to flow (Song of Sol. iv. 16), is evidently a
type of the Holy Spirit ; and masters in Israel were
familiar with the prophecies of Him under this
emblem. The most important of these is in the
vision of the valley of dry bones, where the wind
and the breath (for which the same word is used) are
constantly mentioned. Ezekiel was told to prophesy,
and say to the wind, "Thus saith the Lord God, Come
from the four winds, O breath, and breathe upon
these slain, that they may live." They were merely
dead bodies until the wind came, although the dry
bones had come together, and had been clothed with
sinews and flesh. The Word of the Lord explained
the vision to Ezekiel, and showed him that it represented the putting of His Spirit into them. It is a
picture of the new birth of the earthly nation, and in
speaking of the necessity of the new birth for an
individual the Lord uses the same simile when He
says to Nicodemus, "The wind bloweth where it
listeth, and thou hearest the sound thereof, but canst
not tell whence it cometh and whither it goeth ; so is
every one that is born of the Spirit."

He speaks also of the cloud and the showers, and
this was another Old Testament symbol with which
the Jews were familiar. The Psalmist had prophesied

of One who should come "like rain upon the mown grass; as showers that water the earth "; and in Prov. xvi. 15, we read, "In the light of the King's countenance is life; and His favour is as a cloud of the latter rain;" but though they had the King Himself in their midst they did not recognise Him, they did not discern "the time " that had been predicted.   He was willing to pour out upon them even then the showers of blessing that had been foretold, and to cause "the shower to come down in his season," but they were not ready for it; and so the time of blessing, when He will give them the early and latter rain, still waits in the future for them.

CHAPTER VII

THE LORD'S INCARNATION AND DEATH

THE parables cover the whole period from the first advent of our Lord Jesus Christ in incarnation, to His second advent in glory. His incarnation is implied; His life, ministry, and rejection are described; and His death is prophesied; but most of the pictures represent the time of His absence or the epoch of His return.

The Incarnation.—The incarnation is implied in four of the parables. In that of the wicked husbandmen the Father is seen sending His well-beloved Son, and the Son leaving the Father's house and coming down with the Father's message. But in order to do this He "made Himself of no reputation, and took upon Him the form of a servant, and was made in the likeness of men." In the parable He merely describes Himself as bearing the Father's message, and in His teaching He constantly referred to this. We have many of the conversations between the Son and the husbandmen in John's gospel where He is pre-eminently the sent One. The word is repeated about forty times. He told them that He had come to do the will of His Father who sent Him (chap. vi. 38), that He sought the glory of Him that sent Him, &c.

There is, however, another side of the picture. "God so loved" that He *sent*, but the Son so loved that He *came;* and while the parable of the husbandmen shows how He came in obedience to His Father's will, we are not left without a picture portraying that it was also in accordance with His own desire.

In the parables of the hidden treasure and the pearl of great price the one who sees their preciousness and has set his heart upon them for "joy thereof" sells all that he has, that, in the first place, he may purchase the field in which the treasure is hidden, and secondly, that he may purchase the pearl. The words of the apostle Paul are a beautiful commentary upon these two parables, "Ye know the grace of our Lord Jesus Christ, that though He was rich, yet for your sakes He became poor."

In the parable of the good Samaritan the incarnation is again implied. The thieves had robbed and stripped the man travelling from Jerusalem to Jericho, and wounded him, leaving him half dead, and he thus represents man's condition since the Fall, helpless and dying. The Priest and Levite pass by on the other side: they can do nothing for him, any more than the law and ceremonies can avail to save a lost sinner. Religion cannot help him : it is a Saviour he needs. "But a certain Samaritan, as he journeyed, came where he was: and when he saw him, he had compassion on him." "*But* a certain Samaritan." It reminds us of the passage in Eph. ii., "*But* God, who is rich in mercy, for His great love wherewith He loved us, even when we were dead in sins, hath quickened us together with Christ ;" and Rom. v. 8, "*But* God commendeth His love toward us, in that, while we were yet sinners, Christ died for us."

At the moment of the man's greatest need the good Samaritan appeared. It was "as he journeyed." He was not going on the downward road to Jericho, the place of the curse, as the others were, but it simply says that he journeyed. What a journey it was that the Lord took ! "He saw that there was no man," He "looked, and there was none to help," but He not only looked—the priest and the Levite had done this—He came where the wounded man was. The Lord had compassion on the sinner in his helpless and hopeless condition, and stooped even to his lowest need. To do this He had to become a man. "Forasmuch then as the children are partakers of flesh and blood, He also Himself likewise took part of the same ; that through death He might destroy him that had the power of death, that is, the devil."

But the parable goes no further, for the good Samaritan in putting the man in his own place had not to give his life for him ; He whom he represents has done even this in order to raise the sinner from the depth of ruin to His own throne.

His Life and Ministry.—In the parable of the fig-tree the three years of Christ's ministry on earth are evidently referred to when the owner says to the dresser of his vineyard : "Behold, these three years I come seeking fruit on this fig-tree, and find none." Israel was God's vineyard over which He had spent so much trouble, as we read in Isaiah : "The vineyard of the Lord of hosts is the house of Israel, and the men of Judah His pleasant plant." He Himself was the dresser of the vineyard. "I the Lord do keep it : I will water it every moment, lest any hurt it." All through the three years of His ministry He had done His best to make it fruitful, but though occasionally there had been some signs of promise, they had come to nothing.

By His simile of the children in the market-place He illustrated the treatment He had received. "And the Lord said, Whereunto then shall I liken the men of this generation ? and to what are they like ? They are like unto children sitting in the market-place, and calling one to another, and saying, We have piped unto you, and ye have not danced ; we have mourned to you, and ye have not wept." John the Baptist would not dance to their piping, so they said, "He hath a devil." The Lord Himself would not fast and lament when they mourned, so they said, "Behold a gluttonous man, and a winebibber."

Another aspect of His ministry is represented in the parable of the sower, where He takes the humble place of a field labourer, in striking contrast to that of the King that was to reign.

His Rejection and Death.—The Lord's rejection by Israel was, as we have seen, prophesied in the parable of the wicked husbandmen. They said, "This is the heir; come, let us kill him, and let us seize on his inheritance." The father had said, "It may be they will reverence him when they see him," but they said instead, "When we shall see Him, there is no beauty that we should desire Him; He is despised and rejected of men, a Man of sorrows, and acquainted with grief : and we hid as it were our faces from Him ; He was despised, and we esteemed Him not." So they cast Him out of the vineyard and slew Him, and thus, as the Lord goes on to show, the builders rejected the stone that was by-and-by to become the head of the corner. The death of the Lord Jesus Christ was actually foretold in this parable of the wicked husbandmen. It is remarkable that while so many parables speak of His coming again, this is the only one that clearly speaks of His death. In John xii. we have a beautiful picture of the results of His sufferings on Calvary. "Verily, verily, I say unto you, Except a corn of wheat fall into the ground and die, it abideth alone, but if it die it bringeth forth much fruit." We find throughout the Word a series of types representing the Lord as corn in various forms. The manna, the corn of heaven, speaks of Him who from all eternity was the bread of God, and tells of His incarnation ; the fine flour, of His perfect life ; the old corn of the land and the sheaf of the first-fruits, Christ in resurrection ;

and this figure tells of His death and its consequences. "It became Him, for whom are all things,
and by whom are all things, in bringing many sons
unto glory, to make the Captain of their salvation
perfect through sufferings." He might have escaped
the suffering, but He would have had to abide alone.
Like the servant in Exod. xxi. 4, He might have gone
out free but it would have been by Himself, but as
God had said of the first Adam, "It is not good that
the man should be alone ; I will make him an help-
meet for him." So with the second Adam ; for this
the first "I will" of Scripture may be compared with
the last, which is, "I will show thee the bride, the
Lamb's wife." To win her for Himself He must
suffer on Calvary, dying like the corn of wheat.
He suffered alone that He might not abide alone. As
He by dying for us bore much fruit, so the fifteenth
of John tells us that we may bear much fruit by living
unto Him.

The last sight men had of the corn of wheat was
when it was dropped into the ground to die, but
behold, it has produced the much fruit which is to
be garnered at the " Harvest Home." How has this
miracle taken place ? The corn of wheat has been
like the seed described in Mark iv. It is " as if a man
should cast seed into the ground, and should sleep
and rise night and day, and the seed should spring
and grow up, he knoweth not how." The last sight
the world had of the Lord Jesus Christ was when they
put Him to death. The next time they see Him it
will be to recognise what a wonderful harvest His
dying has produced, "when He shall come . . . to be
admired in all them that believe."

He very clearly foretold His death in the discourse
recorded in John x., for though, as we have seen, the
figure of the shepherd and the sheep resembles that of
the parables, the statement, "The good Shepherd

giveth His life for the sheep," is a plain announcement of His substitutionary death without the veiling of a parable.

There is no actual mention of the *resurrection* in the parables, but it is included in this passage in John xii., and implied in all those which speak of His return.

Many of the latter also tell of His going away, leaving His house, or taking His journey, and all this took place at His *ascension*. They speak of Him as travelling to a far country, yet this is only how it appears to those left behind. He is not really far away, for " the Lord is at hand," but to the world, and even at times to His own disciples, the distance seems to be great.

Twice over in the parables which we have been considering, mention is made of His journeying. In that of the good Samaritan it was His journey to earth in incarnation ; in Mark xiii. and Luke xix. it was His journey to heaven in ascension. " Lo, I come to do Thy will," were His words when He set out on the first ; " Now come I to Thee," He said as He was about to start on the second journey.

CHAPTER VIII

HIS ABSENCE

THE scenes represented in the parables for the most part picture the state of things during our Lord's absence and the events which will happen before He sets up His kingdom; a few of them were applicable to the time when He was upon earth, but the majority are descriptive of the interval between the rejection of the King and the final setting up of the postponed kingdom. We do not find that kingdom described in any of them in its full glory and power.

Some comprehend the *whole* time of His absence, such as those which mention His going away and His return, *e.g.* those which tell of Him as the absent Master. The length of time which will elapse before He returns is differently described according to the requirements of each story. In Mark xiii. He goes for a journey which cannot be accomplished in a day, He will not be back before nightfall, and so He gives the servants their day's work, but they are to stay awake till He returns. His absence is therefore referred to as lasting a day and a night, so as to describe the two duties which He gives to all, working in the day, and watching in the night.

The parable of the talents tells us that the master was absent for "a long time." The story requires this, for otherwise there would not have been sufficient time for the servants to trade with what had been entrusted to them, and the excuse of the one who had hidden his Lord's money might have been that he had not had time enough to trade with it. God's servants will never be able to plead this as an excuse. The trading will be judged according to the opportunities given ; and these begin from the moment a sinner believes, and last till the very time he is called away, or the Lord Himself come. Indeed, we are responsible for all the privileges of our lifetime.

Some have taken the expression "a long time" as a statement by the Lord that His advent was not to be expected for many centuries. The parable was evidently not given to teach this. If the long time were taken literally it would prove just the opposite, viz., that those to whom He spoke were to expect Him in their lifetime, for the master returned to reckon with the very servants to whom he had given the money before he left. But this, of course, is not the purpose of the parable, it covers all the time of His absence, and refers to all who profess to be His servants. The parable of the pounds explains the reason of His absence, while giving an assurance of His return. "A certain nobleman went into a far country, to receive for himself a kingdom, and to return."

There are many lessons to be learnt from the parables about this interval.

In Mark iv. 26, in the parable of the seed cast into the ground, the prominent lesson is the absence of the owner from his field until the time of harvest, when he returns to find that as the fruit of his sowing, the earth has brought forth the blade, the ear, and the full corn, which is now to be gathered into his garner. Until the full corn is ready for the sickle he "waiteth for the precious fruit of the earth, and hath long patience for it."

In the parable of the marriage supper the king and his son are not seen by the guests until the invitation has been accepted and they are assembled at the feast.

In the first part of the parable in Luke xiv. the guests take their seats, choosing their own places before he comes that bade them.

Both parables therefore seem to suggest that the present is the time for giving and accepting the invitation, and for the seating of the guests. In a sense the gospel feast begins for each one as soon as he is saved, but the great banquet represented in these parables cannot really take place till " He that bade thee come." He Himself will then sit down and feast with us.

If we take the good Samaritan as representing the Lord Himself, this parable also suggests the thought of His absence and coming again. After bringing the man to a place of safety, he said to the host, "Take care of him ; and whatsoever thou spendest more, when I come again, I will repay thee." During the Lord's absence those whom He has saved are to be cared for by His servants, and He gives to them the means wherewith to supply their needs.[1] It is not to be done at their own expense but at His, and when He returns He will repay. "No care shown to wounded travellers will be forgotten, He will keep it in His ledger and will repay it to the uttermost farthing, exceeding abundantly."

In Dr Wilson's book of Chinese pictures, in the series representing the parable of the good Samaritan the Chinese artist in his last picture shows the man, as convalescent, sitting at the door of the inn, and eagerly on the look-out for the expected return of his benefactor. Though this is not described in the parable, we may certainly picture to ourselves this conclusion

---

[1] The pence together evidently represent the good Samaritan's provision, but to try and give the "two" a separate definition, as some have done, is to limit the meaning of the detail, instead of explaining it. It has been suggested that this was the same sum as the Atonement Money in Exodus xxx.

to the story, and imagine the meeting between them.

There are several parables which speak of the Lord as an absent Master (Mark xiii. 34–37, Luke xii. 35–48, and Matt. xxiv. 42–51). In these we have a picture of His sudden return to His household, and the result when He finds that He has not been expected. In Mark xiii. some are described as sleeping during His absence; in Luke xii. and Matt. xxiv. the evil servant who says in his heart,[1] "My lord delayeth his coming," is found ill-treating his fellow-servants, and eating and drinking with the drunken, instead of doing his lord's will. This is no true servant, as the Lord explains, but one whose portion is with the unbelievers and the hypocrites. As one has said, "Unkindness to the Lord's people and fellowship with the ungodly are two marks of hypocrites." But the picture in these two parables is not all dark, there are some faithful and wise servants who, having been left by their master in charge of his household, are found at his return giving their fellow-servants their meat in due season; and others are watching for him "that, when he cometh and knocketh, they may open unto him immediately. Blessed are those servants, whom the Lord, when He cometh, shall find watching." It is important to notice the little word *like* in Luke xii. 36. All in the household professed to expect the Master's return, but only the faithful ones lived *like* it.

In Mark xiii. the time of His absence is spoken of as a night season,[2] and this thought is specially prominent in the parable of the ten virgins. It is always dark when He is absent, as when the disciples were

---

[1] In this parable the evil servant only says it in his heart, he does not go so far as to speak out, but Peter tells us that scoffers in the last days will boldly sneer at the idea of expecting Him.

[2] See Appendix I.

alone on the stormy lake, toiling in rowing, and we read, "It was now dark, and Jesus was not come to them." At first the virgins are all sleeping, but when they are awakened by the midnight cry a separation takes place. "The wise and foolish virgins can all stay together while they are asleep. Why should they not? But the moment they trim their lamps comes the question of the oil, and they do not go together any more. . . . The wise virgins prepared for a night season, they counted on a darksome time till Jesus returned. The early freshness had faded, but the reality of supreme delight in Christ and desire after Him had not departed. The vessels were still at the side of the slumbering virgins. The oil had not to be bought but only to be used afresh." [1]

There is a reference to His absence in Matt. ix. 15, when the Lord, in answering John's disciples, spoke of the time when the children of the bride-chamber should mourn because the bridegroom was taken from them. The parables in Luke xii. and Matt. xxv. speak of the return of the bridegroom.

We may thus sum up the parables which most clearly depict the time of His absence.

1. The seed cast into the ground. The sower absent till harvest.

2. The wedding feast and the great supper. The King's son or the host not being present till the guests are assembled.

3. The good Samaritan leaving the wounded man at the inn.

4. The man absent in a far country taking a journey.

5. The household. The lord or bridegroom absent.

6. The virgins. The bridegroom on his way.

7. The talents and the pounds. The master absent for a long time.

This group gives a very complete picture of the

[1] J. N. D.

attitude and duties of His own people, for though, as we shall see in the next chapter, there is in many of them a special reference to His return to the earth, the practical teaching belongs to the whole period of His absence.

During the time of His absence we are to be :—

1. Bearing fruit. 2. Inviting to the feast. 3. Tending the wounded ones whom He has brought to us. 4. Keeping awake. 5. Caring for our fellow-servants. 6. Having our lamps trimmed. 7. Trading with what He has entrusted to us.

It has often been pointed out that the servant who is condemned in the parables of the talents and the pounds is the one who did nothing. He had hidden his Lord's money, and made no use of what had been entrusted to him ; so, too, the foolish virgins suffered because they had neglected to make preparation, and those on the left hand, will also be judged because they have done nothing to show their loyalty to Him.

In many other passages of Scripture we learn that sins of omission are noticed by God. Not to obey is as much a sin as active disobedience. The former is falling short, or missing the mark, the literal rendering of the word for " sin " ; the latter is transgression, or stepping over the boundary. The words " be sure your sin will find you out " were uttered as a warning against a sin of neglect. This passage is generally quoted in reference to acts of crime vainly hidden, but we see from the context that this was not its original meaning. The sons of Reuben, Gad, and the half-tribe of Manasseh promised that if they were allowed to settle on the further side of Jordan, when their brethren went in to possess the land they would help them in conquering their enemies. Moses said if they would do this, the land they wished for should be theirs, but if not, if they did not help their brethren and fight before the Lord, " be sure your sin will find you out " (Num.

xxxii. 23). So again in Judges, in Deborah's song, we read, "Curse ye Meroz, said the angel of the Lord ; curse ye bitterly the inhabitants thereof because they came *not* to the help of the Lord, to the help of the Lord against the mighty." And again in the Psalms we read, "The wicked shall be turned into hell," and not only they, but "all the nations that forget God."

"In one of the apocryphal gospels, 'the Nazarene gospel,' the parable of the talents is altered to suit human ideas, so as not to inflict so severe a punishment on mere sloth. There are three servants : one multiplies his talent ; another hides it ; the third wastes it with harlots and riotous living. The second is only rebuked, the third is cast into prison."[1] So men still change the Word to suit their thoughts.

[1] "Introduction to the New Testament." Dr. Salmon.

CHAPTER IX

HIS COMING AGAIN

IT seems strange that any one who reads the parables should doubt whether the Lord will return to the earth. However different may be the views of prophecy held by Bible students this point is absolutely certain, and is clearly demonstrated in many of the parables, where the Lord shows by the very illustrations He uses that for Him to be absent from His people is just as abnormal as for the head of a household to be absent from home.

It is important to remember that the coming of the Lord both in incarnation and in glory is an era rather than an isolated event. The first of these "comings" extended over thirty-three years. In Micah v. 2, the word is used in reference to His birth, "Thou, Bethlehem Ephratah, . . . out of thee shall He come forth unto me that is to be ruler in Israel." In Zech. ix. 9, His entry into Jerusalem is described as a coming: "Rejoice greatly, O daughter of Zion; shout, O daughter of Jerusalem; behold, thy King cometh unto thee . . . lowly, and riding upon an ass, and upon a colt the foal of an ass."

In the same way what is called His second coming is marked by various events which are alike included in the one great era called in the New Testament the "Parousia," or Presence. It commences with the fulfilment of His promise: "I will come again and receive you unto Myself," as more fully explained in I Thess. iv. 14-17, when all His own will be caught up to meet the Lord in the air.   It will be completed when He comes in glory to judge the world.

Probably none of the parables describe the first stage only, the coming for His saints, for this was revealed later.   They rather describe events on the earth when at His apocalypse, or epiphany (His revelation, unveiling, or appearing) He appears in glory to set up His kingdom.   But as the stories commence with a going away and end with a return, they must include the whole time of His absence, and therefore all the stages of His coming.

To limit the parables to the time of the Lord's appearing in glory on the earth, because they describe the events at the very end, would be like limiting the whole of Isaiah lxi. 1–3 to the same time of judgment immediately preceding His advent, because the passage speaks of "the day of vengeance."   We know that the prophecy embraces the whole period from His first coming to His return to set up His kingdom in the midst of Israel.   "The acceptable year of the Lord" had begun when He said, "This day is this Scripture fulfilled in your ears."   It has lasted nearly two thousand years already, and will be followed by the events of judgment and blessing mentioned in the remainder of the prophecy.   In the same way the parables which describe these events include also, in most cases, the centuries of His absence.

We do not need to study Euclid to know that "the whole is greater than a part," but this important axiom is very often forgotten in the study of the parables.   Some writers seem to believe that the part is greater than the whole, for they say that the primary and, indeed, the only interpretation of many of the parables is Jewish, and that though there may be a general application for us it is quite secondary. The great principles on which God deals with man are larger, far larger, than any application which refers to one dispensation or part of a dispensation, and it is the same with the practical lessons. Whilst acknowledging, therefore, that many details of these parables may refer to the days just preceding the Lord's appearance to set up His kingdom, it is very important to recognise that they have this general teaching for the present time.

We may be quite sure that there is nothing in the parables which is contradictory to the teaching given to Paul about the Lord's return. It was among the things which the Lord could not reveal to His disciples while He was with them, because they were not able to bear it ; but the parables must be read with the epistles, for the epistles are sequels to them. If we see this fact we shall not be so much in danger of accepting wrong theories about the Lord's coming. Many such have been founded on the parables through want of studying together these two portions of New Testament revelation.

For instance, through looking at the subject merely as revealed in the parables, it has been stated that certain events must take place before He comes for His own, and that therefore we must not expect Him now. Paul shows that this is not the case as to His coming to receive us to Himself, though there are many things to be fulfilled before He appears in glory. Viewed as a progressive revelation, the later teaching is seen to be no contradiction, but a more detailed unfolding and expansion of the subject, which could not have been so minutely explained earlier.

One great object of the parables was to make His disciples understand that He was about to leave them, and that He would return. It was hard for them to grasp even these two great truths. They thought that He would set up His earthly kingdom at once ; and they clung to the hope even to the last, as we see by their question, "Wilt Thou at this time restore again the kingdom to Israel?" (Acts i. 6). Till they understood the new condition of things about to be introduced in the dispensation of the Spirit, how could they learn the details concerning His return?

While therefore the incidents described are chiefly connected with the coming to the earth, the attitude enjoined is that which is to be cultivated during the whole time of His absence. The teaching is for us who look for the Lord from heaven as much as for the Jewish remnant, who, in a future dispensation, will look for their Messiah. The fact that these word-pictures describe the public coming to the earth does not make them less applicable to us now; on the contrary, if the later stage be imminent, how much more the earlier one?

The teaching of the Bible, both Old and New Testaments, circles round three great facts, He *is* coming, He *has* come, He *will* come again, and the last of these is one of the chief subjects spoken of in the parables, for whilst only one or two very clearly prophesy His death, fourteen or fifteen at least tell of His coming again.

Not only is it announced as a fact, but the manner of the coming, the result, and many of the incidents connected with it are foretold. We may therefore group them together in connection with these different subjects.

In the parable of the virgins we have a vivid picture of a sudden awakening to the truth of His approach. The midnight cry arouses all from their sleep, and the word is passed from one to another, " Behold, the bridegroom cometh."

There has been almost as much controversy over this parable as over those in the thirteenth of Matthew. Some apply it entirely to the present dispensation, others say that it has nothing to do with us now, but refers wholly to the time when the Church has been taken away and the Jewish remnant are waiting for their Messiah. The parable begins with the word "then," which links it with the preceding chapter. This deals with the era which includes the latter part of Daniel's seventieth week,[1] "the Great Tribulation," or "the time of Jacob's trouble" (Jer. xxx. 7) ; and also the interval between the end of the Tribulation and "the coming of the Son of Man." It is therefore evident that there is a special reference in the parable to this period of Israel's history. But though the special scene may be future, the lesson the Lord would teach is the need of watchfulness during the whole time of His absence ; just as He illustrated the need of importunate prayer in Luke xviii. by a picture belonging to this same period.

It not only contains solemn lessons for the present day, but also suggests the glad hope that He is very near. For long centuries the Church has slept. The very truth of His personal return seems to have been lost, but many in recent years have begun to hear the cry, "Behold, He cometh." The "blessed hope" is more real to the Church than ever before, and from this parable we may expect that a great awakening, of which this may be the commencement, will precede His coming. We know that there was a general expectation at the time of His incarnation, and the hearts of His own are doubtless being prepared, that they may look for Him to return. The truths of God's Word concerning things to come have during the last century been opened up in a wonderful way.

It is interesting to read the words of a devoted

[1] See Daniel ix. 25, 27. A clear and most helpful exposition of this important passage is given in "The Coming Prince," by Sir Robert Anderson, K.C.B. Kregel Publications $3.95

servant of God nearly a hundred years ago. Henry
Martyn wrote on February 29, 1809, " It seems evident
to me that the eleventh of Daniel, almost the whole of
it, refers to future times. But as the time of accom-
plishing the Scriptures draws on, knowledge shall
increase. In solemn expectation we must wait to see
how our God will come."

Many strange theories have been founded upon the
parable of the virgins. If anything is clear in the
story it is that constant watchfulness for the Lord's
coming is enjoined, but some have used it to try
and prove that it is contrary to Scripture to live in
expectation of His return.

Others who do believe in the nearness of the Lord's
coming argue from this parable that when believers
are caught up to meet the Lord, only those who have
reached a certain standard of devotedness or watchfulness will be taken, and the rest will be left behind.
But who is to set the standard ? Which of us could
look forward with joy to the thought of His appearing
if we had not the certainty that each one that belongs
to Him will see Him as He is when He appears, and
in the twinkling of an eye be made like Him ? The
fact that the bridegroom says to the foolish virgins
who are shut out, " I know you not," proves that they
cannot represent believers, for it is said, " The Lord
knoweth them that are His." False professors will be
left behind, but none of those who have passed from
death unto life. There is a tendency in this teaching
of a divided Church to minimise the miracle that takes
place when a soul is born again, and to make out that
there is more difference between life and life abundant
than between death and life. Every saved sinner has
been accepted in the Beloved, and his acceptance
rests not on his own attainments but on the fact that
he is " in Christ Jesus." This is the teaching of the
burnt-offering. Though there may be shrinking back

with shame to meet Him at His coming,[1] and though there may be loss of reward, there can be no doubt that all believers will participate in the joyful event, for it includes all that are "Christ's at His coming."

The apostle Peter speaks of "the *grace* that is to be brought unto you at the revelation of Jesus Christ" (1 Pet. i. 13), and tells us that it is "the God of all *grace*, who hath called us unto His eternal glory by Christ Jesus" (v. 10). It is all grace from first to last. It was grace that opened our eyes to see Him for salvation, and it will be grace that will open our eyes to see Him as He is, for transformation and glorification. "Not of works, lest any man should boast," is as true of the one as of the other. How could we "comfort one another" with the thought of His return, as we are enjoined to do by Paul in 1 Thess. iv. if it were not a settled fact that all we which are alive and remain, as well as all who sleep in Jesus, will be caught up to meet the Lord in the air? In any case it is dangerous to found a doctrine on the details of a parable.

As we have seen in the preceding chapter, there are several other parables which emphasise the unexpectedness of His coming, and the need of watchfulness and preparedness. Especially is this the case in those which speak of the Lord as an absent Master, as in Mark xiii. 34–37 ; Matt. xxiv. 42–51 ; and Luke xii. 35–48.

In the last two passages the suddenness of His coming is compared to that of a thief in the night. This simile is used seven times in the New Testament,[2] but in all of them it is clear that He does not thus come to His own.

---

[1] 1 John ii. 28, Dean Alford's translation.
[2] Matt. xxiv. 43 ; Luke xii. 39 ; 1 Thess. v. 2, 4 ; 2 Pet. iii. 10; Rev. iii. 3 ; xvi. 15.

It has been pointed out that there is a difference between the "house" in Matt. xxiv. 43, and the "household" in verse 45. It is to the one who is occupied with the stuff, the mere externals, that He will come as a thief in the night. In 1 Thess. v. it is clearly shown that it is to the world He will thus come (verse 2), not to the children of light (verse 4), "when *they* shall say, Peace and safety, then sudden destruction cometh upon *them*." In 2 Peter iii. 10, as in the parable, it is to them who say, "Where is the promise of His coming?" men who are "scoffers, walking after their own lusts;" in Rev. iii. 3, the warning is to the sleeping church at Sardis, to which the Lord says, "Thou hast a name that thou livest, and art dead," but He adds, "Thou hast a few names even in Sardis which have not defiled their garments," and to these overcomers He will not return in this unlooked-for manner. The last time the expression is used (Rev. xvi. 15), it is in the midst of the descriptions of the terrible judgments that will be poured out upon the earth before the Lord comes in His glory, and therefore seems to refer to His return to the earth.

It has been said that "there are three kinds of judgment—discriminative between true and false, distributive for rewards, and retributive." The parables show that the Lord's coming will be marked by all three.

I. Discriminative judgment, a division between true and false.[1] The parables vividly depict this solemn separation in a series of pictures. Seven times the scene is described by the Lord in Matthew's Gospel, under different forms, and if a double repetition proves that a thing is "established by God, and God will shortly bring it to pass" (Gen. xli. 32, see pp. 192, 193),

[1] See Appendix II.

how much more emphatic must be a sevenfold repetition !

In the parable of	*There is a separation between*
(1) The tares, Matt. xiii. 24–30, 36–43.	Wheat and tares.
(2) The drag net, Matt. xiii. 47–50.	Good and bad fish.
(3) The marriage-feast, Matt. xxii. 2–14.	Guests with and without a wedding garment.
(4) The household, Matt. xxiv. 45–51.	Good and evil servants.
(5) The ten virgins, Matt. xxv. 1–13.	Wise and foolish virgins.
(6) The talents, Matt. xxv. 14–30.	Profitable and unprofitable servants.
(7) The sheep and the goats, Matt. xxv. 31–46.	Sheep and goats.

This final division is represented as taking place—

(1) "In the time of harvest," or "the end of this age."

(2) "At the end of the age."

(3) "When the king came in to see the guests."

(4) "When He cometh."

(5) When "the bridegroom came."

(6) When "after a long time the lord of those servants cometh."

(7) "When the Son of Man shall come in His glory."

There is a very marked progress of revelation in this series. The last picture shows plainly who it is who thus makes the separation. It is not merely "a certain king," as in Matt. xxii.; but *the* King, the Son of Man to whom the Ancient of days delivers the kingdom (Dan. vii. 13, 14).

The result of the separation and the alternative destinies are described in these words—

(1) "Gather into my barn;" "the kingdom of their Father."	"Cast into a furnace of fire."
(2) "Gathered into vessels."	"Cast away;" "the furnace of fire."
(3) "The wedding."	"Cast into outer darkness."
(4) "Ruler over all his goods."	"Cut off" (*marg.*); "portion with the hypocrites."
(5) "In with Him to the marriage."	"The door was shut."
(6) "The joy of thy Lord."	"Outer darkness."
(7) "The kingdom prepared for you."	"Everlasting fire prepared for the devil and his angels."

Three of these parables refer to the furnace of fire (1, 2, and 7 on the list), while three others (3, 5, and 6) speak of those who are left outside in the darkness. In five of them (1, 2, 3, 4, and 6), the same expression is used to represent their awful condition, "weeping (or wailing) and gnashing of teeth." It is not by accident that this is so often repeated, and the words are also found in Matt. vii. 12, and Luke xiii. 28, making a sevenfold repetition of the phrase.[1] The words have been thus defined, "Weeping is the expression of sorrow, gnashing of teeth the expression of wickedness (Acts vii. 54). If the condemned soul carries its sorrow it carries its enmity too for ever."[2] To this we might also add that wailing seems to suggest hopeless despair.

Two of these parables give a glimpse of the company in which the lost will have to spend their eternity (4 and 7); the hypocrites, or, as it is in Luke xii., the unbelievers, and those for whom the fire was prepared, the devil and his angels. In comparing this twofold

[1] Matt. viii. 12; xiii. 42, 50; xxii. 13; xxiv. 51; xxv. 30; and Luke xiii. 28.
[2] J. G. Bellett.

destiny it is striking to notice, in the last on the list, how the Lord used the word "prepared." The kingdom was specially prepared for the blessed of the Father, but the fire was prepared for the devil and his angels, not for man. It reminds us of the careful use of the same word in Rom. ix. 23, where the apostle speaks of " the vessels of mercy which He had afore prepared unto glory," and in the preceding verse of "the vessels of wrath fitted to destruction." It does not say that *He* had fitted them to destruction. God prepares His own for glory, and prepares the glory for them, whatever form it may take, but He does not prepare hell for the lost, nor fit the lost for it. It is prepared for the devil and his angels, who fits his own, or helps them to fit themselves, for their own place, though that he does his best to make men disbelieve.

From the seven scenes represented in these parables we can gather what will be the various marks of difference between the two classes. There will be no difficulty in that day, of discerning "between the righteous and the wicked ; between him that serveth God, and him that serveth Him not." (Mal. iii. 17, 18). When He maketh up His jewels all will be clear, for this is the time of which the prophet Malachi spoke. He uses the same symbolic language (chap. iv. 1, 2), where he speaks of the day that "shall burn as an oven," when "all the proud, yea, and all that do wickedly, shall be stubble." Thus the Old Testament closes,[1] and John the Baptist repeats the same prophecy. We may add to the seven parables the figure used by him in Matt. iii. 12, where he speaks of the wheat and the chaff being separated when the Reaper's fan is in His hand, and the wheat being gathered into His garner and the chaff cast into unquenchable fire.

In the first of the seven pictures the tares are

---

[1] See Appendix II.

distinctly stated to be the "children of the wicked one;" they have passed as children of the kingdom (comp. Matt. viii. 12, and xiii. 42), but they are cast out as "things that offend, and them which do iniquity;" they are those who have never been born again.

(2) The bad fish represent the wicked, the good fish the just.

Wedding feast

(3) The man without the wedding garment was bound hand and foot, and taken away because he lacked one thing. The other guests were not all good for they are described as "bad and good." Their fitness to sit down at the feast did not depend on their own characters but on their willingness to receive the king's invitation and the king's provision. The man's refusal of the latter proved that he was not amongst the "chosen."

(4) The servant who begins to smite his fellow-servants, and to eat and drink with the drunken, is appointed a portion with the hypocrites or un-believers, showing that he was himself a hypocrite and an unbeliever.

(5) The foolish virgins were those who were not "ready," they had no oil.

(6) The servant who hid his lord's money was "wicked and slothful" and therefore "unprofit-able."

(7) Those on the left hand of the King were those who had done nothing to prove their loyalty to Him by their treatment of His brethren.

The fact that evil is mixed with good in all these cases shows that they cannot refer to the Church in its heavenly aspect. As viewed in God's sight it is composed only of those who are members of Christ's body, of His flesh and of His bones, those who have passed from death unto life; and such could never be compared to tares, bad fish, men without

a wedding garment, foolish virgins, hypocritical servants, or, lastly, to goats.

These parables must therefore refer to something
which is viewed from an earthly standpoint, whence
the real and false cannot be distinguished.   It is
probable that they have a twofold application, first,
as to the practical teaching relating to professing
Christendom in which it is so often impossible
to distinguish between mere professors and real
possessors. In this aspect they would include the
Church, for all true possessors now are members
of the Church and must be professors also.   It has
been well said, " There is only one way of getting out
of the professing Church, viz., by ceasing to profess."
Secondly, many of these parables give a picture of
the condition of things when the Lord comes to earth
to set up His kingdom.

At the first stage of His coming when His saints are
caught up to meet Him in the air, there will be no
immediate judgment of the wicked as here described,
when the Son of Man will gather out of His kingdom
" all things that offend, and them which do iniquity."
At His coming for His saints it is they who are
gathered out, and gathered unto Him, but at His
appearing in glory it is the wicked who are gathered
out. The passage, " One shall be taken, the other left,"
is often used in reference to the taking up of His
own, but from the allusion to the flood in the days
of Noah, which took them all away, it is evident that
it speaks of His coming to the earth, when one shall
be taken away for judgment, and the other left to
share in the blessings of the kingdom.

There is nothing in these parables to indicate, as some
would teach, that those who have been once saved
can be finally lost.   Those upon whom the doom falls
seem indeed for a time to be numbered amongst the
Lord's own people, but it is by a mere lip profes-

sion, they are not acknowledged by the Lord Himself. He will profess that He does not know them. Yet they are judged according to their own profession, and their condemnation is all the greater. The foolish virgins to whom the bridegroom said, " I know you not," were but hearers of the Word and not doers. The words in Matt. vii. 21–23 are very similar to those in Matt. xxv., " Not every one that saith unto Me, Lord, Lord, shall enter into the kingdom of heaven. . . . Many will say to Me in that day, Lord, Lord, have we not prophesied in Thy name ? and in Thy name have cast out devils ? and in Thy name done many wonderful works ? And then will I profess unto them, I never knew you : depart from Me, ye that work iniquity." Their estimate of their lives was " many wonderful works ; " His estimate that they had worked iniquity. What an awful awakening in that day, when those things which have been accounted wonderful works appear in their true light. In the parable that follows the Lord pictures the " wonderful works " under the simile of a house built upon the sand.

It is also clear that the unfaithful or " evil servant " in the twenty-fourth of Matthew was never a true servant. He was judged not merely because he was not ready for his master's return, but because by his conduct in smiting his fellow-servants, and eating and drinking with the drunken, he had shown that he had no heart for his lord ; and so his lord cut him off and appointed him a portion with the hypocrites. He pretended to be a servant, but used the position he had assumed to ill-treat his fellow-servants. This was his attitude to those within the household. He had no fellowship with them, but had to go outside for the company in which he found himself really at home. His condemnation was that he was doomed to stay with them for ever.

The man who hid his lord's talent was also by profession a servant, and was judged accordingly, but he did not know his lord's heart. The true servant of God must be first a child born into the family, for true service springs from sonship. . In a sermon on this parable Mr. Spurgeon said, " Forced service is not desirable. God wants not slaves to grace His throne. A servant who is not pleased with his situation had better leave; if he is not content with his Master he had better find another. . . . He was condemned to be *as he was*, for hell, in one light, may be described as the great Captain's saying, 'As ye were.' . . . In another world there is permanence of character; enduring holiness is heaven, continual evil is hell. This man was outside of the family of his lord. He thought his lord a hard master, and so proved that he had no love for him, and that he was not really one of his household. He was outside in heart, and so his lord said to him, 'Remain outside.' Besides that, he was in the dark : he had wrong notions of his master ; for his lord was not an austere and hard man, he did not gather where he had not strawed, nor reap where he had not sown. Therefore his lord said, 'You are wilfully in the dark ; abide there in the darkness, which is outside.' This man was envious ; he could not endure his master's prosperity ; he gnashed his teeth at the thought of it. He was sentenced to continue in that mind, and so to gnash his teeth for ever. This is a dreadful idea of eternal punishment, this permanence of character in an immortal spirit : 'He that is unjust, let him be unjust still.' While the character of the ungodly will be permanent, it will also be more and more developed along its own lines ; the bad points will become worse, and, with nothing to restrain it, evil will become viler still."[1]

[1] C. H. Spurgeon, No. 1,541, " Unprofitable Servants."

Each of these pictures is terribly solemn when studied singly ; but when the same truths are repeated seven times, how awful the reality they depict !

II. *Distributive Judgment.*—Turning to the brighter side of the picture, we see that at the Lord's coming there will be a distribution of *rewards;* and the parables show the principles on which they will be awarded, and tell us something of their character.   The faithful and wise servant who, during the absence of his lord, served him as ruler over his household, is to be made ruler over all his goods.   The servants who traded with the talents were made rulers over many things. The same words of commendation were addressed to the man who had made the five talents into ten, and the one who had made the two talents into four : "Well done, good and faithful servant ; thou hast been faithful over a few things, I will make thee ruler over many things ; enter thou into the joy of thy lord." This last word summed up everything, it was the greatest reward that could be given to them.   It is not said, however, that the "many things" were to be equal in both cases.   Probably they were in the same proportion as the "few things" in which they had showed themselves faithful.

It is suggestive that in both these parables the reward is closely allied in character to the service rendered.   He who was faithful as ruler over the *household*, is made ruler over *all* things ; he who is faithful in a *few*, is made ruler over *many* things. In the parable of the pounds, the nature of the reward is more definitely described.   The servant who gains ten pounds from the one pound entrusted to him is given authority over ten cities ; the one who gains five pounds is placed over five cities.   This is in accordance with the story of him who went away to receive for himself a kingdom and to return.   There is no such mention in the Matthew parable, where the scene described is merely that of a master reckoning with his servants. Here again, as in the other two instances in Matt. xxiv., xxv., the servants are rewarded for faithfulness. We are not told the result of the trading of the other seven servants; there were ten altogether, but these are set forth as samples.

The judgment of the nations in Matt. xxv. is not really a parable; but it must be included amongst them, on account of its describing the same events, and because of the figurative language which links it with the parables of the Shepherd. It commences with the simile. The King will separate the nations "as a shepherd divideth his sheep from the goats" (verse 32); the next verse continues the figure, and says, " He shall set the sheep on His right hand, but the goats on the left." The description that follows is that of a real scene, it is more than a parable.

Those on the right hand are commended because of their devotion to His brethren, and we may be quite sure that they possess the other marks belonging to His sheep. Some have argued from this picture that men will be blessed hereafter according to what they have done, and not according to what they have believed. From other Scriptures we know that this is not the teaching. The works prove the faith. The key to this passage is probably to be found in Revelation. (See pp. 260, 261.)

By comparing Scripture with Scripture, we learn that there are to be three great judgments. The first, the judgment-seat of Christ; the second, the judgment of living nations; the third, the Great White Throne. The first will take place at His coming to the air for His saints; the second at His coming to the earth with them; and the third after the millennium. Only saved ones will stand before the first, only lost ones before the last; but at the second both classes will be represented. At the first, rewards will be given, at the last, doom will be pronounced, at the middle one, there will be both rewards and sentences of judgment.

When at this second judgment the Lord sets up His throne upon earth, the scene will be on a much smaller scale than those which precede and follow it; for at the first *all* the saved ones up to the time of His coming to the air will be judged according to their works, in order that they may receive commendation. It will be no question of salvation, for their presence there, either as raised or changed ones, will prove that they are saved. And at the last *all* the dead in trespasses and sins from the beginning of time will appear to receive their condemnation. At the second the Lord deals with those alive at His coming to set up His kingdom on the earth, not with those alive when He comes to the air. It is possible that those martyred in the time of antichrist for refusing to worship him may receive their rewards at this time, as we know from Rev. xx. 4, that they will be raised at His coming in glory, for they are to take part in the first resurrection.

As we have already seen, the parables which describe His session in judgment deal chiefly with the second and central scene. But although He chooses this as a sample it seems impossible to limit the teaching to the condition of either the righteous or wicked who have lived during the period between the first stage of the Lord's coming and His return to earth. Here again the whole is greater than its part. The underlying principles apply to all His judgments and all His rewards, although only one scene in His administration is pictured. He will adjudicate the rewards for works done by believers now, in the same way as He will reward those who have passed through the Great Tribulation. " Every man according to his works " covers each of the great sessions whether it is a question of reward for works, of position in heavenly or earthly glory, or of final destiny. In studying these pictures we may therefore take the bright side to include the rewards that have gone before, and the dark side the doom that will follow after.

With reference to the latter, other passages seem to suggest the possibility that though sentence is pronounced when He comes to set up His kingdom, it may not be carried out till after the millennium, when according to Rev. xx. the rest of the dead will be cast into the lake of fire.

The *retributive* judgment has already been referred to, and is also considered in connection with Israel (pp. 161–163).

After speaking of the rejected corner-stone, the Lord added these solemn words, which seem to include judgment on Israel beginning from that time, and judgment on the world at His coming again : " Whosoever shall fall on this stone shall be broken ; but on whomsoever it shall fall, it will grind him to powder." Mr. David Baron has thus expressed it : " Eighteen hundred years ago Christ crucified became a stumbling-block to the Jewish nation. Israel fell *on* the stone and they were broken, but there is hope in their end, for the broken fragments of the Jewish nation will, according to God's own promise, be gathered together from the four corners of the earth and be made whole again ; but as to hypocritical professed Christendom the stone will fall *on* them." It will be like the stone in Dan. ii. 34, 45, " cut out of the mountain without hands," which will break in pieces the image. The stone here represents the kingdom which the God of heaven will set up in those days, which will destroy the other kingdoms.

It was the husbandmen themselves who pronounced their own judgment. This is shown in Matthew's account (chap. xxi. 40). "When the lord therefore of the vineyard cometh, what will he do unto those husbandmen ? They say unto Him, He will miserably destroy those wicked men." He might have said, like the master in the other parable, " Out of thine own mouth will I judge thee, thou wicked servant" (Luke xix. 22). Some of His hearers exclaimed, " God forbid" (Luke xx. 16), but the parable had no real effect in making them see their danger. " The same hour" they hurried away to fulfil the prophecy, and when they had accomplished it, they cried, " His blood be on us and on our children."

Several of the parables describe the Lord's return as a time of *harvest*, and this figure also suggests the largest and most inclusive view. The taking up of the Church is not the harvest, but it is a part of the " first-fruits;" and though the " first-fruits " be not the harvest, they are included in it, for it represents the ingathering from the field of the world of all that is precious to the Lord.[1]

It is even possible to reap two harvests in the same year if the ground is made fruitful by the latter rain. It is prophesied of the land of Israel, " Behold, the days come, saith the Lord, that the ploughman shall overtake the reaper, and the treader of grapes him that soweth seed " (Amos ix. 13). The barren land will thus become so fruitful that there will be a double harvest. This will be true also of the coming of the Lord. There will be a harvest in one aspect when He comes to the air, and another when He comes to the earth. The sower will go forth immediately the first sheaves have been garnered. The remnant of Israel will sow the seed anew after the close of this dispensation.

Will the harvest be the end of everything as to the

---

[1] This subject is considered in connection with Old Testament types, pp. 178–180.

field of the world? Surely not, any more than in the field of an earthly landowner. Some of the seed gathered out of the field during one year is used the following springtime for sowing it once again, and may we not also conclude that it will be so with God's ingathering. We have only a few hints about the ages to come, but these suggest that the harvest of time will be the seed for eternity.

His coming will also be a time of *rest* from earthly labour. This is suggested in the parable of the labourers in the vineyard, who, when even was come, were called to receive their hire; and also in the passage in Luke xvii. which speaks of the servant " by-and-by when he is come from the field." Field labour will then be over, there will be no more weary toil, though His servants shall serve Him throughout eternity.

It will be a time of *sorrow* to those who are not ready, but it will be a time of great *joy* to those who are expecting Him. The latter is graphically described in the picture of the return from the wedding in Luke xii. 36; a figure which represents better than any other the scene of the greatest possible rejoicing for a loyal household.

Thus we see that the coming of the Lord is brought before us in the parables as a time of division, reward, retribution, ingathering, rest, sorrow, and joy.

CHAPTER X

THE KINGDOM

THE first mention of the Lord's reign is in the song of Moses on the shores of the Red Sea. Never before had Israel been manifested as a nation, for they had been born in a night—the Passover night.

It was God's purpose to reign in their midst, but on account of their sin the fulfilment of this purpose had to be postponed. In wishing to be like other nations, they asked for a king to reign over them, and when they did so God said, "They have rejected Me, that I should not reign over them" (1 Sam. viii. 7; x. 19). He granted their request, as we read in Hosea xiii. 11, "I gave them a king in Mine anger, and took him away in My wrath." But we see how, after Saul had been set aside, God overruled the failure of His people which He had already foreseen (Deut. xvii. 14–20); and choosing David, a man after His own heart, promised that his kingdom should be without end, and that the coming Messiah-King should be of his seed (Psa. cxxxii. 11; John vii. 42).

We read that "Solomon sat on the throne of Jehovah as king" (1 Chron. xxix. 23), but the prophets told of a future day when a "greater than Solomon" should come and take the kingdom, who would be not only son of David, but Son of God.

> " A little while and David's Son
> On David's throne shall reign."

This was the kingdom foretold by Daniel and the other prophets. David himself speaks of it in the second Psalm, where he tells of Jehovah proclaiming, "Yet have I set My King upon My holy hill of Zion;" "My King" in contrast to the kings of the earth, who "set themselves . . . against the Lord, and against His Anointed" (verses 2, 10).

When He came the same nation that had in Old Testament times rejected Him as *God*, refused Him again, and said, "We will not have this *man* to reign over us." Thus once more the kingdom was postponed.

The King whom Israel rejected in the days of Samuel was the very same whom they refused in the days of His flesh. Isaiah in vision saw "the King, the Lord of Hosts," and John tells us that this was the Lord Jesus, for he says, "These things said Esaias, when he saw His glory, and spake of Him." The King who sent Isaiah to carry His message to Israel (Isa. vi. 9, 10) speaks the very same word Himself in Matt. xiii. 14, 15. How little the disciples realised that the Jehovah of the Old Testament was the One known to them by the name of "Jesus." By-and-by He will be known to the world as Jehovah, and by this very name.

When we read the fortieth of Isaiah in the light of the first part of Matthew, we seem to have a suggestion of what actually took place. In verse 3 there is the prophecy of the preaching of John the Baptist, one of the few Old Testament passages quoted in all the four Gospels. In New Testament language the message, "Prepare ye the way of the Lord," was "Repent ; for the kingdom of heaven is at hand." In Isaiah the simile of the King's forerunner is continued, and there is a description of the preparation which would naturally follow a proclamation of the King's approach. A road would at once be levelled, straightened, and smoothed as described in verse 4. It was at the same time a command and a prophecy. The command was disobeyed but the prophecy stands ; for though on hearing the voice of John, the nation did not at once prepare the way of the Lord, the time will come when the King's highway will lead right through the nation, and then " the glory of the Lord shall be revealed."

In the sixth verse is there not a hint at least of this failure of Israel to respond to the herald's cry? "The voice said, Cry. And he said, What shall I cry? All flesh is grass, and all the goodliness thereof is as the flower of the field : the grass withereth, the flower fadeth, because the Spirit of the Lord bloweth upon it : surely the people is grass." Judgment fell upon the nation because they rejected their King. "The grass withereth, the flower fadeth ; but the Word of our God shall stand for ever." Though man is like the perishing flower of the grass, "which to-day is, and to-morrow is cast into the oven," the corn to which the Word is compared in the parable of the sower does not fade away and end in being burned, but it ripens for the garner, and goes on producing fresh harvests.

In the light of New Testament history and pro-phecy, therefore, after the prediction of John's preach-ing in verse 3, we can trace a suggestion of the events which followed it. Thus we shall see in the opening verses of Isaiah xl. the proclamation of the King's approach and of the glory of His reign (verses 4, 5) ; the change of message in verse 6 on account of the rejection of the King by Israel ; the consequent judg-ment that falls upon them (verse 7); and the good seed of the Word which is now scattered broadcast (verse 8).

The change of God's dealings with Israel and the world, in consequence of the former's rejection of Messiah, is very clearly shown in the forty-ninth of Isaiah, and the setting of Matt. xi. 28 is very beauti-

ful when studied in connection with this chapter.
We are there permitted to overhear a wonderful
dialogue between two of the Persons of the Trinity.

The speaker is the Messiah Himself, and He is
addressing the Gentiles—" the isles "—telling them of
the conversation that had taken place. First, He
mentions how He was chosen and fitted by God
(verses 1, 2) ; then He repeats what Jehovah has said
to Him (verse 3), for a greater than Israel is here.
In verse 4 He tells of His reply to Jehovah, "Then
I said, I have laboured in vain, I have spent My
strength for nought." In the fifth and sixth verses
we have Jehovah's answer, "It is too light a thing
that Thou shouldest be My Servant to raise up the
tribes of Jacob, and to restore the preserved of Israel ;
I will also give Thee for a light to the Gentiles that
Thou mayest be My salvation unto the end of the
earth " (R.V.).

These words were addressed "to Him whom man
despiseth, to Him whom the nation abhorreth," and
they speak of blessing to the world during the time of
Israel's rejection. According to the A.V., verse 5
reads "though Israel be not gathered," and the R.V.
(*marg.*) renders it " but Israel is not gathered," as if
the Messiah were still mourning over His rejection
by the chosen people. We know that the Gentiles
will be blessed when Israel is gathered, but this seems
a prophecy of the grafting in of Gentile branches,
a suggestion of the mystery finally revealed to the
apostle Paul (Eph. iii.).

As we read the closing verses of Matt. xi. we seem to
hear this conversation going on between the Father
and the Son. It is true that we do not read of
the voice from heaven speaking to Him as in John
xii. 28, 29, but *He* heard it, for in verse 25 we are told
that He "*answered*" His Father, implying that He
had first been listening to His voice.

As the Lord Jesus reproaches the cities for their unbelief, we seem to hear Him saying at the same time to His Father, "I have laboured in vain, I have spent My strength for nought." He grieves because they will not allow Him to gather them, as He did again at the close of His ministry when He said, "How often would I have gathered thy children together." Can we not hear the Father's voice comforting Him who was despised and abhorred by the nation, by telling Him that He was now to be "a light to the Gentiles, and My salvation to the end of the earth"? Is it not this which calls forth the praise of the twenty-fifth verse? "At that season Jesus answered and said, I thank Thee, O Father, Lord of heaven and earth, that Thou didst hide these things from the wise and understanding, and didst reveal them unto babes; yea, Father, for so it was well-pleasing in Thy sight" (R.V.). Then He turns to those around Him and says, "All things have been delivered unto Me of My Father."

Now the blessing is for "whomsoever"[1] He will, and we can thus understand His next words, "Come unto Me, *all* ye," not only the lost sheep of the house of Israel, as in the tenth chapter (verses 5, 6). The gospel of the kingdom is "Repent, for the kingdom of heaven is at hand," the gospel of the kingdom in mystery is "Come unto Me, all ye." The twelfth chapter shows us the final public rejection by the nation, and the parables in Matthew xiii., especially that of the sower, teach how in consequence of this, the living seed is sown broadcast throughout the field of the world.

It has often been pointed out that the expression "the kingdom of heaven" only occurs in Matthew's

---

[1] The first, "whomsoever," represents divine sovereignty (xi. 27), the second, "whosoever," shows man's responsibility (xii. 50). "Whomsoever He willeth" always goes before "whosoever will."

Gospel, and to explain this many theories have been suggested. Some teachers have affirmed that "the kingdom of heaven" and "the kingdom of God" are quite different in meaning, others have said that the latter is more comprehensive. Mr. David Baron says that from Talmudic literature it may be seen that the words "the heavens" were constantly substituted by the ancient Jews for the Name of "God," and even for "the Name."

Is there not possibly a reference to this in Matt. v. 34; xxiii. 22? The Lord seems to say that although the Jews intentionally avoided the Name of God and substituted the word "heaven," it was just the same. "He that shall swear by heaven, sweareth by the throne of God, and by Him that sitteth thereon."

It may be that this, in measure, explains how it was that the sphere of Divine rule was substituted for the mention of the One who wields the power.

Many of the same things are said of both "the kingdom of heaven" and "the kingdom of God." While we are told in Matthew iv. 17, that the Lord preached "The kingdom of heaven is at hand," in Mark i. 15, it is "the kingdom of God;" and in Luke xxi. 31, it is the latter which "is nigh at hand" when the Lord is about to return.

The childlike spirit is needed for each (Matt. xviii. 3; Mark x. 15; Luke xviii. 17). Trusting in riches will shut out from both (Matt. xix. 23, 24; Mark x. 23–25; Luke xviii. 24, 25). The least in either is said to be greater than John the Baptist (Matt. xi. 11; Luke vii. 28). The Lord said of the little children " of such is the kingdom of heaven " in Matt. xix. 14; and "of such is the kingdom of God" in Mark x. 14; Luke xviii. 16. The promise is to the poor in spirit in both cases (Matt. v. 3; Luke vi. 20).

The parables of the leaven and the mustard-seed illustrate both, and they and the parable of the sower are spoken of as amongst the mysteries of the kingdom of heaven, and also amongst the mysteries of the kingdom of God.

"The kingdom of heaven is at hand" implied not merely that God's kingdom was to be established in the *hearts* of men, but that the Messiah-King, the God-Man who was seed of David as well as Son of God, was about to take the throne of Israel, and that the visible and earthly would also be the heavenly kingdom. It was something new, something which had never before taken place, but which had been long foretold, and it meant a great deal more than was revealed to Nebuchadnezzar—that "the heavens do rule."

This declaration, "the kingdom of heaven is at hand," is made three times in Matthew's Gospel (chaps. iii., iv., x.), first by John the Baptist, then by the Lord Himself, and then by the disciples, who were told to make the proclamation to none but Israel. This was the gospel of the kingdom preached by our Lord (Matt. iv. 23 ; ix. 35); and again to be preached in the future immediately before His return to the earth (xxiv. 14). But Matthew's Gospel, which tells us first of the genealogy of the King, of the birth of the King, of the credentials of the King, of the proclamation of the kingdom, has to tell us in its eleventh and twelfth chapters of the King's rejection by the nation. Instead of taking upon Himself kingly majesty He assumes the humble guise of a sower, and then for a time retires from the scene. With this change of condition the expression the "kingdom of heaven" seems to bear a different meaning. It is now the kingdom in mystery, not in manifestation; no longer is Jerusalem the centre, it is world wide in extent, for as soon as the King has been rejected He shows in the incident in Matt. xii. 46-50, that He acknowledges no longer mere brethren after the flesh, but by His gracious "whosoever" enlarges the circle to include both Jew and Gentile.

The King is the Messiah of Israel, but "He came unto His own, and His own received Him not." Some of the natural branches of the olive tree were therefore broken off and the wild olive branches were engrafted in their place.

Instead of the sowers being sent forth to Israel only, as in Matt. x. 5, 6, the seed is to be scattered through the whole world, for the field in the first parable of Matt. xiii. must be as wide as that in the second, which our Lord plainly tells us is "the world" (verse 38). During the time of the mysteries of the kingdom of heaven while the rejected King is gone into the "far country," *evil* is *permitted* to mix with the good as we see in the parable of the wheat and the tares, and of the leaven; while in that of the mustard-seed the birds of the air, which in the parable of the sower represented "the evil one" and his messengers, are allowed to lodge in the branches. But when the kingdom is finally set up, evil will be *purged out*, the angels will be sent to gather out of His kingdom "all things that offend, and them which do iniquity;" just as in type Solomon had to visit in judgment those who rebelled against his father before reigning as prince of peace.

The parables of the kingdom of heaven evidently do not therefore represent the kingdom as it will be when the King is reigning in power; they tell us either of the whole period of His absence, or of the time just before He returns.

The following parables are introduced by such words as "The kingdom of heaven is like." In the last the words are added in italics :—

(1.) The Wheat and the Tares.   Matt. xiii. 24–30 ;
     36–43.
(2.) The Mustard-seed.   „   xiii. 31–32.
(3.) The Leaven.   „   xiii. 33.
(4.) The Hidden Treasure.   „   xiii. 44.
(5.) The Pearl of Great Price.   „   xiii. 45–46.
(6.) The Net.   „   xiii. 47–50.
(7.) The King and His Servants.   „   xviii. 23–35.
(8.) The Labourers in the Vineyard.   „   xx.   1–16.
(9.) The Marriage Feast.   „   xxii. 1–14.
(10.) The Ten Virgins.   „   xxv.   1–13.
(11.) The Talents.   „   xxv.   14–30.

The parable of the sower is not so introduced, and it has therefore been stated by some that it does not belong to this special series ; but the explanation shows that it was given that the disciples might know the mysteries of the kingdom of heaven.

It is indeed the key to all the other parables, and only by understanding it aright can their true meaning be seen (Mark iv. 13). The householder is a scribe "instructed unto the kingdom of heaven" (Matt. xiii. 52).

The parable of the wicked husbandmen does not come in this list, for it is largely historical, and speaks of Israel in Old Testament times as well as in New. If it had dealt with the subsequent history of the vineyard when it had been taken from the husbandmen, and had described it under the new cultivation, it would have come under the period of the mysteries of the kingdom, but this is not its subject.

In the parable which follows in Matt. xxii. the history begins with the announcement to them that were bidden, that the feast was ready. It implies the Old Testament invitation, but does not dwell upon it.

By the majority of earlier expositors the dispensational character of the parables was almost entirely ignored and only the moral and spiritual lessons expounded.

Those who are so taken up with the prophetic and dispensational aspect of the parables that they ignore the other side of their teaching, tell us that the parables in Matthew's Gospel have nothing to do with the present dispensation. To follow either line of teaching to the exclusion of the other must be wrong. Let us rather take both, going as far in the one direction as in the other, and learning from the parables both spiritual and dispensational lessons. While it is quite evident that the Church is not synonymous with the kingdom, as so many writers on theology seem to suppose, we must not assume that they are in no way connected.

"The Royal Family" is not "the British Empire," but no one would say that the Royal Family has nothing to do with the British Empire, for it is included in it. True, the former stands in closer relationship to the king, but that relationship implies very intimate connection with the Empire over which he reigns.

It seems as incorrect to state that the Church has nothing to do with the kingdom of heaven parables as to say that these parables refer to the Church exclusively. It might just as well be said that the Church is not in the eleventh chapter of Romans, for the subject is Gentile privilege during Jewish dispersion, but we know that this is the very key to the present dispensation.

In God's sight "the Church which is His body" is unmixed with evil. It is composed only of those who are united by living faith to Christ, and no false professors can be members of His body.

In this its *heavenly* aspect it is true to say that the Church is not the subject of these parables,[1] but in

[1] With the exception possibly of the pearl and the treasure, which some think refer to the Church.

its *earthly* aspect, from man's side, it is impossible for us to eliminate the evil from the good.

Those who profess to belong to the kingdom will be judged accordingly, as we see in several of the parables.

The passages where the expression "The kingdom of heaven" is used, may be grouped under four heads, describing :—

The kingdom in *power*, in *patience*, by *possession* and *profession*. They give two aspects of the kingdom—manifestation and mystery ; and two kinds of subjects—nominal and real. The threefold proclamation comes under the first heading, though it also shows that repentance is a necessary preparation for truly belonging to the kingdom. The parables belong to the second division, but also describe the two classes, and the other passages about entering, possessing, or taking rank in the kingdom, refer to its subjects.

Three times in the Psalms (xviii. 44 ; lxvi. 3 ; lxxxi. 15), we are told that during the millennial reign of Christ there will be those who only "yield feigned obedience ;" so also there are, in the days of the mysteries of the kingdom, those who nominally profess allegiance, and thus include themselves in the kingdom of heaven although their hearts have never acknowledged His sway.

It is impossible to refer the words "The kingdom of heaven" *only* to the Messianic kingdom as prophesied in the Old Testament, for it is used in the parables in connection with the time of His absence ; nor will it do to state that it *only* applies to the time of the King's absence, for the proclamation of its nearness and the promises concerning it at the beginning of Matthew's Gospel require the King's presence.

We are therefore driven to the conclusion that the expression bears both meanings, first referring to the time of the King's manifestation, then after

His rejection to the time of His withdrawal and
return.

The scrupulous pains taken by the Jews to avoid
mentioning the name of Jehovah was but a symptom
that they had lost contact with Him, and it is possible
that the use of the expression by our Lord implied
this.   His words were very strong : " Ye hypocrites !
well did Esaias prophesy of you, saying, This people
. . . honoureth Me with their lips ; but their heart is
far from Me."   When such was their condition He
could not reign in their midst, and there is probably
on this account an analogy between the expression
"The kingdom of heaven" and two titles which are
given to Jehovah in the Old Testament, viz., "The
God of heaven" and "The Lord of the whole
earth."

In that remarkable passage in Deut. xxxii. 8, 9, we
read : "When the Most High divided to the nations
their inheritance, when He separated the sons of
Adam, He set the bounds of the peoples according to
the number of the children of Israel.   For the Lord's
portion is His people, Jacob is the lot of His inheritance."   Both history and geography have been determined by God's purposes towards Israel.

When as a nation they crossed the river Jordan and
entered the land, God for the first time assumed the
title of "Lord of all the earth" (Joshua iii. 11, 13),
and it has been pointed out that this title is only given
in association with Israel in the land.   In the five
other passages where it is found (Isa. liv. 5 ; Micah
iv. 13 ; Zech. iv. 14 ; vi. 5 ; Psa. xcvii. 5) the prophets
are looking forward to a time when the people have
returned and Messiah's reign will have commenced.

During the captivity, in Ezra, Nehemiah, and
Daniel, Jehovah is constantly called "The God of
heaven."   The kingdom is in abeyance, and though
"The Most High ruleth in the kingdom of men"

(Dan. iv. 17, 25, 32), and "the heavens do rule" (verse 26), the "kingdoms of this world" have not yet "become the kingdoms of our Lord, and of His Christ." When this has taken place the throne will once more be set up in Jerusalem, and the closing word of the last song of degrees, the benediction of Psa. cxxxiv., will be possible: "The Lord, that made heaven and earth, bless thee *out of Zion*." Meanwhile during the times of the Gentiles He is the God of heaven, and it may be that in the same way we have mention in these parables of "the kingdom of heaven" as the place of His authority, instead of denoting the character of it as in other passages where it is used. The King is seated not on the earthly throne that was promised, but on the right hand of His Father in heaven, waiting for the time when He will come to set up His kingdom.

The hidden rule from heaven has taken the place, for the time being, of the manifested rule upon earth. But if this analogy exists between the Old Testament titles and the expression "kingdom of heaven," it seems only to do so when the kingdom in mystery is referred to.

Besides these two expressions, there are others which should also be noticed. The disciples were to see the "kingdom of God" in power (Luke ix. 27; Mark ix. 1), or, as Matthew tells us, "the Son of Man coming in His kingdom" (xvi. 28), and this was probably fulfilled at the transfiguration when they caught a glimpse of the kingdom in miniature.[1]

In the model prayer, "Thy kingdom come," the disciples were taught to pray for the kingdom of the Father, and when the wheat is garnered the righteous will "shine forth as the sun in the kingdom of their Father" (Matt. xiii. 43).

[1] See 2 Peter i. 16.

In Luke xxii. 16, 18, the Lord speaks of eating and
drinking "in the kingdom of God," in verse 30 He
says in "My kingdom," and in Matt. xxvi. 29, "in My
Father's kingdom."

Col. i. 13 (*marg.*), tells us that we have been "translated into the kingdom of the Son of His love."

Eph. v. 5, speaks of "inheritance in the kingdom of
Christ and of God," and Rev. xi. 15, of the time when
"the kingdoms of this world are become the kingdoms
of our Lord ; and of His Christ." Many other passages
might be quoted, but these seem to prove that the
different expressions are used according to the
different relationships of the King and the several
portions or aspects of His realm. *He* is the same in
all, but He is presented as the Messiah or Christ in
"the kingdom of heaven," as God or Son of God in
"the kingdom of God ; " as the Son of the Father in
"the kingdom of the Father," and "the kingdom of
the Son of His love ;" as the God-Man in "the
kingdom of the Son of Man."

Those who say that this dispensation is not included
in "the kingdom of heaven" will say that we have
nothing to do with Him as Messiah, but it was to the
Messiah that the promise was given in the forty-ninth
of Isaiah and elsewhere, of being a light to lighten the
Gentiles, and it is on the ground of this promise that
during the Church dispensation He can "visit the
Gentiles, to take out of them a people for His Name."

In the thirteenth of Matthew the Evangelist interposes an explanation of the reason why the Lord
from this time spoke in parables, prefacing the
very remarkable quotation from Psalm lxxviii. 2,
by the words, " *That it might be fulfilled*, which
was spoken by the prophet, saying, I will open
my mouth in parables ; I will utter things which
have been kept secret from the foundation of the
world."

This is striking, for several reasons. First, it asserts the prophetic character of the Psalms, a most important truth which is entirely ignored by "higher critics." Then, again, we learn that the prophetic character was of such high order that what was foretold had to be fulfilled ; and also the words give us a clue to the interpretation of the parables. If they were spoken concerning something that had been hidden from the foundation of the world the subject could not be the final Messianic kingdom or its triumphant supremacy over the kingdoms of this world. This was no secret, but, as the apostle Peter proclaimed in the temple, it was to be "the times of restitution of all things, which God had spoken by the mouth of all His holy prophets since the world began." He was referring to the restoration in the jubilee year in Israel, a beautiful type of the coming jubilee when the Lord Jesus Christ would return to His family and to His land (Lev. xxv. 10–13). Peter continued, "Yea, and all the prophets from Samuel [1] and those that follow after, as many as have spoken, have likewise foretold of these days" (Acts iii. 19–24).

The mysteries of the kingdom, veiled to the people, and unveiled to the disciples in these parables, cannot, therefore, refer to the Messianic kingdom in its manifestation. The apostle Peter refers, however, in his Epistle to something which had been kept secret, into which the prophets had inquired and searched diligently, "which things the angels desire to look into" (1 Pet. i. 10–12). He shows that what they could not understand was the manner of time which was to elapse between "the sufferings of Christ and the glory that should follow." This is the time of the kingdom in mystery and the subject of the parables.

[1] The first mention of " Messiah " as " His King," "His Anointed," is in 1 Sam. ii. 10.

The Psalm which is introduced by the words quoted by Matthew, recapitulates the failures of Israel, and ends with the choosing of David the hepherd to feed His people, and with his reign over them. Is it not suggestive that this dark picture of Israel's history—representing the very things which the apostle tells us happened to them as ensamples for us—should be linked with the parables which tell of the failure and corruption that mark the history of those who profess to be His people in the period of the Lord's absence?

The time covered by the mysteries of the kingdom seems to include all other "mysteries," and it may be that the expression also includes them. It has often been pointed out that the "mystery of godliness" (1 Tim. iii. 16) probably speaks not only of the God-Man, but, especially in the last phrase, includes the Church, which is His body. (1) "Manifest in the flesh," at the incarnation; (2) "justified in the Spirit," by the resurrection; (3) "seen of angels," who witnessed it; (4) "preached unto the Gentiles," because of Israel's rejection; (5) "believed on in the world" out of which He was taking a people for His name; and (6) "received up into glory." If the Lord alone were referred to it would seem as though this last clause would have been placed before the preaching to the Gentiles.

Many of the mysteries of which the apostle speaks range themselves round these six facts. In Rom. xvi. 25, 26, he speaks of "the revelation of the mystery" in connection with the fourth and fifth, "made known to all nations, for the obedience of faith."

In Rom. xi. 25, 26, we have a mystery of the kingdom which is a key to the understanding of Matt. xiii., viz., "that blindness in part is happened to Israel, until the fulness of the Gentiles be come in;" and it explains also the fourth clause in the passage in Timothy, "preached unto the Gentiles." This, too, is closely linked with Paul's *great* mystery;[1] the mystery of the Christ, Christ and His members, "the Church which is His body;" or as he expresses it in Eph. iii. 3–10, "that the Gentiles should be fellow-heirs, and of the same body, and partakers of His promise in Christ;" and that he was to "preach among *the Gentiles* the unsearchable riches of Christ" (see also Col. i. 26, 27).

In 1 Cor. xv. 51, there is the mystery that "we shall not all sleep, but we shall all be changed," and this corresponds with the last fact in 1 Tim. iii. 16, "received up into glory."

Paul was a "steward of the mysteries of God" (1 Cor. iv. 1), and his preaching included all the mysteries of the kingdom. His fourfold testimony is given in Acts xx. 21, 24, 25, 27. (1) Repentance toward God, and faith toward our Lord Jesus Christ;" (2) testifying "the gospel of the grace of God;" (3) "preaching the kingdom of God;" and (4) declaring "the whole counsel of God" (R.V.).

"The mystery of His will" (Eph. i. 9–10) refers to the time of ingathering and manifestation, when the treasure and the pearl which cost Him so much will be displayed before the universe.

Paul speaks in 2 Thess. ii. 7, of another mystery, which is described in the parable of the leaven. "The mystery of iniquity doth already work," and he tells us that it will culminate in the manifestation of antichrist. As one has said, "The mystery of *godliness* is God humbling Himself to become man," this is the beginning of the one; and "the mystery of *iniquity* is man exalting himself to become God," this is the culmination of the second.

---

[1] The word "*great*" is used in this connection twice (1 Tim. iii. 16, and Eph. v. 32).

Another mystery was revealed to John in vision. "Mystery, Babylon the Great" (Rev. xvii.). There is surely an analogy between this and the parable of the mustard-seed. A tree was in Dan. iv. 10–12, 19–22, typical of the literal Babylon and its king. The mystic Babylon and literal Babylon of future days (Rev. xvii. and xviii.) will both be included in this mystery of iniquity ; and of Mystery Babylon we read, it "is become the habitation of demons, and the hold of every foul spirit, and a cage of every unclean and hateful bird," reminding us of "the birds of the air" who "come and lodge in the branches" of the mustard-tree.

"The mystery of the seven stars" must belong to the period before the millennial reign has set in ; whether the opening chapters of Revelation refer to the state of things in the time of the seer, to the history of the Church now, or to a future time,— indeed, they seem to bear this threefold interpretation. It is a vision of a night season, for the stars in His hand can only be seen while He hides His face, which is "as the sun shineth in his strength," and then only is it that the lamp-stands are needed. The apostle tells us also that he was in the kingdom and patience of Jesus Christ, a contrast to the manifestation of the kingdom.

When at last the mighty angel swears "by Him that liveth for ever and ever . . ." that there shall "be delay no longer . . . then is finished the mystery of God, according to the good tidings which He declared to His servants the prophets" (Rev. x. 6, 7, R.V., *marg.*). All the mysteries of the kingdom will then have come to an end. This, we are told, is to be "in the days of the voice of the seventh angel, when he is about to sound ;" and in the following chapter (xi. 15) we read, "The seventh angel sounded ; and there were great voices in heaven, saying, The

kingdoms of this world are become the kingdoms
of our Lord, and of His Christ ; and He shall reign
for ever and ever." "The Lord hath prepared His
throne in the heavens ; and (at last) His kingdom
ruleth over all."

"Learn to think imperially," was Mr Chamberlain's
message at the Guildhall a short time ago. "Person-
ally," he said, "I am totally unable to separate this
great city—the metropolis of the empire—from the
kingdom of which it forms a part."

This should be our attitude towards the kingdom
of our Lord and Saviour Jesus Christ. The kingdom
is one, though, as we have seen, the aspects under
which it may be considered are very numerous
and the relationships very varied. It is possible
for an Englishman to be entirely occupied with his
own concerns, his own parish, or city, or county ;
or with Great Britain alone, instead of thinking of
the Empire as a whole ; so, too, a Christian may
have very limited views. We whose citizenship is
in heaven, need to "think imperially." We must
not consider only our personal salvation or spiritual
blessings, nor must we be interested merely in our
own little corner of the field or in its mission work
in foreign lands. It is not enough even to try and
include in our thoughts the whole of God's people
and their labour for God, or to look back on all
Church history. We should take even larger views
than these, and see that the period of this dispensation is but one small part of God's plan,
and that it is no more the whole kingdom than
this great metropolis [1] is the whole British Empire.
We need, by the teaching of God's Spirit, to
learn something of His future plans if we are to
"think imperially," and to understand that the
time is coming "when the kingdoms of this world"

---

[1] Israel or Jerusalem might rather claim to be His metropolis.

will "become the kingdom of our Lord; and of His Christ." To enter truly into dispensational teaching is to cease to think selfishly of our personal privileges in Christ, or even of those of the Church merely. We have been translated out of darkness into the kingdom of His dear Son, but the present aspect of His kingdom is only a tiny portion of the great empire over which He will one day hold sway. May He give us grace to "think imperially."

CHAPTER XI

THE THIRTEENTH OF MATTHEW

THE parables in the thirteenth of Matthew form a group by themselves, and may be compared and contrasted in many ways. The innumerable books and pamphlets that have been written on this important but most difficult chapter may, generally speaking, be classified according to the three lines of teaching which they represent. The majority of writers treat these parables merely as to their moral and spiritual teaching, taking them independently, and thus missing much of their intention. Of the other two methods of interpretation, which resemble one another in treating the parables dispensationally, one school looks on them as pictures of the time of the Lord's absence, some writers among them viewing them as consecutive representations of the condition of Christendom; while by the third class they are pronounced to be entirely Jewish, having nothing to do with the present dispensation.

Is it not more than probable that there is much truth in all three lines of teaching,—the spiritual lessons, the pictures of the present state of things, and the future meaning for days to come, when the Church has been removed? To take the latter interpretation to the exclusion of the others is as wrong as to take only the spiritual lessons, ignoring all dispensational teaching.

In looking at the parables in Matt. xiii. as consecutive pictures there certainly seems an analogy between the condition of things depicted in the first four, and the early chapters of Church history. There was first the broadcast sowing, then the mixture of tares with the wheat ; the abnormal growth of professing Christianity, such as took place in the days of Constantine ; and the leaven permeating the meal through the instrumentality of the woman.

These characteristics were very marked in the centuries before the " dark ages " of the Church's and the world's history, but this method of interpretation fails when it comes to the fifth and sixth parables, the hidden treasure and the pearl, for it is only by great ingenuity that they can be made to represent the Reformation and other periods. The details of the two parables must for this be reversed, the finder and seeker taken to represent men instead of the Lord Himself.

If there is consecutive teaching in the chapter, the break at the end of the fourth parable claims notice, when the Lord ceased speaking to the multitudes and addressed His disciples alone. Even if we accept it thus far we must also see that all the four were true pictures of the professing Church in the days of the apostles. There was then the sowing of the seed broadcast, so that Paul could say that the gospel had been preached " in all the world " ; the enemy began at once to introduce the tares ; there was a rapid growth ; and the leaven, the mystery of iniquity, had already begun to work.

We see also that all four pictures represent the condition of things now, in ever-increasing measure. In these days of gospel privilege and freedom, the Word has been scattered broadcast in a way that was impossible formerly, but it is also true that the tares have multiplied as well. The mustard seed too is larger than ever, and there is room for an ever-increasing number of birds. The leaven has been spreading rapidly, and there is no doubt that the whole lump is becoming leavened.

This does not at all interfere with the view held by some, viz., that the whole has reference to the days to come, when the Lord will again have taken up Israel preparatory to the establishing of His kingdom on earth.

As we have seen in the preceding chapter, the actual kingdom, as prophesied of old, is not described in these parables ; they lead us no further than the King's arrival on the scene, and the acts of judgment preparatory to the reign of peace. They no more represent the kingdom itself than 1 Kings ii. describes the reign of Solomon. That chapter only tells us of the purging out of all things that did offend, and of them which did iniquity. The interval between the rejection of Messiah and His return may be divided into three eras. First, the days of the apostles, then the long ensuing period until the taking up of the Church, and lastly, the interval between the two stages of His coming.

Though we cannot harmonise interpretations which are actually opposed to one another, such as leaven representing good and evil, it is more than probable that successive interpretations are in many cases needed in order to grasp the full meaning of the picture.

Attention has often been called to the suggestive break in the middle of the chapter. The parables in the first group were spoken to the multitude when the Lord "went out of the house and sat by the seaside. And great multitudes were gathered together unto Him, so that He went into a ship and sat, and the whole multitude stood on the shore." [1] The conversation with the disciples, in which He explained His reasons for speaking in parables, and interpreted

_____

[1] The sea in Scripture often represents the world.

the parable of the sower, also took place in the
ship ; but the second group was spoken in the house
to them "that were about Him with the twelve"
(Mark iv. 10).

It is generally stated that there are seven parables in
Matt. xiii.—four spoken to the multitude on the shore,
and three to the disciples in the house. This is
true so far as the most familiar and generally accepted
parables are concerned ; but just as there are only
seven notes in the scale, and yet an eighth is required to
make the octave repeating the first note in another
key, so after the seven parables, there is an eighth which
completes the group. It seems strange that this should
be so constantly overlooked. It is not shorter than
those of the leaven and the treasure, and refers like
them to the kingdom of heaven. A question from the
Lord and an answer from the disciples come between
it and the remainder of the group, but these do
not break the sequence, but rather prove its connection with all the rest. "Jesus saith unto them,
Have ye understood all these things ? They say
unto Him, Yea, Lord. Then said He unto them,
Therefore every scribe which is instructed unto the
kingdom of heaven, is like unto a man that is an
householder, which bringeth forth out of his treasure things new and old." It has been said that
this is only an analogy, but it is evidently included in
the parables. The first group of four closes with the
words, "All these things spake Jesus unto the multitude in parables" (verse 34). The second group of
four is concluded by similar words, "When Jesus had
finished these parables, He departed thence" (verse 53).

The illustrations in a book may vary in the method
of their production, or in the medium used ; they
may be coloured, or only in black and white ; they
may be outline sketches, or copies of photographs,
maps or diagrams, woodcuts or engravings ; but the

importance is in the illustration, not in its form.
In the same way the figurative language under which
" His doctrine " was presented may be in the form of
parable, metaphor, analogy, or simile—indeed, most of
the parables are analogies. The chief importance lies
in the teaching enfolded in the figure rather than in
the form in which it is pictured.

The contents of the chapter may thus be enumerated, *first*, the parable of the sower, followed by
three parables introduced by the words, " Another
parable put He forth unto them," or " spake He ; " and
commencing, " The kingdom of heaven is like," or
" likened to." Then after the dismissal of the multitude, there are *three more*, each introduced by the word
" again," and beginning like the other three ; and *lastly*,
the little parable of the householder, not exactly
like the others in form, but very important as to
subject. It covers all the preceding seven, for it
shows the use which is to be made of the teaching
they contain. It also gives a key to their interpretation, for the " things new and old " are plainly the
things contained in the preceding parables, and
therefore the mysteries of the kingdom must include
both. Some teach that the kingdom parables refer
only to the earthly kingdom prophesied of old, and that
the new is entirely excluded, while others see only
the present dispensation ; but there are things new and
old in His teaching, and we must recognise them both
as equally true and equally important. Possibly it
also suggests that the successive interpretations
already alluded to may be in the same parable.
The first group is therefore comprised of $1 + 3$
parables, the second of $3 + 1$. These central triplets
may be again subdivided into $1 + 2$ and $2 + 1$; for
the first in one group, the tares, and the last in the
other, the net, are strikingly alike in many ways, and
the two pairs must be contrasted.

The first parable, that of the sower, is easier to understand than the two groups of three which follow it ; it is indeed a key to the whole parabolic teaching of our Lord, and for many reasons it seems naturally to head any list of the parables. We have seen from its position in Matthew's Gospel that it marks a great epoch in the history of Israel, and the life of our Lord. The King has been rejected, and the command to His disciples is revoked. He no longer bids them go only to "the lost sheep of the house of Israel." The sphere of labour is now the field of the world. The position of the "whosoever" at the close of the twelfth chapter is most instructive, for it immediately follows the description of the nation's condition as depicted in the parable of the unclean spirit, and was uttered in connection with His repudiation of earthly relationships. When told that His mother and brethren stood without, perhaps wishing to recall Him to His home, He answered, "Who is My mother ? and who are My brethren ? And He stretched forth His hand toward His disciples, and said, Behold My mother, and My brethren ! For whosoever shall do the will of My Father which is in heaven, the same is My brother, and sister, and mother."

From this time forth the Lord spake in parables, as we have seen. But besides this, the parable of the sower seems to furnish a clue to the understanding of the other parables. The private interpretation given to the disciples shows us how much meaning there is in all of them, but more than this the Lord said, "Know ye not this parable ? and how then will ye know all parables ?" (Mark iv. 13). He probably did not mean merely that it was the simplest of all, but that to understand the parable of the sower thoroughly was to understand the change of dispensation which was about to take place. The promised kingdom was to be postponed, it could not yet be set up on earth as foretold by the prophets; and the King who should reign was about to take the humble position of a sower. None but His own would understand the change, but in this and the following parables He made known to the disciples the mysteries of the kingdom, and a mystery in Scripture means a secret revealed.[1]

The explanation of the parable of the tares,[2] which our Lord added in private to the disciples, is the fullest explanation given of any parable except that of the sower, and yet it still presents many difficulties.

Although the two parables are alike in many respects, there are differences. The seed in the former represents the Word of God, in the latter those who have received the Word, so that, while in the second "the field is the world," in the sense of the place of their habitation, in the first "the field is the world" as in John iii. 16, "God so loved the world." In the one the enemy catches away the good seed, and in the other he sows tares.

Though it is not related in the first parable we know that the enemy follows the sower of the Word with his basket containing another kind of seed— the seed of error—which he tries to scatter wherever the good seed of the Word falls.

"The tares are the children of the wicked one." What a solemn word is this, and how contrary to the modern doctrine of the universal Fatherhood of God. There were those who were called sons of Belial in Old Testament times; there are two men who are specially mentioned as children of Satan— Cain and Judas—and the Lord said to the Jews, "Ye are of

---

[1] The parable of the sower is considered amongst those which bring before us teaching respecting the Word of God (pp. 279–284).

[2] Or darnel. "Tares" could easily be distinguished from wheat, but the darnel, which is supposed to be the plant referred to, appears in its earlier stages to be almost exactly similar to it.

your father the devil." In Matt. xxiii. 33, the scribes and Pharisees are addressed by the Lord as "serpents, generation of vipers." They were the actual seed of the serpent. The beloved disciple (1 John iii.) clearly describes the different marks of the two families, and shows how tares and wheat may be distinguished. In their early stages the two may be mistaken, but as they grow the ripening fruit shows which is which.

The enemy had begun his work even while the Lord was Himself on earth. He had to say of His twelve disciples, "And one of you is a devil."

The scattering of the good seed is the work of the great Sower Himself. If He were to keep the precious grain in His basket, there would be no increase and no harvest, and so He scatters the children of the kingdom throughout His field that there may be a glorious ingathering. In the persecution that arose after the death of Stephen we might have thought it was Satan who had succeeded in dispersing the Church at Jerusalem when "they were all scattered abroad throughout the regions of Judæa and Samaria, except the apostles;" but this parable teaches us that it was really the heavenly Sower, according to His own purpose, planting His seed-bearers in different furrows of the field.

It is important to notice that the field is the world, and not the Church. The parable has nothing to do with the church discipline to which the Apostle Paul refers in 1 Cor. v. It does not teach that false professors, when proved to be false, are still to be counted amongst true believers, nor does it teach, like Rome, that heretics are to be put to death. The servants, in asking permission to cut down the tares, asked to destroy them, and this would mean taking them out of the field altogether, which was distinctly forbidden. For the same reason, the binding of the tares in bundles cannot take place while they are still growing in the field.   Some have supposed that this is already going on in the associations of evil that are formed amongst men.   In the harvest field the corn is not tied up till the sickle has been thrust in, and then the sheaves are made up according to the time of reaping and the place where it has grown.   So we read that the owner of the field said, "Let both grow together until the harvest : and in the time of harvest I will say to the reapers, Gather ye together first the tares, and bind them in bundles to burn them; but gather the wheat into my barn."   To try and define how the bundles are made up is to create difficulties.

Some have suggested a difficulty in the fact that the tares are bound first, but in the instructions to the servants the tares are only to be gathered when the wheat is ready for the sickle.   It is the condition of the wheat which determines the time for gathering and binding the tares.   Then the reapers are told to bind them "to burn them," in order that they may be burned when the time comes.   Though the tares will be gathered out of the kingdom at the beginning, the actual burning may not take place till the great final judgment, except in the case of those who have been chief amongst them—the beast and the false prophet.   The order, first the tares and then the wheat, reminds us of "one shall be taken, and the other left," the one taken away for judgment, as the context and illustration clearly show, the other left for the kingdom (Matt. xxiv. 37-39).

The name given to this parable by the disciples is suggestive.   They said, "Declare unto us the parable of the tares of the field."   They had understood that the history of the tares was the chief subject in the picture, and this the Lord's explanation proved. There was first the origin of the tares, then the growth of the tares ; there was the letting alone of the tares till the harvest, then, when that day came, the binding in bundles ready for burning, and after the ingathering, the casting of the bundles of weed into the fire. The history of the wheat is not the prominent feature of the story; it is, comparatively speaking, incidental. Many have been the varied interpretations as to who are represented by the wheat. Some see in it the Church, others see all God's children, others see only Jews. The Church alone cannot be meant, for the parable takes us right on to the time of the Lord's coming in power to set up His kingdom, and for the same reason the harvest cannot mean only the taking up of the Church, though this may be included as a preliminary. The Lord Himself will gather us to meet Him in the air, but He will send forth His angels finally to gather in His wheat.

Our Lord, in John xii., compares Himself to a corn of wheat which, if it die, bringeth forth much fruit. May not the wheat in this parable represent the "much fruit" borne by that single "corn of wheat," which is in turn sown in the earth that it too may bring forth fruit? Ever since His days the two kinds of grain have been sown and have grown side by side; by-and-by they will be finally separated.

A harvest was never all gathered in one day. In Israel the first ripe ears that were cut were waved before the Lord as the sheaf of the first-fruits, and this represents Christ and His Church. "Christ the first-fruits (or, as some read it, 'the Christ'), afterward they that are Christ's at His coming." The real harvest "at His coming," is the time specially described in the parable.

To assume that the parable of the tares refers only to the time after the Church has been taken up is to imply that there is nothing growing for God in the field of the world. We know that the early part of this parable exactly describes the condition of things now, wheat and darnel growing together.

The fact that the taking up of the Church is not the subject of the parable does not imply that this dispensation is not included.   An Israelite of old who had conformed to the Mosaic law, and had waved the sheaf of the first-fruits, would probably not mention it in speaking of the harvest.   It was the preliminary of·the ingathering.

As we have seen, the taking up of the saints was not understood as the first stage of His return till it was revealed to Paul ; but in the light of this fuller knowledge we understand that before the whole field is reaped there will be a first-fruits presented to God.

The *second pair* of parables in the thirteenth of Matthew consists of the mustard-seed and the leaven. In both of these we have a collective aspect of the mysteries of the kingdom of heaven, whereas in the former pair individuals were described.   There is first the reception of the good seed in individual hearts and then the sowing of good or bad seed ; represented by individual " children of the kingdom," and " children of the wicked one."   In the mustard-seed it is viewed as one object, and in the leavened meal as one.

Two very opposite views of these parables have been taken by theologians.   The one school sees in both a figure of the spread of the gospel, a picture of unmixed good, and this, almost without exception, was the interpretation given by older writers. [1]   The other class of Bible students view the two parables as

---

[1] In the opening sentence of Neander's "Church History" we find a good illustration of the way in which these parables have been generally applied, and yet the historian shows in the succeeding volumes that the rapid spread of the Christian religion was not an unmixed blessing, and that there was a development of evil at the same time.   He thus commences his introduction : "It shall be our purpose to trace, from the small mustard grain through the course of the past centuries, lying open for our inspection, the growth of that mighty tree which is destined to overshadow the earth, and under the branches of which all its people are to find a safe habitation.   The history will show how a little leaven, cast into the mass of humanity, has been gradually penetrating it."

showing unsatisfactory results ; they detect in them a prophecy of the progress and admixture of evil, and of seeming failure in that which at the beginning was only good. Which of these two lines of teaching is correct ? Taking the parables separately, apart from their context and from the rest of Scripture, it is easy to see how the more popular interpretation was arrived at ; but comparing the pictures with other passages in Scripture, it is impossible to take this optimistic view.

What mystery of the kingdom does the mustard-seed represent ? In Old Testament language we often find kingdoms of earth and their kings represented by trees. Nebuchadnezzar, in Dan. iv., and Assyria, in Ezek. xxxi., are compared to great spreading trees ; but the mustard-seed in its abnormal growth is merely "a garden shrub outdoing itself." It looks like a tree, but what is the good of it ? Its fruit, a little pungent seed, is attractive to the birds of the air, good for flavouring, but very different from the nourishing wheat. In the first parable the birds of the air represented " the wicked one," according to Matthew ; " Satan," in Mark ; " the devil," in Luke ; and it is more than likely in this third parable that they have the same significance.

In the early centuries of Church history, when persecution had failed to exterminate the light of the gospel, Satan tried by other means to weaken its power and mar its testimony. The Church became mixed with the world and soon strove after political power. It wanted to be like the other kingdoms, and indeed to rule over them. Various historians, viewing the spread of so-called Christianity from different standpoints, look upon this growth as a triumph or as a disaster, and in their contrary opinions represent the two lines of interpretation of the parable. Was the so-called conversion of Constantine a triumph or a calamity ?

It is often stated that our Lord compares faith to a mustard-seed, and that therefore the comparison in Matthew xiii. is good ; but a closer study of the two passages about faith (Matt. xvii. 20, and Luke xvii. 6) will show us that He compares faith to some unknown force able to produce an earthquake. Faith has greater power than gunpowder, dynamite, or gun-cotton, for a tiny amount no larger than a mustard-seed would be sufficient to remove a mountain or uproot a tree ; and not only could it produce an earthquake which destroys, but could transplant the tree and set up the mountain again in the sea. Thus the Lord did not compare faith to a mustard-seed. If it were stated that a piece of gun-cotton the size of a pea would produce such and such an effect, this would not be making a comparison between destructive gun-cotton and a harmless pea. It is merely a simple means of denoting something very small in size.

As we compare the mustard-seed with the trees of the wood, we are reminded of the bramble in Jotham's parable that wished to rule over the other trees, and invited them to come and put their trust in its shadow. Here we have a herb that tries to be a tree. It endeavours to be like the trees of the wood. Much mischief was done by the Church wanting to assume political power and constantly struggling for supremacy.

The next parable also, that of the leavened meal, has been taken to represent both the spread of good and the spread of evil. Those who take the first as its meaning say that this is the one occasion in the Bible when leaven is used as a symbol of good, and they read, " The kingdom of heaven is like unto leaven," and ask how can it be likened to what is evil ? But in reading the verse we must not stop there. It is the whole incident that resembles the kingdom in mystery. In a subsequent parable we do not read, " The kingdom of heaven is like unto a certain *king*," and stop there. We quite understand that it is likened to the whole story of the marriage-feast.

Leaven was to the Jews the symbol of evil, and as such had to be put out of their houses at the time of the Passover, that they might keep the feast of unleavened bread. There could be no two opinions amongst them as to its signifying evil, and as so often pointed out, the Lord emphasised this by warning His disciples against the leaven of the Pharisees, Sadducees, and Herodians; and Paul used the same simile to denote evil doctrine (Gal. v. 9) ; and evil walk (1 Cor. v. 6). Its twofold aspect is summed up in his warning against "filthiness of the flesh and spirit" (2 Cor. vii. 1).

A woman, in Scripture, generally seems in symbolic language to represent a system or a people. The woman with the light in the fifteenth of Luke is taken to represent the Church, and the woman here, though very differently occupied, seems also to signify the professing Church. What is she doing ? Is she simply making bread, or is there not a deeper meaning in the parable ?

It has often been remarked that the first mention of a word or expression is always suggestive. This law has been thus stated, "The only unfailing method of interpreting Scripture is the structural method. Where do you first hear of any matter, and where the end of it ? Then compare the beginning and the end in order to get a firm grasp of the general character of all that intervenes." This is suggestive when applied both to the leaven and the "three measures of meal." The first allusion to leaven is in Gen. xix. 3, where Lot baked *unleavened* bread for his angel visitors ; the next is in Exod. xii. 8. Both incidents seem to suggest that leavened bread was the habitual food of these two countries.

We may be quite sure that our Lord had some reason for naming the quantity as "three measures," and by looking at other instances where it was used we probably have a clue to the interpretation of the parable.

The first time we read of "three measures of meal" is in Gen. xviii. 6, where Abraham prepared refreshment for the Lord. The smallest amount that might be offered as a meal-offering according to the law of Moses was an omer, the tenth part of an ephah (Exod. xvi. 36). Three-tenths was the most usual offering, and it is seven times mentioned in Num. xv. 9; xxviii. 12, 20, 28; xxix. 3, 9, 14.

The "measure" here spoken of was the third part of an ephah, and therefore three measures were equal to an ephah. This same amount was offered as a meal-offering by Gideon (Judges vi. 18, 19), and by Hannah (1 Sam. i. 24); and this is also the quantity commanded for the meal-offerings in the prophetic chapters of Ezekiel, where the ephah, or three measures of fine flour, is mentioned seven times—Ezek. xlv. 24 (twice); xlvi. 5, 7 (twice), 11 (twice).

When we study the parable in the light of all these passages it seems very probable that there is some reference in the three measures of meal to the meal-offering, of which it is distinctly commanded, "No meat-offering which ye shall bring unto the Lord, shall be made with leaven" (Lev. ii. 11). This is the view taken by Mr. F. W. Grant, who says, "The woman is doing what the Word of God prohibits, she is putting leaven in the meal-offering. . . . The meal-offering speaks . . . of Christ as the food of His people, of which they partake in communion with God. . . . Christ, the bread of life, is what the professing Church has had entrusted to her for her own sustenance and for the blessing of others. The doctrine of Christ is her most precious deposit, and the maintaining this in purity her great responsibility. Alas! she has adulterated it with leaven. . . . And here distinctly 'the woman's' form appears in that which Scripture itself stamps as 'the mother of harlots and abominations of the earth' (Rev. xvii.), she who, claiming emphatically to be the 'Church,' at the same time assumes the power of adding to it her own authoritative interpretations."[1] This seems a terrible picture, but it was a true prophecy of what was very soon to commence in the professing Church.

There is still another interpretation which may be suggested for the meal, also an aspect of the meal-offering. It may be looked upon as symbolic of the Church itself. The good seed in the parable of the sower is the Word—either the written or the incarnate Word; in that of the tares it represents the receivers of the Word; and in like manner the meal may have any of these three significations. The corn of wheat which is Christ Himself brings forth the harvest of His own; Christ is the first-fruits, afterward they that are Christ's at His coming, and so we may look on the meal (another form of the grain) as Himself, His Word, or His people. This last is the meaning given to it by the apostle who compares the Church to a loaf in 1 Cor. x. 17, "We being many are one loaf," and in the same Epistle he speaks of the possibility of the whole lump being leavened (1 Cor. v. 6). This view seems most appropriate when the parable of the leaven is compared with that which immediately follows.

It may be objected that this interpretation makes both the woman and the meal represent the same thing, but if it were so the double symbolism would be quite in accordance with types and parables (pp. 295, 296). The same thing might be said of such a passage as Rom. xii. 1, where the offerers and the offerings are the same persons, "I beseech you therefore, brethren, by the mercies of God, that ye present your bodies a living sacrifice."

[1] "The Numerical Bible." F. W. Grant.

Whether the parable represents the professing Church as preparing food for herself, or a meal-offering for God, and whether that meal-offering is Christ alone or Christ and His Church, we cannot say. In either case what she needed was the Spirit's power, the *oil* instead of the leaven. This was always to accompany the meal-offering, the cakes were either to be "mingled with oil or . . . anointed with oil" (Lev. ii. 4). In Ezek. xlvi. 11, we read that a hin of oil was to be presented with every ephah brought as a meal-offering, "to temper with the fine flour," or to moisten it. That which is to be presented to God must be filled and anointed with the Spirit, and what the Church has needed from the first has been the Spirit's indwelling and anointing power. Had this truth been recognised the mystery of iniquity would not have succeeded in its permeating work.

While the apostle Paul evidently gave a present interpretation to the parable of the leaven, a study of Lev. xxiii. suggests a future application as well. It may be connected with the two leavened loaves which formed the second first-fruits of Pentecost, "the oblation of the first-fruits" (Lev. ii. 12). The interpretation of the parable probably includes these various meal-offerings.

In these four parables there is a marked increase in the form which the evil takes. In the first, birds of the air hurriedly catch away certain seeds; in the second, the enemy sows tares deliberately, though secretly; in the third, there is no concealment, the birds of the air make their home in the shrub before the eyes of all; and in the fourth, the woman is not in the least ashamed of mixing leaven into the meal, in fact, she is rather proud of it, and is quite under the impression that she is actually improving it. In the first and third, there are the birds of the air; in the second and fourth, the actual addition of evil.

The parable of the mustard-seed describes the outward growth of the branches; and the parable of the leavened meal, the inward permeating of evil principle.

The setting of these two parables in Luke xiii. suggests their interpretation. It was a moment of seeming success following a miracle—"All His adversaries were ashamed; and all the people rejoiced for all the glorious things that were done by Him." But the Lord knew their hearts. The very men who had rejoiced to-day, would to-morrow join in the cry, "Crucify Him, crucify Him." So when they rejoice He mourns over Jerusalem (verse 34; see also xix. 37, 41; John xii. 12–15, 27).

He foresaw that there would be times when the cause of Christianity would seem to be very popular and would gain great applause, but He estimated this at its right value; and He knew also that when it gained in popularity it would lose in purity.

At first the evil is recognised as such, afterwards it pretends to be good.

> "Thus sin triumphs in Western Babylon,
> Yet not as sin, but as Religion."[1]

Our Lord's heart must have been grieved as He spoke of the sad condition of things which He foresaw, but we are reminded of the words of the prophet, "He shall not fail nor be discouraged;" and so turning now to His disciples He leads them apart, and shows them the bright side of the picture, the Godward aspect, faith's view.

The *third pair* of parables in this wonderful chapter presents to us a very different picture. If we had only the preceding parables we might be inclined to ask, "Is the kingdom of heaven a failure?" But when we go inside the house with our Lord He shows us the other side, and we can use the words of David, "When

---

[1] "The Church Militant."   George Herbert.

I thought to know this, it was too painful for me, until I went into the sanctuary of God ; then understood I." We look around us at the professing Church of Christendom and see the worldliness, the divisions, the errors, and we do not wonder that the question is asked, " Is Christianity a failure ? " But the King brings us into His chambers and there teaches us something of " the riches of the glory of His inheritance in the saints." The revelation He here gives is not for the crowd without, but for His own people ; none but they could understand His love and His grace.

The parables of the treasure trove and the costly pearl have been interpreted, like the preceding ones, in very opposite ways. The almost universal explanation of both used to be, and still is, according to many, that Christ Himself is the treasure and the pearl, that we must sell all we have in order to possess Him

Others who think the seven parables are a consecutive series of pictures see in these two the Reformation period, when the precious truths of the Gospel were discovered afresh. Either of these interpretations, however, seem inconsistent with the rest of the chapter and with the details of the parables themselves. The man in both is the same as He who in the second parable was proclaimed to be the Son of Man. He it is who sells all that He has to obtain the treasure and the pearl, for in each case He must become poor to gain possession of that on which He has set His heart.

Varied interpretations are given to these two parables by those who agree that the seeker is the Lord Himself. Some hold that the treasure is the Church, others think that it is Israel, or the remnant, and others that it represents all the redeemed of whatever dispensation.

In the interpretation of a former parable we are

told that the field is the world, and in Lev. xxvii. 16, we read the value of a field was estimated " according to the seed thereof." It was valued according to the harvest that could be reaped. In this parable His estimation was according to the treasure thereof, and we know that the price paid was His own blood. It is striking that the Lord calls it *a* field, not His field, as in the second parable. It becomes truly His after He has bought it.

In the same way some take the pearl of great price to represent Israel, and others think that it is the Church.

In the first of this pair of parables the treasure, though collective, is probably made up of units of precious things, such as coins, or jewels, or both. In the second there is but one object ; and so it may be that we have in the treasure a partially individual, and in the pearl an entirely collective, view. The two pictures together seem as though they may represent different aspects of the same thing, not one Israel, and the other the Church, but both alike, either the Church or all the redeemed, purchased by His own blood. This is probably an instance of double symbolism, the use of which is explained by Joseph in Gen. xli. 32 (see pp. 192, 193).

Both parables are very short and are evidently intended to emphasise the two truths, the costliness of the treasure or pearl, and the delight of the purchaser. Both stop at the same point, the completion of the purchase. We are not told what became of either the treasure or the pearl when they had passed into the possession of Him who paid the price.

Though we must not as a rule put into a parable what is not there, we are tempted to ask several questions. As to the treasure hid in the field, we should like to ask how it came there, why was it hidden, and who hid it ? What led the man to dig in that particular spot ?   Did he know that the treasure was there ?   If he had had no previous claim to it would the transaction have been perfectly fair to the owner of the field ?   Did not the field belong to him once ?   To be buried in the earth is not the natural place for a treasure, and the story seems to imply that it had been hidden on purpose.   May we not, from facts revealed in other parts of Scripture, assume something like this — a usurper had taken possession of the field, knowing nothing of what was safely concealed, but He who found it knew before that it was there.   He knew exactly where to look for it, and when He found it He rejoiced at its safety, and determined to buy back the field.   The field, we know, is the world, and the Lord paid the price for the whole, not that He might gain possession of Israel only, but that He might have all His redeemed, every one for whom His death paid the price ; not the Church merely, for that would exclude the multitude whom no man can number, who pass through the Great Tribulation ; and not the remnant only, for He did not buy back the field merely in order to gain possession of the 144,000.

The purchase price was paid on Calvary, but the parable goes no further.   It tells us nothing of what became of the treasure.   We may be quite sure that though it was necessary to hide it again for a little while, the man would lose no time in taking it out of the earth and putting it in its proper place.   It would only remain concealed " until the redemption of the purchased possession."   (See pp. 198–200.)

Is not the wonderful prayer in the seventeenth of John His intercession for the treasure hid in the field ?   He there pleads for the company whom He seven times mentions as " those whom Thou hast given Me."   They belong to Him by double right, given by the Father, and then purchased by

Himself. He speaks of them as being left in the world, like the treasure in the field, and prays that they may be kept. He embraces in His pleading all His own, those who should later believe on Him through the testimony of the earlier disciples. The prayer goes further than the parable, for whereas the latter ends with the treasure still in the field, the seventeenth of John looks on to the day when it will be lifted out, and raised to the position for which He secured it. "Father, I will that they also, whom Thou hast given Me, be with Me where I am : that they may behold My glory."

His work of redemption includes the bodies as well as the spirits of His people. Each one is precious to Him, and in a literal sense they will be buried in the field, only till they hear the voice of the archangel, and are raised or changed at His coming. Then the treasure will no longer remain hidden, but at the resurrection will take the place which He always meant it to have. His prayer and purpose will then be accomplished. They will behold His glory, and they will add to His glory.

In John xv. 19, we read, " Ye are not of the world, but I have chosen you out of the world." Is not this truth foreshadowed in the parable ? The treasure is very different from the soil around it. Once the gold was in a vein running through the field, forming part of it ; the gems were lying among the other stones, but a Master-hand has made the treasure what it is. The gold had to be dug up, refined, and engraved, or impressed with the king's image, while the gems had to be sought and found, cut and polished. It is difficult to say which of the two parables is the more beautiful. What a glimpse they both give of the Lord's wondrous love ! In the second we are specially told that the purchaser was a merchantman. He was a connoisseur, and knew all about pearls. He would not be taken in by a sham pearl, or be disappointed in it afterwards because he detected some flaw. He did not grudge the price for he knew the value, and never regretted his purchase.

We should like to know much more about that precious pearl. After the merchantman had bought it what did he do with it ? It has been said that in the pearl there is the thought of personal adornment, but a merchantman would not invest all his capital in one pearl in order to wear it himself. He buys for some one else. We have many instances in history of what would probably follow. Such a treasure would only be fit for the king, and the merchantman would take it to him that he might put it among the crown jewels and wear it in his own diadem. The merchant- man knows that he will be well repaid for his outlay. One pearl worth all his fortune ! Who but a king could wear such a gem ? No wonder the parable ends here. We should need another to complete the story, for the merchantman *is* the King who says, " They shall be Mine, saith the Lord of hosts, in that day when I make up My jewels " (*marg.*, special treasure).

This view of Finder and Seeker is much more in harmony with the teaching of the rest of the chapter than that which singles out the two parables from the series, and takes them as a picture of the precious- ness of Christ to a seeking sinner, and to one who finds Him. We may say, " I've found the pearl of greatest price," and may rightly compare Him to something that is worth all beside ; but the details of the parable do not agree with such an interpre- tation. If we adopt it we are obliged to break the sequence, and treat them as individual pictures, not as part of a series. The seven parables of the thir- teenth of Matthew each represent some great whole. There may be difference of opinion as to what that whole is, but it seems clear that none of them represent merely the experience of individuals. In the first and second, and possibly the fifth (the sower, the tares, and the treasure), the complete picture is made up of many individuals, but each picture needs the various groups or classes of persons.

The first gives the view which is patent to all ; the second requires a practised eye to detect the difference ; the estimate of the third would be according to what you are looking for—if you only want a shade or shelter, you may be satisfied, but you will not find fruit or stability, or evergreen beauty. The fourth represents a great change which some might think an improvement, but which God looks on as evil. What men approve, God may disapprove.

Then in the fifth and sixth we have first *God's view*, and then faith's view, which is by-and-by to be recognised by all the universe. The hidden treasure possibly suggests a look into the past, and shows how its preciousness was discovered by Him even when the treasure was hidden in the field. The priceless value of the pearl when exhibited would be acknowledged by all, and it seems to look onwards to the time when He will come to be admired in all them that believe, and when the gem He has won from the ocean of the world shall be the wonder of the universe.

The estimate of the draught of fishes cannot be made till the net is drawn to land, and the fishes are sorted. Even the most practised fisherman cannot judge of his haul till the net is emptied.

The eleventh of Leviticus shows how the fish may be divided. " Whatsoever hath fins and scales in the waters " were accounted clean and good, and might be eaten by Israel ; " All that have not fins and scales . . . shall be an abomination unto you." One of the early fathers wrote, "Those fishes above accursed float in the deep, not swimming on the surface like the rest, but making their abode in the mud, which lies at the bottom."[1]   Other writers have given the same kind of interpretation.   Respecting fins and scales, one wrote : " A Christian needs spiritual capacity to enable him to move onward through the scene with which he is surrounded, and at the same time to resist the influence.   If we seem to be able to keep the world out, and yet have not the motive power, we are defective."

This seventh parable is in some respects the most difficult of the series.   Viewing them to some extent chronologically it has often been taken to represent the widespread preaching of the gospel by the Jewish remnant after the close of this dispensation, the witnessing of the 144,000 of Rev. vii., which will result in the ingathering of the multitude which no man can number.   It may be that this is the correct interpretation, but one difficulty opposed to this view is that those who divide the good from the bad fish seem naturally the same as those who cast in the net, and the interpretation of the parable shows that these are the angels.   There is a good deal in the Revelation to suggest that angelic agency will be united with Jewish testimony, and it may refer to this preaching of the kingdom (Rev. xiv. 6).   Others again see in it a picture of the judgment of the living nations of Matt. xxv.

Might not this parable, however, point to the last event in Israel's history and in the mysteries of the kingdom, prior to the final setting up of the kingdom in power ; viz., that which is referred to in Matt. xxiv. 31, when "He shall send His angels with a great sound of a trumpet, and they shall gather together His elect from the four winds" (Isa. xxvii. 13), purging out the rebels from the midst, according to Ezek.

---

[1] Epistle of Barnabas.

xx. 38, so that they do not enter the land (see also Isa. xxvii. 13).

In Jer. xvi. 16, the same figure is used in connection with bringing the children of Israel again into their land : " Behold, I will send for many fishers, saith the Lord, and they shall fish them ; " and this harmonises with the above suggestion.

The sea into which the net is cast is evidently symbolic of the nations, as we read in Rev. xvii. 15, " The waters which thou sawest, . . . are peoples, and multitudes, and nations, and tongues."

The series in one aspect closes with this parable, for there is a break between it and the eighth picture, which, as we have seen, embraces all the others. If, however, the parable of the net speaks of the time of the end, when the kingdom is about to be set up, that of the householder and his storehouse carries us beyond the present time, and beyond the kingdom ; for surely it will be always true of those whom God instructs, that they will have full treasuries, and will be constantly bringing out of them the things new and old which He has given.

But the importance of the eighth parable is seen when we couple them together in other ways. Not only may we compare the first and second, the third and fourth, the fifth and sixth and so on ; but, placing the two groups side by side, there are striking harmonies between the first and eighth, the second and seventh, the third and sixth, and the fourth and fifth.

It may be argued that it is fanciful thus to compare them, that such combinations would be endless, but some of them are so striking that the first objection will be met to the satisfaction at least of those who expect to see many wonderful lessons in these gems of divine teaching.

As to the variety of comparisons being endless, it is very possible, just as there are unnumbered melodies to be brought out of a few notes. Let us not be content to play only scales, important though they may be.

The eighth parable in the thirteenth of Matthew is very like the octave in musical harmony. It is the complement of the first note of the scale, and as we listen to it thus, we hear how it repeats it.

The sower and the householder both speak of the treatment of God's Word by the individual recipient. The one tells how it is to be received into the heart and to be allowed to bear fruit, the other gives a different simile. The heart is here likened not to prepared soil, but to a treasury; and the householder brings out his stores for the benefit of others. The fruit represents a Godward aspect, whereas the food of the household speaks of a manward use of the supplies. In the parable of the sower, the fruit-bearing is shown to be understanding, receiving, and keeping the Word. The parable of the householder proves that the best way of keeping it is to give it out to others.

The sower sows in the field of the world—the instructed scribe feeds the household. Here we have symbolised very clearly the work of the evangelist, and the work of the pastor and teacher. Neither the first parable nor the eighth in the chapter commences with the words, "The kingdom of heaven is like," but they are both connected with the kingdom. That of the sower is the key to the understanding of the mysteries of the kingdom,—that of the householder shows the use that is to be made of the mysteries when they are thus understood.

It needs but a glance to see the intimate connection between the second and the seventh parables, the tares and the net. Both show good and bad, side by side at first, and then divided; both were explained by the Lord in the words, "So shall it be at the end of the age ; " both describe the work of the angels in separating the wicked from the just ; both describe the doom of the wicked, the "fire " where there shall be wailing and gnashing of teeth.   In the one the world is represented as a field, in the other as a sea.   In the one the angels are reapers, in the other they are fishers.

The next couple is formed by the third and sixth, the mustard-seed and the pearl, and the contrast is very suggestive.   Both grow from something very small ; the shrub from the little mustard-seed, and the pearl from a tiny bit of sand that has come inside the shell of the oyster.   But what a different result The pearl never assumes very large dimensions, but its value may be almost priceless, and the two parables together teach that *size* is not everything.   The value is not to be estimated thus.

In the fourth and fifth parables, the leaven and the treasure, we notice one point in common ; there is something hidden in both, but the purpose is very different.   In the one the woman hides the leaven in the three measures of meal ; in the other the man hides the treasure in the field.   The one who instigates the first action is surely the devil, but it is the Lord who hides the treasure.   When Satan hides, it is for mischief, and in order to destroy ; when God hides, it is for blessing, and in order to preserve.

The meal in the first instance was precious and holy, as Paul says, "The lump is holy" (Rom. xi. 16) ; but all through man's history, when anything precious is entrusted to him, he spoils and corrupts it.   The Lord has His ways of hiding so that neither man nor devil can touch it.   The devil, through the agency of the woman, succeeded in leavening the meal, but he has never been able to reach the treasure.   Gladly would he gain possession of it had this been possible.

The comparison of the leaven and the treasure suggests a harmonious interpretation for these two much controverted parables, viz., that which the apostle adopts when he speaks of the Church as the one loaf. In one aspect the Church has indeed become leavened throughout, permeated entirely by the leaven of doctrine and conduct ; but in the other, God's own aspect—for only He can see it hidden beneath earth's soil—it is His own peculiar treasure. This comparison suggests that these pictures represent two aspects of the same object rather than two entirely different objects.

⁼ The first four parables all show mistakes into which a merely human estimate may lead us.

We might think that the seed received into the rocky soil was going to yield a good harvest, that the tares were really wheat, that the mustard-seed was a great success, and that the meal was much improved. If we fell into these mistakes it would be in the first two cases by judging hastily, and in the other two by viewing the matter from a human standpoint.

The harmony between the second, fourth, and seventh is most striking, for they are the three in which evil is introduced under the figures of tares, leaven, and bad fish. The chord of the fifth and the eighth is very beautiful, for it describes two kinds of treasures. The parable of the treasure hid in the field tells of the treasure which *the Lord* has in His people, that of "the householder" speaks of the treasure which *we* have in Him and in His Word.

The more we pray over this chapter and the longer we study it, the deeper will be our conviction of its marvellous character. Not only was the speaker of the parables divine, but He Himself must have inspired the Evangelist to record them in this perfectly harmonious manner.

The first four parables were spoken to the multitudes on the shore of the sea of Galilee. The sixth, the pearl, and the seventh, the net, speak of another sea, typified by the seas of earth, but they give the view from its further side—eternity's shore. The pearl and the fish have been drawn out of the waters, and are viewed from the heavenward side.

Studied as a whole, we have in this wonderful chapter a great battle scene, the contest between good and evil, between the power of God and the power of Satan. The first Messianic prophecy was a prediction of this great contest. " I will put enmity between thee and the woman, and between thy seed and her seed ; it shall bruise thy head, and thou shalt bruise His heel." Every clause in this wonderfu. germ prophecy is illustrated in the parables. In many of them, as in Matt. xiii., the adversary of the woman's seed himself appears on the scene, and his seed is seen in constant antagonism to her seed. In the parable of the tares he is called " *His* enemy,"— the avowed opponent of the owner of the field.

Two parables in Matt. xiii.—the first and the second —distinctly speak of the work of the enemy, and we can trace his influence in others ; two—the tares and the net—tell of the work of the angels at the end of the age, and though at times it seems that Satan has succeeded in his malicious attempt, the final victory will be with the Stronger than he. There will be a plenteous harvest, a precious treasure, and a peerless pearl which will well compensate for all that the Lord has suffered ; " He shall see of the travail of His soul, and shall be satisfied."

It is this contrast which marks the two central groups of three parables. Man may see something of the triumph of Satan in the pictures shown to the world in the first triplet, but in the last three God has revealed to His own people His view of the ultimate victory.

CHAPTER XII

ISRAEL'S HISTORY

WE have been taught that a parable is an earthly story with a heavenly meaning, but it might also be said of the majority that they have an earthly meaning as well. This is specially the case with those which relate to the history of God's earthly people.

Reference has already been made to some of the events in Israel's history which are foretold in the parables, but it is helpful to sum them up and link them together. It greatly adds to the interest of studying the parables to recognise their Jewish character. In some of them this is clearly indicated by the explanation given, or by the attitude of the listeners; as, for instance, when the chief priests and Pharisees "knew that He had spoken against them."

1. There is first a reference to two facts in Israel's *past*, viz., the withdrawal of God's immediate presence and the sending of the prophets. These are pictured in the journeying of the owner of the vineyard "into a far country" after planting his vineyard, and in the sending of the messengers. The first made the second necessary. The householder no longer lived on his property, he no longer came into his garden to eat of his pleasant fruit, but had to depute his servants to receive it for him.

A prophet is an intermediary, and the need of such an one to come between two parties who do not speak face to face, implies distance between them. He may act for both, for who so likely to have

the ear of the king as he who carries his messages ?
God told Abimelech in vision to ask Abraham to pray
for him, "for he is a prophet" (Gen. xx. 7). When
Moses thought himself unable to speak to Pharaoh,
God allowed Aaron to be his "prophet" (Exod.
vii. 1). He would not have needed a spokesman if
he had not been unwilling to carry the message
himself.

When at Sinai the children of Israel feared to hear
God's voice, they prayed for an intermediary, "Speak
thou with us, and we will hear ; but let not God speak
with us, lest we die" (Exod. xx. 19). Thus Moses became the greatest prophet that ever lived until He
came of whom he was a type : "A prophet shall the
Lord your God raise up . . . like unto me ; Him shall
ye hear." If Jehovah had spoken directly to the
people there would have been no need of a prophet.

The sending of prophets to Israel is referred to in two
of the parables, namely, those of the wicked husbandmen and of the marriage supper. In the former we
read that "When the time of fruit drew near, he (the
householder) sent his servants to the husbandmen,
that they might receive the fruits of it. And the
husbandmen took his servants, and beat one, and killed
another, and stoned another. Again he sent other
servants more than the first : and they did unto them
likewise." This reminds us of what we read in 2
Chron. xxxvi. 15, "The Lord God of their fathers sent
to them by His messengers, rising up betimes and
sending ; because He had compassion on His people,
and on His dwelling-place : but they mocked the
messengers of God, and despised His words, and
misused His prophets, until the wrath of the Lord
arose against His people, till there was no remedy."
And if He was wroth when the messengers were but
men like themselves, how much more when it was
His own Son that they treated thus ? As Mr.

Spurgeon has said, "He was God's ultimatum."
When He had come, there was no need of any
other prophet, and so as He increased, John, the last
of the prophets, must decrease, and pass from the
scene.   The yielding of the fruit of the vineyard
was estimated according to the treatment of the
messengers sent to receive it, and according to the
reception of the well-beloved Son.   In the other
parable, the fig-tree had brought forth no fruit for
three years because Israel had not received Him.   He
came to His own vineyard, and His own tenants
received Him not.

In the parable of the marriage-feast the Old Testament prophets are represented by the first set of
servants who went forth to call to the wedding.

2. The *reformation* of the people under the preaching of John the Baptist is probably indicated in the
parable of the unclean spirit in Matt. xii. 43–45, which
clearly refers to Israel, for the Lord says, "Even so
shall it be also unto this wicked generation."

The house was only emptied, swept, and garnished,
so that although Satan had gone out, he came back
again with seven other spirits worse than himself.   Reformation is not enough, there must be indwelling,
whether it be in an individual or in a nation.

After Israel's return from captivity idolatry was
abhorred ; and at the preaching of John the Baptist,
"There went out unto Him *all* the land of Judæa and
they of Jerusalem, and were all baptized of Him in the
river of Jordan, confessing their sins."   But they did
not listen to John when he said "that they should
believe on Him that should come after him, that is, on
Christ Jesus" (Acts xix. 4).   They did not recognise
that John was only the voice, the messenger preparing
the way for Him.   When He came they would not
receive Him, and as their house was empty Satan
came back.

3. They had made great *profession* of obedience to God. They said to Moses, " All that the Lord hath spoken we will do ; " and to Joshua, who had begun to doubt their protestations, they affirmed, " Nay ; but we will serve the Lord." Their subsequent history shows how they failed, and this is described by the Lord in the parable of the two sons. Israel was like the son who said to his father, " I go, sir, and went not."

4. The *blindness* of Israel's leaders is shown in the little parable of the " blind leaders of the blind " (Matt. xv. 14), and in the allusion to the cloud and the wind. " Can the blind lead the blind ? shall they not both fall into the ditch ? " (Luke vi. 39). The Pharisees thought that they saw, but were really blind (John ix. 39–41). They had refused to see, and they had become judici- ally blinded. Thus was fulfilled the prophecy in Zeph. i. 17, " They shall walk like blind men, because they have sinned against the Lord." Again and again the Lord charged them with being blind (see Matt. xxiii. 16, 17, 19, 24, 26).

They knew that the cloud from the west indicated a coming shower ; they could tell when the land was thirsting for rain ; but while they could see this they could not see Him, or feel their need. So He said to them, " Ye hypocrites ! ye can discern the face of the sky, and of the earth : but how is it that ye do not discern this time ? " (Luke xii. 54–56).

5. We next see *Israel's rejection of their Messiah*. This has already been noticed in connection with many of the parables which speak of our Lord's incarnation, rejection, and death, and it is especially described in the parables of the marriage-feast, the nobleman and his servants, the wicked husbandmen, and the corner-stone. Those that were bidden *despised* the invitation of the king to the marriage of his son ; the servants of the nobleman *hated* him ; the husband-

men *slew* the son of the owner of the vineyard ; the builders *rejected* the corner-stone.   The husbandmen, as we have seen, *refused* to give the fruit to the owner of the vineyard whether the messengers were his servants or his son.   In all three Gospels the parable is followed by the account of the Pharisees trying to entrap our Lord in His words by asking Him whether it was lawful to pay tribute or not.   He asks for a penny, and having made them acknowledge the superscription upon it, He says, " Render to Cæsar the things that are Cæsar's, and to God the things that are God's." This was the very thing which they themselves had not done.   The parable which He had just uttered condemned them for having refused to render to God the things that belonged to Him.   " It is a mistake to consider this as simply settling the rights and distinguishing the jurisdiction of the civil and spiritual powers.   The Gentile yoke had come, as their father Jacob had long before prophesied (Gen. xlix. 14, 15). Israel had accepted fellowship with the Gentile, and Cæsar's coin was only the sign of this. . . . Let them give Cæsar his own, but let them give God His own also.   When they really do this there will be no question at all to settle as to Cæsar." [1]

6. It may be that reference is made to Israel in Luke xii. 58, 59, and Matt. v. 25, 26.   " When thou goest with thine *adversary* to the magistrate, as thou art in the way, give diligence that thou mayest be delivered from him ; lest he hale thee to the judge, and the judge deliver thee to the officer, and the officer cast thee into prison.   I tell thee, thou shalt not depart thence, till thou hast paid the very last mite."

Instead of making peace whilst they were in the way with Him, by their rebellion and rejection they made their Messiah their adversary, and neglected to become reconciled to Him.   By-and-by He will be

[1] F. W. Grant.

their Judge, and like the debtor in the parable, Israel will be delivered to the tormentors till he shall have paid all that was due to Him. In Isa. lxiii. 10 we read, " They rebelled, and vexed His Holy Spirit : therefore He was turned to be their enemy."

7. The *unfruitfulness* of Israel during the time of the Lord's ministry, and His patience with them, are beautifully pictured in the parable of the fig-tree.

8. In the same parable we have also His *intercession* for the barren tree which yielded no fruit for Him during the three years of His ministry among them. When the owner said, " Cut it down ; why cumbereth it the ground ? " He prayed, " Lord, let it alone this year also, till I shall dig about it, and dung it ; and if it bear fruit well, and if not, then after that thou shalt cut it down." He prayed on the cross, " Father, forgive them ; for they know not what they do ; " and in answer to that prayer Peter and the other apostles were sent with a fresh proclamation to them.

9. *The second opportunity* which was thus given to Israel is shown in this parable. The Book of the Acts gives the history of "this year also," not a literal year, but an "acceptable year of the Lord," which was granted to the fig-tree in answer to the prayer of the dresser of the vineyard. One of the most important subjects in the Acts is the gradual turning away from Israel ; it is the history of the transitional period before this dispensation (in which there is neither Jew nor Gentile) is finally set up. In the early part of the Acts the proclamation is to the Jew *only*, those converted, being Jews or proselytes; and to the very last chapter, after heathen Gentiles have been brought in, it is still to the Jew *first*, even when the preacher is the great Apostle of the Gentiles. But after finally turning from them in the last chapter, we find in the Epistle to the Romans that there is in this dispensation *no difference*.

As a nation the fig-tree was no more fruitful during this added year of grace than during the three years of the Lord's presence and personal ministry among them; and the closing chapter of Acts seems to describe the cutting down of the tree foretold by John the Baptist when he said, "Now also the axe is laid unto the root of the trees." Under a slightly different simile—an olive- instead of a fig-tree—the eleventh chapter of Romans shows that the cutting off is not final, but that by-and-by Israel will once more bring forth fruit to God. Though the tree has been cut down there still remains a root which will spring into life once more. It was not uprooted. There is a passage in Job which is very beautiful in this connection. "There is hope of a tree, if it be cut down, that it will sprout again, and that the tender branch thereof will not cease. Though the root thereof wax old in the earth, and the stock thereof die in the ground; yet through the scent of water it will bud, and bring forth boughs like a plant" (Job xiv. 7–9). When "the river of God which is full of water" flows near to Israel the tree will begin to bud (see Isa. xxxii. 15).

This second offer of mercy to Israel is also implied in the parable of the marriage feast, for in Matt. xxii. 4, after the first invitation has been rejected, we read, "*Again* he sent forth other servants, saying, Tell them which are bidden, Behold, I have prepared my dinner; my oxen and my fatlings are killed, and all things are ready; come unto the marriage. But (occupied with what they already possessed, or with what they had in anticipation) they made light of it, and went their ways, one to his farm, another to his merchandise." By-and-by when they have recognised their Messiah they will confess how they have "turned every one to his own way." In the corresponding parable in Luke, the servant goes into the city, before passing on to the highways and hedges.

10. The next verse (Matt. xxii. 6) describes *their enmity to His messengers* in the persecution which the disciples endured, the stoning of Stephen, the murder of James, and the threatenings and slaughter which followed. "The remnant took His servants, and entreated them spitefully, and slew them."

11. Then follows a clear prophecy of the *destruction of Jerusalem*. "But when the king heard thereof, he was wroth : and he sent forth his armies, and destroyed those murderers, and burned up their[1] city." The armies were led by Titus, they were made up of Roman soldiers, but they were "His armies," doing His work. The destruction of Jerusalem took place only about five years after the close of the Book of Acts, when Paul for the last time turns from his nation, and the solemn prophecy of Isaiah vi., partially fulfilled in the time of our Lord, and quoted in each of the Gospels (Matt. xiii. 14, 15; Mark iv. 12; Luke viii. 10; John xii. 39, 40), takes full effect.

According to this parable the destruction of Jerusalem marked the final stage of the rejection of Israel. Their lengthened time of probation had been forty years, for it took place just forty years after the crucifixion, and this fact seems to give an added force to the words quoted in the Epistle to the Hebrews[2] towards the end of this period. The writer and the Psalmist referred to the forty years' provocation in the wilderness; but here again it might have been said, "Forty years long was I grieved with this generation."

12. We see from this parable, and from Paul's action in accordance with it, that not until this *final turning away* from Israel is the invitation given broadcast, not

---

[1] Not *His*. Comp. Matt. v. 35.
[2] Heb. iii. 7–19; Ps. xcv. 7–11.

only to the Jews rich in privileges, but to the Gentiles who had hitherto been poor compared to them. The servants go forth with the message to all whom they can find in the highways and hedges. Those who had first received the invitation are set aside, for the master of the house says, " I say unto you, That none of those men which were bidden shall taste of my supper."[1] In Matthew, the king says to his servants, "The wedding is ready, but they who were bidden were not worthy."[2] The same expression is used in Acts in one of the great crises of the book when " Paul and Barnabas waxed bold, and said, It was necessary that the Word of God should first have been spoken to you : but seeing ye put it from you, and judge yourselves unworthy of everlasting life, lo, we turn to the Gentiles " (Acts xiii. 46).

13. In Luke xix. we have another picture of the events which were to take place after the ascension of the Lord. The nobleman had gone " into a far country, to receive for himself a kingdom, and to return. . . . But his servants hated him, and sent *a message after him*, saying, We will not have this man to reign over us." They had said this very plainly when on Calvary they had crucified their King, but at the stoning of Stephen a final message was sent after Him which could not be misunderstood.

It may be that had the Jews received the proclamation at Pentecost, He would have returned immediately. Peter seems to have expected it when he pleaded with them to repent, "That so there may come seasons of refreshing from the presence of the Lord, and that He may send the Christ who hath been appointed for you, even Jesus : whom the heaven must receive until the times of restoration of all things, whereof God spake by the mouth of His holy prophets" (Acts iii. 19–21, R.V.). Israel's jubilee would

[1] Luke xiv. 24. [2] Chap. xxii. 8.

then have set in, and the absent One would have returned to "His family" and to "His possession"; for it is to this type, the blowing of the jubilee trumpet, and the "restitution of all things" in the fiftieth year, that reference seems to be made (Lev. xxv.).

When Stephen saw the Lord, he said, "Behold, I see the heavens opened, and the Son of Man standing on the right hand¦of God." It is thought by many that He was *standing* as though to receive the final answer of the people. In Hebrews i. and elsewhere we read of His *sitting* at the right hand of God, and the 110th Psalm tells us that this will be His attitude until His enemies have been made His footstool. Then the time will have come when the Master of the house will have "risen up" (Luke xiii. 25), just before He is about to take His seat on His own throne; and the solemn words at the end of the parable will be fully accomplished— *His* answer to their "message "—"Those Mine enemies which would not that I should reign over them, bring hither and slay them before Me " (Luke xix. 27).

14. The leading out from Judaism is taught in John x. As we have seen, the word in the preceding chapter where the Jews *cast out* the man who had received his sight (chap. ix. 34, 35) is the same as that used of the Lord *putting forth* His sheep (chap. x. 4). The tenth chapter of John has new meaning when we see in the opening verses the change of dispensation to which our Lord evidently referred. The following interesting explanation has been given of the various doors spoken of in verses 1, 2, 7, and 9 :—

"The door into the sheepfold" (verses 1, 2). "In the Jewish fold, besides the sheep of Christ, there were others not of this fold" (verses 3, 26). We are taken in thought to a sheepfold in which the sheep are kept all night, a porter watching at the door. In due time on a new day the shepherd comes to lead

out his own sheep, for there may be more than one
flock in the fold.   The shepherd seeking his own
flock enters in by the door, the only recognised way
of getting in.   A thief or a robber would climb up
some other way, to get in surreptitiously for his own
ends, and not for the welfare of the sheep.   Now the
Lord is the Shepherd here intended ; He entered the
fold, which is here Judaism, and entered by the door,
that is, He conformed to all the rights and ordinances
of that day which God appointed for Israel.   Born
under the law, He was circumcised the eighth day,
and subsequently, at the purification of His mother,
was presented to God in the Temple, then He was
baptized of John in Jordan, the only one so baptized
who had no sin to confess. . . . Within the fold He
found Himself among the sheep.   They owned Him,
for He spake and they heard.   In time He would lead
them out of the fold, going, however, as He here says,
before them.   But till He had died, Judaism was
owned of God, so the fold was not to be left.

"'The door of the sheep' (verses 7 and 8).   He
had just spoken of leading out of the fold (verse 3).
Attempts had been made previously to do that, but
without success, and now the reason is vouchsafed
that Christ, and Christ only, is the door of the sheep.
There is no way out of the fold of Judaism but by
Him. . . . Efforts had been made (Acts v. 36, 37), but
each attempt ended disastrously both for leaders and
followers, and proved that they were not of God. . . .
So after the Lord's death and the coming of the Holy
Ghost . . . the door of the fold being opened, thousands came out.   Before that, those characterised by
the Lord as thieves and robbers might rise up, but
the sheep did not hear them.   The time to relinquish
Jewish ground had not come, and no way out of
Judaism for those placed under it by birth has God
ever sanctioned save by Christ the door of the sheep.

Only as Jews hearkened to Him have they divine authority for leaving the Mosaic ritual and the teaching of the synagogue.

"Christ 'the door' (verse 9). But led out of the fold, whither should they go ? Now He presents Himself in another character, 'I am the door : by Me if any man enter in, he shall be saved.' The door by which they can enter in for blessing, not the door of the sheep in verse 7. Grace and its provisions are for any, for all who will accept them." [1]

15. The *jealousy* of the Jews at the Gentiles receiving favour is probably shown in the parable of the two debtors in Matt. xviii. A certain king which would take account of his servants, finds when he begins to reckon that one of them owes him an enormous debt of 10,000 talents.[2] The king, however, has compassion on him and forgives the debt. Forgetting the mercy that he himself has received, that servant goes out, and finding a fellow-servant who owes a trifling debt of one hundred pence, he harshly insists on payment, and instead of forgiving as he has been forgiven, thrusts him into prison.

The practical teaching is evident, but there is probably more than this in the parable. "The debt of the Jews in crucifying the Lord Jesus was so enormous that it could not be paid. It was forgiven in answer to the Lord's prayer, 'Father, forgive them ;' but the Jews were angry at the Gentiles who owed them but a little debt receiving mercy, and therefore they have been delivered to the tormentors and will have to pass through the Great Tribulation." When in Acts xxii. 21, Paul spoke of having been sent to the Gentiles, they could not restrain their rage. They "lifted up their voices and said, Away with

---

[1] " Tracings from the Gospel of John." C. E. Stuart.
[2] It is supposed that the 10,000 talents would equal between £2,000,000 and £3,000,000 ; and the 100 pence about £3.

such a fellow from the earth ; for it is not fit that he should live, and . . . they cried out, and cast off their clothes, and threw dust into the air." Referring to this in 1 Thess. ii. 15, 16, he writes, that they " both killed the Lord Jesus, and their own prophets, and have persecuted us ; and they please not God, and are contrary to all men ; forbidding us to speak to the Gentiles that they might be saved, to fill up their sins alway ; for the wrath is come upon them to the uttermost."

The elder brother in the parable of the prodigal evidently represented in the first place the Pharisees who murmured because the Lord received sinners. But the Pharisees were representatives of their nation, and therefore some have seen in this a picture of Israel.

Thus Dean Burgon wrote, " Under the image of a son who remained in his father's house the favoured descendants of Abraham are set before us, while the rest of the world is portrayed in the person of another son who goes into a far country and there wastes his substance with riotous living. . . . In the embrace which the father (while yet the offending but repentant son is a long way off) runs to bestow, behold *how* God loved the world." The conduct of the father towards the elder brother, "Therefore came his father out and entreated him," reminds us of Jer. ii. 35, " Behold, I will plead with thee because thou sayest, I have not sinned."

16. *The covenant of works.*—In the parable of the labourers in the vineyard in Matt. xx., there seems to be a comparison between grace and the covenant of works. The Jews may be represented by those hired at the beginning of the day who are displeased, and murmur when they see those called at the eleventh hour, receiving in grace that for which they had laboured. The agreement with those hired

early in the morning (verse 1) seems to point to the
covenant of works, whilst those hired at the eleventh
hour would represent those received on the ground of
grace, although the suggestion that they were hired
at all precludes the gospel idea of free grace.

In Matt. xxi., xxii., there are three parables clustered
together : the two sons to whom the father said, " Go
work in my vineyard;" the husbandmen; and the marriage of the king's son. "The people were convicted
in these three under the law ; under the ministry of
John the Baptist and the Lord Himself ; and under
grace."

17. Their reception of *Antichrist.* In the parable
of the unclean spirit, we are shown the reason why
Israel will be prepared to receive Antichrist. The
unclean spirit returns to his house with the seven
other spirits worse than himself. The Church possessed by the Spirit becomes the dwelling-place of
the Trinity, but Israel indwelt by Satan receives the
trinity of evil, the dragon, the beast, and the false
prophet (Rev. xvi. 13). It has been said that "Satan
now deceives Israel with Deism because he would
have them reject the Lord Jesus. When it serves
his purpose he will make them worship the image
of Antichrist as easily as he tempted them to idolatry
of old." Truly, that last state of the nation will be
worse than the first.

18. The *judgments* which are to fall upon Israel are
represented under many similes. Beginning at the
destruction of Jerusalem, they culminate in the time
of Jacob's trouble, the Great Tribulation which is immediately to precede the coming of the Lord. In the
parable of the debtors and the adversary, they are
cast into prison till they shall have paid their debt ;
in connection with the corner-stone, they are broken
by falling upon it ; in the parable of the marriage
supper, we are told that their city will be destroyed,

and the rebels slain. This is also mentioned in the parable of the pounds, while the cutting down of the fig-tree is referred to in Luke xiii., reminding us of John the Baptist's warning, "Now also the axe is laid unto the root of the trees."

It seems also that the parable of the rich man and Lazarus pictures the terrible doom of the unbelieving nation. Rich in privileges, surrounded with blessings, they had thought nothing of the perishing ones at their gates, shut out from so much that they enjoyed. God's purpose for Israel was that they should be the centre of enrichment for the other nations, as is beautifully expressed in Solomon's prayer, "That all people of the earth may know Thy name, to fear Thee, as do Thy people Israel." But instead of acting on this principle, they proudly shut themselves within their gates, leaving the Gentile, with his sores and his hunger, unheeded. Lazarus desired "to be fed with the crumbs which fell from the rich man's table." This expression reminds us of the story of the Syrophœnician woman who addressed the Lord as Son of David. He had to teach her that on this ground she could not claim blessing. "It is not meet," He said, "to take the children's bread, and to cast it to dogs." Then came her beautiful answer, "Truth, Lord: yet the dogs eat of the crumbs which fall from their masters' table." The Lord did not deny her the crumbs she begged for, but answered and said unto her, "O woman, great is thy faith, be it unto thee even as thou wilt," and the crumb from His hand was as sufficient as it ever is. She was content to take her place among the dogs, yet she received the blessing whilst Israel's favoured sons missed it altogether. The rich man in the parable in Luke xvi. seems specially connected with Israel from the answer of Abraham, whom he addressed as father Abraham. He had asked that one might be sent to his five brethren, but he replied, "They have Moses and the prophets; let them hear them." Thus, it seems that one line of teaching in the parable is that though Israel had refused to share their riches with the Gentiles, yet the unbelieving nation would be cast out, and would see the despised Gentiles in Abraham's bosom acknowledged by the Father of the faithful as his children. The word of Abraham respecting the rich man's brethren was truly applicable to Israel. "If they hear not Moses and the prophets, neither will they be persuaded though one rose from the dead." Our Lord said to them, "Had ye believed Moses, ye would have believed Me; for he wrote of Me." Israel rejected Moses and the prophets, and when the One of whom they spake rose from the dead, they were not persuaded. Another Lazarus was indeed raised, but the Lord Himself was the only One who rose; He was also able to take His life again, and yet when He did so they were not persuaded.

19. The final judgments are to be preceded by *the budding of the fig-tree*. "When his branch is yet tender, and putteth forth leaves, ye know that summer is nigh: so likewise ye, when ye shall see all these things, know that it is near, even at the doors" (Matt. xxiv. 32, 33; Luke xxi. 29–31). The fig-tree is several times used as a symbol of Judah, and before the events foretold in Matt. xxiv. shall befall them, the Jewish people are to show fresh signs of life, and this will indicate that the events prophesied by the Lord are very near. The tree has in recent years begun to shoot forth, and on all sides we see signs of fresh life among the Jews. Scattered throughout the world their eyes are beginning to turn to their own land as the Zionist movement clearly shows. Whether their present schemes are successful or not, it is a very

remarkable thing that delegates should be gathered from so many countries.   Better still, there are indications of a greater readiness to receive the Word of God, the only true source of fruitfulness.   From such signs we, too, may surely "know of (our) own selves that summer is now nigh" for Israel.   From Isa. xviii. 5, we see that the budding of the vine of Israel will be followed by much pruning, "For afore the harvest, when the bud is perfect, and the sour grape is ripening in the flower, He shall both cut off the sprigs with pruning-hooks, and take away and cut down the branches." This pruning will be "the time of Jacob's trouble."

20. *Their sorrows avenged.*—The parable of the unjust judge in Luke xviii. teaches us that God will by-and-by avenge the sorrows of His chosen people.   The widow here is evidently a picture of Israel suffering at the hand of her adversary.   The vengeance for which she pleads is probably in connection with the restoration of her property (see p. 198), but He will avenge their sorrows on those who have persecuted them.   As we read in Zech. i. 15 : "I am very sore displeased with the heathen that are at ease : for I was but a little displeased, and they helped forward the affliction."   This final vengeance will be poured out, at the coming of the Son of Man, in answer to the cry of His own elect, the believing remnant, for whose deliverance He will suddenly appear, as is so beautifully described in Psalm cxviii. The cry ascends to God even while the nation is in unbelief, just as they cried to him out of Egyptian bondage, before He had revealed Himself to them ; and even now He says, "I know their sorrows."   The parable ends with the sad question, "Nevertheless, when the Son of Man cometh, shall He find faith on the earth ?"   Will not the remnant who cry day and night for His help be but small compared with

the unbelieving nations of Christendom who fóllow
the lead of Antichrist in trying to exterminate Israel,
and say with him, "Come, and let us cut them off
from being a nation " ?

It is noticeable that in this series of parables
relating to Israel, great prominence is given to the
thought of fruit-bearing. In the parable of the husbandmen we see them bringing forth fruit for themselves, and refusing to give it to the rightful owner ;
in the parable of the fig-tree there is no fruit; in
symbol the literal fig-tree was cursed by the Lord,
and immediately withered ; and finally we have the
tree budding again.

It is possible that the words of our Lord at the
close of the parable of the husbandmen anticipate
the time when Israel will once more become the
fruitful vineyard of the Lord. "Therefore say I unto
you, the kingdom of God shall be taken from you,
and given to a nation bringing forth the fruits thereof."
Allusion is made to this in chap. xv., as probably
referring to the change of dispensation ; when turning
from Israel God takes up Jew and Gentile alike (Rom.
xi.). Some might object to this view on account
of the vineyard being given to a nation, but Paul in
the same passage, speaking of Israel being for the
time cast off, quoted Deut. xxxii. 21, as applicable
to the present dispensation. "Did not Israel know ?
First Moses saith, I will provoke you to jealousy by
them that are no people, and by a foolish nation I
will anger you" (Rom. x. 19). God is looking for
fruit from His vineyard now, but it is probable that
this parable also looks forward to the time when this
dispensation being closed, God will once more take
up the nation of Israel, no longer under a covenant
of works as when the vineyard was "let out" to
them (Matt. xxi. 33, 41), but under the new covenant
of grace as expressed by the word "given" (verse 43).

There are in the parables several allusions to a "city," and these naturally lead us to think of Jerusalem.

(1) In Matt. v. 14 there is a city lighted and shining. "A city that is set on a hill cannot be hid." Jerusalem was the favoured city which was meant to be a light to the world. The days will come when God's purpose will be carried out, and it will be said to Israel, "Arise, shine : for thy light is come ;" the exhortations in Matt. v. 14, and Isa. lx. 1, may now be applied to the Church, which was intended to be God's light-bearer in a dark world (Eph. v. 8, 14).

(2) In Luke xiv. there is a city invited to the feast. After those that were bidden have rejected the message the servant is sent into the streets and lanes of the city, before he goes into the highways and hedges. When the nation had rejected their Messiah, the disciples were sent forth to witness for Him, "beginning at Jerusalem," and it was in that guilty city that the Holy Spirit gathered on "the same day . . . about three thousand souls."

(3) In Luke xix. there is the other side of the picture, the rebelling city, for we read that " His citizens hated him, and sent a message after him, saying, We will not have this man to reign over us." It was in Jerusalem that Stephen was stoned.

(4) In Matt. xxii. 7 there is the destroyed city.

(5) In Luke xviii. 2, 3, the widow who cries for vengeance belongs to "a certain city," and probably represents the city and the nation.[1]

Thus we see that the parables cover the whole history of Israel, past, present, and future, from the

[1] See also the city mentioned amongst Old Testament illustrations (Deut. xxi. and Ezek. ix., pp. 186, 201). The city may be taken in its larger sense as symbolising the world. The invitation is sent out into the world, the world has rebelled, and by-and-by when the Lord reigns upon the earth it will be like the city set on a hill, a centre of light in the universe (see also p. 212).

time when the first messengers were sent, until the days when the kingdom will be set up, and Israel will at last bring forth fruit unto God.

The question may be asked, What then, has this to do with us? We may answer this inquiry in two ways. It is of the utmost importance for us to understand God's dealings with Israel. The Old Testament prophecies are a sealed book until we do so ; and that which is of such deep interest to God Himself will surely be full of interest to those who are in communion with Him.

But having seen this dispensational and prophetic character of the parables, we need not dismiss them as having no personal teaching for ourselves. A spiritually minded Bible student would not doubt that the true interpretation of the book of Exodus is the typical teaching contained in the scenes there recorded, as we learn from the apostle Paul.

It has sometimes been stated that the wilderness experiences refer only to God's people, because *all* the children of Israel were redeemed by blood ; *all* had partaken of the paschal lamb ; and, as the apostle expresses it, *all* had been "baptized unto Moses in the cloud and in the sea."

But while this is doubtless one aspect of the types, we need not limit them to those who have been redeemed by blood. We may unhesitatingly make a much wider application, for we have the Lord's own warrant for it. He used the scene in Num. xxi. in the widest sense possible when He said, "As Moses lifted up the serpent in the wilderness, even so must the Son of Man be lifted up ; that whosoever believeth in Him should not perish, but have eternal life. For God so loved the *world*." Could He have made a more universal application? The bitten Israelites, though in one sense God's people, were thus typical not merely of backsliders but of all sinners, and so with many other types. The object lessons were given to a redeemed people, but they were for the whole world. A surgeon who is giving ambulance lectures needs some one on whom to demonstrate.

If the Lord used the scene in Num. xxi. in this world-wide sense, we may also use the picture of the leper in Lev. xiii. as a representation of man by nature. We may see even in the offerings a complete picture of God's provision, giving different aspects of the work of Christ, for God Himself, for the believer, and for the seeking sinner ; for the teaching of the brazen altar has brought a gospel message to many.

In the same way the parables which refer to Israel's history are full of warnings for the unsaved and the saved, for individuals and communities, for the world and the Church. The fact that there is in them a reference to Israel's past, or a prophecy of Israel's future, does not prevent our taking them thus. For instance, the parable of the unclean spirit was used by the Lord to give a picture of the last state of that generation (or race) ; but it is a solemn warning to men now, against being satisfied with mere reformation. The house of Israel that was swept and garnished under John's preaching, is also a picture of one who has broken off evil habits for a time, without receiving Christ into his heart. He has thus only made room for the evil spirit to return with his companions, and the man's last state is worse, instead of better, than the first. It also contains a solemn lesson for professing Christendom ; whilst the barren fig-tree is a warning to a fruitless world, a fruitless sinner, a fruitless Church, or a fruitless believer. The parable of the husbandmen is an admonition to those from whom God now expects fruit. The apostle Paul urges the Gentile branches that have been grafted into the olive-tree not to boast, but to take heed lest they also should be cut off.

" Behold therefore the goodness and severity of God : on them which fell, severity; but toward thee, goodness, if thou continue in His goodness; otherwise, thou also shalt be cut off." The Lord Himself, speaking to the Church in Ephesus which had left its first love, says: " Remember, therefore, from whence thou art fallen; and repent, and do the first works; or else I will come unto thee quickly, and will remove thy candlestick out of his place." The warnings of the parables are equally applicable to any from whom God expects fruit-bearing or light-giving, and in the same way all the parables which refer to Israel's history are full of practical teaching.

CHAPTER XIII

OLD TESTAMENT SYMBOLISM

HE who in the New Testament spake "many things in parables" is the same who, by His Spirit, moved "holy men of God" to write the Old Testament, and at times spake to men in dreams and in visions of the night. We may therefore expect to trace the same mind running through them all. In the Old Testament generally, as well as in its types, and parables, and visions, we find many things which illustrate and throw light on the Lord's parables in the Gospels. As we study them together we are more and more impressed with the testimony they give to the marvellous unity of Scripture. We are also better able to place ourselves in the position of our Lord's hearers who, familiar with the symbolism of the Old Testament, could understand something at least of His meaning.

It would need many volumes to exhaust this subject; but it is helpful to notice some passages which are specially connected with New Testament parables. We may draw our illustrations from general symbolism, typical substances, Levitical laws and institutions, Old Testament incidents and characters, the Psalms, and the parables of Solomon.

Probably all to whom the parables were addressed, whether the disciples, the scribes and Pharisees, or the crowds, had some perception of typical teaching underlying the Levitical ritual; and knew at least that there was a spiritual significance in the ceremonies commanded. A hint of this is found in Deut. viii., where, speaking of the manna, the Lord tells the people that it was given to them in the wilderness in order to teach them that "Man doth not live by bread only, but by every word that proceedeth out of the mouth of the Lord doth man live." Even in Old Testament days, therefore, they knew that the manna represented more than ordinary food, and typified to them the spoken and written Word. It needed the Lord's own commentary in John vi. to show how fully it pointed to Himself, the Incarnate Word.

When He spoke of building on a rock their thoughts would probably go back to the song of Moses (Deut. xxxii.), where God Himself is so often called their Rock. Moses gives Him this title immediately after speaking of the doctrine that should distil as the dew, and thus expresses His stability, His faithfulness, and His truth.

When the Lord spoke of the wicked husbandmen who refused to yield the fruit of the vineyard to the one to whom the vineyard belonged, the Pharisees could not fail to understand that He referred to them. They must have remembered the many passages in which Israel is compared to a vineyard, and especially the song in Isa. v., where it is described in almost identical language. "Now will I sing to my well-beloved a song of My beloved touching His vineyard. My well-beloved hath a vineyard in a very fruitful hill; and He fenced it, and gathered out the stones thereof, and planted it with the choicest vine, and built a tower in the midst of it, and also made a wine-press therein." In the parable we read, "There was a certain householder, which planted a vineyard, and hedged it round about, and digged a wine-press in it, and built a tower." The song in Isaiah also speaks of the hedge. His audience had no difficulty in understanding to whom both passages referred, for the prophet added the explanation, "The vineyard of the Lord of hosts is the house of Israel, and the men of Judah His pleasant plant." He who mourns over the fruitlessness of the vine in Isaiah, the "Well-beloved," as He is so beautifully called, bears the same title in the parable. "Having yet therefore one son, his well-beloved, he sent him also last unto them." He who grieves in the Old Testament, dies in the New.

The eightieth Psalm gives the earlier history of the vine, the transplanting from Egypt, the setting of the plant in the new soil of Canaan, the clearing of the land that room might be made for it, and its rapid growth. It also gives the extent of the vine, "She sent out her boughs unto the sea, and her branches unto the river," thus describing the boundaries of the land of promise, from the great sea to the river Euphrates.

It has often been pointed out that the vine, as in Hosea x. 1; Joel i. 7; the fig as in Jer. xxiv., and the olive as in Jer. xi. 16, 17, are constantly used as symbols of Israel and Judah. The fig-tree seems specially to be connected with Judah. The fertility of their land showed itself in the fruitfulness of these trees, and God's blessing was thus manifested (Deut. viii. 8; Lev. xxvi. 4, 5). When He turned His face from them their trees failed to yield fruit, or the fruit was consumed by locusts and worms (Deut. xxviii. 38–42; Amos iv. 9); when once more He blesses them their land will again become fruitful. Its condition has always corresponded with that of the people, and thus the literal trees were often used as figures of the nation. The parable of Jotham sets forth something of the difference between the three trees. The *fig* is famed for its sweetness. If it bring forth nothing but leaves it might as well be cut down, as in the parable, or withered, as in the miracle. The *vine* is also grown for its fruit and for the "wine which cheereth God and man" (Judges ix. 13). The fruit of the vine brings joy to Him and to us, as we learn of the true vine in John xv. 11, "That My joy might remain in you, and that your joy might be full." The *olive* tree was represented by Jotham as saying, "Should I leave my fatness, wherewith by me they honour God and man?" From it comes the oil for the light, and it is therefore used in connection with testimony for God. But Israel, intended to be God's witness to the world, failed in their testimony. In Old Testament days He looked to them to bring sweetness, joy, and honour unto Him, and He expects these things from His people now, as we see from John xv., Rom. xi., Gal. v., &c.

Having seen the change of symbolism which has taken place in this dispensation, we may use many of these passages typically for ourselves as well as historically or prophetically for Israel.

In Isa. xxvii. 2, 3, there is another song of the vineyard, which reminds us also of John xv., where the Lord says, "My Father is the husbandman." "In that day sing ye unto her, A vineyard of red wine, I the Lord do keep it; I will water it every moment: lest any hurt it, I will keep it night and day." This prophecy of future blessing is as full of teaching for us as their past history has been. Ezek. xv. is important as a commentary on the same passage, for it shows that a vine is planted with one object, that of fruit-bearing, and that if it fails in this it is useless.

When Jacob blessed his sons, he said, "Joseph is a fruitful bough, even a fruitful bough by a well, whose branches run over the wall." A greater than Joseph is here described, the true Vine, whose branches were to spread over the wall of partition, and whose heavily-laden boughs were to bless and refresh the world.   It is one of the passages which, like so many of the parables, seems to bear both present and future interpretations.

I.—TYPICAL SUBSTANCES

The Lord often introduces into His teaching the mention of substances which by their use in the Old Testament ceremonials are proved to have a spiritual meaning—such as leaven, meal, oil, wine, and salt.   No detail in His pictures was without significance, no detail in the types was unnecessary, and we may therefore assume that they teach the same lessons whether we find them in the types of the Old Testament or the parables of the New.

Oil is a familiar type of the Holy Spirit.   It was offered with the meal-offering, signifying the anointing and fulness of the Spirit in the perfect life of the Lord Jesus, and the need of His presence in any offering that is acceptable to God.   There was oil for the light, the power for shining ; there was the anointing oil with which Aaron and his sons were dedicated to the service of the Tabernacle, typifying the anointing of the Holy Spirit ; it was present in the holy ointment which was compounded of precious spices and oil, denoting the preciousness of the Lord Jesus revealed by the power of the Spirit, "Thy Name is as ointment poured forth."   We might refer to many other passages about the oil. The teaching of the types suggests that in the parable of the ten virgins the oil for the light may refer to the Holy Spirit.

The story of the widow's pot of oil is very beautiful in connection with this parable.   The wise virgins had vessels with oil in them, but while they were asleep they did not use the supply.   The widow might have thought the promise of the prophet but poor provision, yet it was only as she kept on pouring it out that she found a plentiful supply. Supposing she had said to the prophet, " I know I have the pot of oil, but I want something more, this is not enough, I need a whole tankful of oil to pay my debts." Had she thus despised the pot of oil, she would never have found out that the tankful was already there in the little pot, she must continue pouring, to discover how much she had. This kind of pouring out of the Spirit is one which the Church needs very much. Many of us are longing for great manifestations of power, for a great revival, but are we not in danger of leaving the pot of oil on the shelf while we ask for a tankful ? When the virgins wakened from their sleep they began to make use of their vessels of oil, and their lamps began to burn brightly. If every believer were "filled with the Spirit," if the Church unitedly and really believed that the promise had been fulfilled, He shall "abide with you for ever," could He not put forth His mighty power in a way that He has never done before ? He would not speak of Himself, but would manifest the Lord Jesus Christ. " He did not many mighty works there because of their unbelief," albeit He was with them, and this is true of the Holy Spirit as it was of the Lord in the days of His flesh. He also might ask, " Have I been so long time with you, and yet hast thou not known Me ? " We know as little of His glory as the disciples knew of the Lord Jesus before He was transfigured. What we want is a transfiguration rather than a fresh bestowal, and if such a revelation were granted, the result would be the same as when the Lord Himself was transfigured ; *His* glory would shine out, not the glory of the Spirit. Like the disciples, we should see "Jesus only."

In the parable the oil and wine of the good Samaritan are used in ministering to the wounded man. We have seen in the Lord's interpretation of the parable of the tares that nothing was introduced without intention, and it is not likely that He who had Himself commanded in days gone by that oil should be used in the service of the tabernacle, should have introduced it here without some meaning. The Epistle to the Hebrews shows that even in the details of the types we have "the Holy Ghost signifying" some spiritual lesson.

The oil in this parable reminds us of the condition of Israel as described under the figure of a sick and wounded man, "wounds, and bruises, and putrifying sores : they have not been closed, neither bound up, neither mollified with ointment," or "oil" (*marg.*), Isa. i. 6. This was the condition of the man who fell among thieves, till the good Samaritan, "as he journeyed, came where he was."

In the types *wine* speaks of joy and strength, as in the drink-offerings and in the passages to which reference has been made. Its mention in this parable reminds us of the words, "Give strong drink unto him that is ready to perish, and wine unto those that be of heavy hearts."

Salt is several times mentioned by the Lord in His figurative utterances, and we learn its meaning also from the types. It was to be provided for offering with the sacrifices, "salt, without prescribing how much" (Ezra vii. 22). It *prevents* corruption, while leaven which *causes* corruption, and honey which easily ferments, were forbidden. This, then, gives the key to its typical signification, it is that which prevents corruption. But this is only a negative definition. It seems to represent judgment upon, or testimony against, sin. The Lord uses it in this sense several times, as when He says, "Ye are the salt of the earth." The righteous by their lives are intended to be a living testimony against sin and thus to hinder corruption, but if the salt have lost its savour it will fail in its purpose, it will be just as useless as the life of a Christian who ceases to witness against sin.   If the Holy Spirit fill a believer He will work through him in convicting the world of sin.   In another place the Lord says, " Have salt in yourselves, and have peace one with another." If there be self-judgment there will be forbearance, and so if there be salt in ourselves there will be peace for others.

The apostle gives another lesson, " Let your speech be alway with grace, seasoned with salt." Gracious-ness which takes no note of sin is not to be admired or cultivated.   It may sometimes seem more easy, more pleasant, more polite, to take no notice of wrong things said or done in our presence, but there must not be grace without salt.   There must be either silent or spoken testimony against sin.

A short time ago, in the daily papers, there was an interesting report of an investigation into the causes of leprosy in the East.   A well-known surgeon, after careful observations in India, had returned to give the result of his researches.   He believed that it was largely caused by the eating of fish which had not been properly salted ; and he was convinced that if there were *more salt* there would be *less leprosy.* Whether this be a medical fact or not, it is a striking illustration of a great spiritual truth.   Leprosy in the Word of God typifies sin in its activity, for it repre-sents it in its corruption and repulsiveness.   If there be judgment on sin as symbolised by the salt, there will be less sin in activity, leprosy will not break out either in the individual or in the community.   We read of dark periods in our own history, and that of other nations, when society became utterly corrupt. Open sin was indulged, instead of being judged, and so things became worse and worse, and outward splendour could not hide the hideous disease. There is no health in a nation or in an individual if there be no salt.

II.—LEVITICAL INSTITUTIONS AND LAWS

The feasts.—The chapter which describes the feasts of the Lord (Lev. xxiii.) is one which should be carefully studied with the parables. There are many analogies between the series of yearly festivals and the parables in the thirteenth of Matthew. The chapter in Leviticus commences with a reference to the sabbath, the weekly rest which ran all through the other feasts. It was distinctly stated to be "a shadow of things to come" (Col. ii. 17), and this is equally true of the great convocations of the Levitical year which follow. They were a wonderful panorama in type of the whole time between the passover—the cross; and the feast of tabernacles—the millennium.

Immediately after the passover there is the feast of unleavened bread, which naturally reminds us of the parable of the leaven (pp. 130, 234). Then there is an account of two feasts which have to do with the harvest, the feast of first-fruits and the feast of ingathering. They are thus described in Exod. xxiii. 16, " The feast of harvest, the first-fruits of thy labours, which thou hast sown in the field : and the feast of ingathering, which is in the end of the year, when thou hast gathered in thy labours out of the field." Both of these are very suggestive in connection with the parables.

The sheaf of the first-fruits was waved "on the morrow after the sabbath" which immediately followed the passover, and thus the very day of the Lord's resurrection was foreshown. It was the beginning of the first resurrection, of which the first-fruits is a type. We know that there are three stages even in this beginning of God's harvest. Christ Himself was "the first-fruits; afterward they that are Christ's at His coming" to the air and to the earth. Those who will have been "beheaded for the witness of Jesus, and for the Word of God, and which have not worshipped the beast," are to be included in the first resurrection (Rev. xx. 4).[1]

If the chapter in Leviticus is, as we believe, a chronological history in type, the question naturally arises, Where does the present dispensation come in? The apostle Paul gives us the answer in his reference to the keeping of the feast of unleavened bread. The feast of weeks, the Pentecost of this chapter, has never really been fulfilled. There was a partial anticipation of the feast, just as there was a representation of the kingdom in miniature on the Mount of Transfiguration; but through the rejection of Israel the clock of time has been put back, and the next date on the calendar postponed. The waving of the sheaf of the first-fruits occurs during the feast of unleavened bread, and the next event is the offering of the second first-fruits (verses 16–20), and then the harvest.

All would be included in the harvest from the first sheaf to the last ear that was gleaned from the field, as is shown by the passage already quoted in Exod. xxiii. 16.

This type also reminds us of the corn of wheat in John xii. 24. There could be no first-fruits unless the seed had been "sown in the field." There must be death before there can be resurrection. The first-fruits could not be offered to God apart from this, for

---

[1] Some tell us we should include the Church with "Christ," and read this passage (1. Cor. xv.), "The Christ the first-fruits, afterward they that are Christ's at His coming" (to the earth), omitting the separate mention of those that are His at His coming to the air.

the handful was to be burnt upon the altar where the blood of the sin-offering had been outpoured, and the burnt-offering had ascended as a sweet savour to God. This was Cain's mistake, he tried to offer the first-fruits without the blood.

The first-fruits offering was a meal-offering and came under the laws of Lev. ii. ; vi. 14–23. Neither leaven nor honey must accompany it, but oil, frank-incense, and salt. A meal-offering was always offered in connection with the sheaf ; and the grain beaten out of the ears, after having been waved before the Lord, might be offered in different ways. It might be made into a cake, and it is to this that the apostle seems to refer in Rom. xi. 16, " If the first-fruit be holy, the lump is also holy." The meal-offering is described as " a thing most holy of the offerings of the Lord made by fire " (Lev. ii. 10). After fifty days "a new meal-offering" of two loaves was offered, called the "oblation of the first-fruits" (Lev. ii. 12). They were to be baken with leaven, and be-cause of its presence they could not be burnt upon the altar, but must be accompanied with a sin-offering. Does not this give a word of encouragement as regards the parable ? Though the woman has added the leaven, God does not altogether reject it, for He has provided the sin-offering.

The only other leavened cake which was allowed to be presented was the thanksgiving offering in Lev. vii. 13, and here too the leaven is met by blood. One cake out of the whole oblation was to be offered "for an heave-offering unto the Lord, and it shall be the priest's that sprinkleth the blood of the peace-offerings."

Clean and unclean animals. — Reference has been made (page 141) to Lev. xi. and Deut. xiv., which enumerate the clean and unclean animals. Several writers have shown that the characteristics which rendered some clean and others unclean denote different things to be imitated or avoided.

Besides the fish, there are directions about four-footed animals which might be eaten. "Whatsoever parteth the hoof . . . and cheweth the cud." "The inward life and the outward walk must go together. A man may profess to love and feed on the Word, to study and ruminate, but if his footprints along the pathway of life are not such as the Word requires he is not clean. On the other hand, a man may seem to walk with pharisaical blamelessness, but if his walk be not the result of the hidden life it is worse than useless."

Then as to the birds, those which are untamable were unclean (verse 13); those that feed on carrion, and those that belong to the night. It is easy to see the spiritual counterpart of these things. Then there are those in verse 20 with power to soar but preferring to creep, and in Deut. xiv. 19, those whose nature is to creep, but who pretend to fly. Some might say that it is fanciful to see meanings in all these things, but it is certain that hidden away in the Mosaic laws there are many parables. The same symbolism is repeated several times in Scripture, and we have the Lord's own example for comparing different kinds of animals to classes of men. Not only have we an instance of this in the parable of the net, but in the acted parables of the two miraculous draughts of fishes (p. 224).

In the book of the Acts we have a parable in vision founded on the same teaching.

The apostle Peter on the housetop in Joppa saw a sheet let down from heaven wherein were all manner of four-footed beasts of the earth, and wild beasts, and creeping things. When he heard the words from heaven, "Rise, Peter; kill, and eat," he replied, "Not so, Lord; for I have never eaten anything that is common or unclean." He must have recognised the

voice, and we see by his reply that he was the old
Peter still.[1]   Again the voice spake to him, "What
God hath cleansed, that call not thou common."   It
was soon made plain to Peter that the unclean
animals in the vision represented Gentiles, and he
learnt by it that it was no longer the unlawful thing
he had imagined "for a man that is a Jew to keep
company, or come unto one of another nation, but
God hath shewed me that I should not call any man
common or unclean."   A further dispensational lesson
has been suggested here.   "This vision which instructed Peter in the fact that God had sanctified the
Gentiles might also have told him that God had made
heaven and not earth the place of their calling, and
the scene of their hopes.   The vessel let down from
heaven and then taken up denoted that the Church
had been of old written in heaven and hid there with
God, but now for a little season was manifested here,
and in the end was to be hid in heaven again, but this
part was reserved for Paul to disclose."

Peter shows by his epistle that henceforth he saw
fresh meaning in Leviticus xi.   We may be quite
sure that he studied the book of Moses with new
interest.   His vision had not taught him to discard
the directions about the clean and unclean animals,
for he quotes from the very chapter in 1 Pet. i. 16,
"As He which hath called you is holy, so be ye
holy in all manner of conversation; because it is
written (in Lev. xi. 44), Be ye holy; for I am holy."
In the next verse he speaks of the Father "who without respect of persons judgeth according to every
man's work."   He still found that the laws were a call

---

[1] "There is a very curious expression . . . If Peter had said ' Not so,
there would have been a clear consistency in his tone.   But ' Not so, Lord,
is an odd jumble of self-will and reverence, of pride and humility, of contradiction and devotion.   Surely when you say ' Not so,' it ought not to
be said to the Lord, and if you say ' Lord,' you ought not to put side by
side such an ascription ' Not so.' "—C. H. SPURGEON.

to holiness, but understood that this was not merely holding aloof from outward defilement, it was an avoidance of habits and characteristics that are abhorrent to God ; not a separation outwardly from sinners, but inwardly from sins.

The law of leprosy.—The law of leprosy in Lev. xiv. concerning a house in which the plague had appeared seems specially to refer to the nation of Israel which is so often compared to a house. We have seen this in connection with the parable in Matt. xii. 44, where the unclean spirit says, " I will return into my house from whence I came out ; and when he is come, he findeth it empty, swept, and garnished." The type tells of a house which is to be left empty, to be deserted, shut up, partially pulled down, or if the evil still spread, entirely destroyed.   Should the priest, however, return and find it healed, the same rites are to be performed as in the case of the healed leper.

All these different conditions of the house are striking pictures of Israel's history. We may compare verses 36–40 with the words concerning the temple in the time of our Lord, for we know that the history of the nation was symbolised throughout by the history of the temple (see Matt. xxiii. 37, 38).

"The priest shall command that they empty the house" (verse 36).

"Your[1] house is left unto you desolate" (Matt. xxiii. 38).

"The priest shall go out of the house to the door of the house, and shut up the house seven days" (verse 38).

"And Jesus went out, and departed from the temple" (Matt. xxiv. 1), typical of His finally leaving the nation.

"Then the priest shall command that they take away

[1] Not "*My* house" as in Matt. xxi. 13, or "*My* Father's house" as in John ii. 16.

the stones in which the plague is, and they shall cast them into an unclean place without the city" (verse 40).

"There shall not be left here one stone upon another, that shall not be thrown down" (Matt. xxiv. 2).

The leprous house in verse 42 was not to be entirely broken down, "They shall take *other* stones, and put them in the place of those stones ; and he shall take *other* mortar." This reminds us of Rom. xi., where the same thing is symbolised by a different figure ; the cutting off of the natural branches of the olive tree, and the grafting in of *other* branches from the wild olive. Israel's rejection has made way for the bringing in of the Gentiles, Gentile stones having been built in with Jewish stones to make a new habitation.

But we find another picture, viz., that of a house which had to be pulled down. This is a figure which is used in many Scriptures concerning Israel, but they also tell us that the house is to be rebuilt (see Rom. xi. 1, 2). "I will build them as at the first" (Jer. xxxiii. 7 ; Ezek. xxxvi. 36, &c.). "To this agree the words of the prophets ; as it is written, After this I will return, and will . . . build again the ruins thereof, and I will set it up : that the residue of men might seek after the Lord, and all the Gentiles, upon whom My name is called, saith the Lord, who doeth all these things" (Acts xv. 15–17). As the apostle shows also under the figure of the olive, it will mean blessing for the world. To suit the type we might say, " If (the shutting up or the pulling down of the house) be the reconciling of the world, what shall (the reopening or the rebuilding) of (it) be but life from the dead ? "

In Psalm li. there is a cry for cleansing from one who acknowledges himself to be defiled as a leper (the whole Psalm is wonderfully beautiful when linked with Lev. xiv.). After speaking of his individual need, which is but a picture of the condition of the nation, the Psalmist prays for the rebuilding of the city : " Do good in Thy good pleasure unto Zion : build Thou the walls of Jerusalem." This verse at the end of the Psalm has perplexed many writers. They have said that it could not have been written before the captivity as the walls were not broken down until then ; that therefore it was not written by David, or that this verse at least must have been added. But David was a prophet (Acts ii. 30), and if he could by the Spirit fore-tell the sufferings of Messiah, he could also prophesy concerning Israel's future. By studying the Psalm with the type in Lev. xiv., we see how appropriate is the reference to the broken down walls at the close, for the chapter that begins with the individual leper, ends with the law concerning the house.

When the Lord thus returns to bless His people, the house of Israel will be like the dwelling-place spoken of in verse 48. The priest, having left it shut up and empty for seven days, will return once more. " Then the priest shall pronounce the house clean, because the plague is healed." In the antitype His return is the remedy. His presence alone can cure the leprosy when He will "arise with healing in His wings " (Mal. iv. 2), fulfilling His promise, " Behold, I will bring it health and cure " (Jer. xxxiii. 6).

The same offerings were prescribed for the healed house as for the individual " in the day of his cleans-ing." They were an acknowledgment of past leprosy that had been cured, and a means of cleansing from its defilement. When the children of Israel have been restored they will loathe themselves in their own sight (Ezek. xxxvi. 31). They will know that they have been saved from their uncleanness as from leprosy (verses 29, 33), and the nations will see that the house has been rebuilt. They will acknowledge, as in Isaiah liii., that their restoration is owing to the death and resurrection of Him who died and rose "according to the Scriptures," as typified by the two birds and the running water. When this provision has been accepted by Israel the house will once more be made fit for habitation, so that the owner can return to His dwelling. Their King will dwell in the midst as never before. "So shall ye know that I am the Lord your God dwelling in Zion" (Joel iii. 17). "The name of the city from that day shall be, Jehovah Shammah, The Lord is there" (Ezek. xlviii. 35).

There is a wonderful picture in Deut. xxi. 1–9 of *a guilty city*, and the means by which its guilt is removed. One is found slain, lying in the field of the world, and the question has to be settled, Who is guilty? It has been said that it is "the only inquest in the Bible, typical of God's inquest over the death of His Son." "The city which is next unto the slain man" is pronounced guilty, and provision is made to remove the guilt.

This is one of the beautiful double types with which the Old Testament Scriptures abound. The finding of the dead body in the field brought home the guilt, the slain heifer removed the guilt, and both typified the Lord Jesus. There is an evident application for every sinner, and also a picture of Israel's crime and Israel's pardon.

We have seen that the figure of the city is often used in connection with their history in the parables (page 166). While it is there represented as shining or rebelling, as being invited and destroyed, it is here typified as guilty of the death of the Lord Jesus. Jerusalem was literally the city "next unto the slain man." All heaven knows the spot which is stained by His blood, for it is still noted for the crime. The angel speaking of it to John called it "the great city . . . where also their Lord was crucified" (Rev. xi. 8, R.V.). But the same chapter which shows that God will require the death of His Son, also shows God's provision for removing that guilt. The heifer was to be slain by the elders of the city, and they were to wash their hands over it, "And they shall answer and say, Our hands have not shed this blood, neither have our eyes seen it." Israel in the future will not be able to offer this plea, they have already said, "His blood be on us, and on our children," but still the sacrifice has been provided to remove their guilt. When they look on Him whom they have pierced, and mourn because of Him, the rest of the prayer will be wonderfully appropriate, "Be merciful, O Lord, unto Thy people Israel, whom Thou hast redeemed, and lay not innocent blood unto Thy people of Israel's charge. And the blood shall be forgiven them."

The cleansing by the water of purification and the ashes of the red heifer, of which the ritual is prescribed in Num. xix., is a type which seems specially to apply to Israel.[1] They are now "unclean by a dead body" (Hag. ii. 13, 14), but the day is coming when according to promise He will "sprinkle clean water" upon them (Exek. xxxvi. 25), and after the mourning of Zech. xii. 10, there will be "a fountain opened to the house of David, and to the inhabitants of Jerusalem, (the guilty city) for sin and for uncleanness" (chap. xiii. 1).

In Deut. xxii. 9, the sowing of the field or vineyard with *mixed seed* was forbidden, and the reason is "lest the fulness (*marg.*) of thy seed which thou hast sown, and the fruit of thy vineyard, be defiled." The enemy

---

[1] See "The Study of the Types," pp. 74–78.
Kregel Publications

who sows the tares knows that this will be the result, the good seed will assuredly be defiled.

There is a promise in Deut. xxv. 15, in connection with *weights and measures*. "Thou shalt have a perfect and just weight, a perfect and just measure shalt thou have ; that thy days may be lengthened in the land which the Lord thy God giveth thee." The blessing in the gospel is promised to those who use an overflowing measure (Mark iv. 24 ; Luke vi. 38). We are not merely to give to others that to which they are legally entitled, but having freely received, we should freely give. The difference between the dispensations of law and grace is well illustrated in this double command. A *just* measure is expected under law, an *overflowing* measure under grace. "Length of days" was the reward in Old Testament times, spiritual "riches and honour" under New Testament teaching.

The instructions given in Deut. xxii. 1–3 are a beautiful supplement to the parable of *the lost sheep*. "Thou shalt not see thy brother's ox or his sheep go astray, and hide thyself from them ; thou shalt in any case bring them again unto thy brother. And if thy brother be not nigh unto thee, or if thou know him not, then thou shalt bring it unto thine own house, and it shall be with thee until thy brother seek after it, and thou shalt restore it to him again. In like manner shalt thou do with . . . all lost thing of thy brother's, which he hath lost, and thou hast found, shalt thou do likewise ; thou mayest not hide thyself."

The good Shepherd is not ashamed to call us brethren, for He is the "First-born among many brethren." He is the well-beloved Son, we are the sons, and though reverence would prevent our addressing Him as brother, and would rather prompt us to call Him Lord, yet in this little parable-type we may surely see a picture of Him. It suggests that we may help the good Shepherd when we see any of His sheep that have gone astray. In one sense, He does not need us, and yet He condescends to let us join Him in His blessed work, and "the head" never says to "the feet, I have no need of you." We may try and draw the wandering sheep to our own dwelling, and keep it there till He seek after it. The skilful soul-winner endeavours to gain an influence over the lost one that he is longing to lead to the Saviour. And by showing love and sympathy one is often able to bring the wandering sheep to his own house, that the good Shepherd may find it. But the warning is given against being satisfied with merely finding the lost one; this is not enough, we must not rest satisfied till it is restored to the Shepherd. To win to ourselves without winning to Christ would be poor work indeed.

It was in the spirit of this command that John the Baptist was so willing to see his disciples leave him that they might follow his Lord. When men came to him, and pointed out how all were following the One to whom he had borne testimony, his answer was very beautiful, "He that hath the bride is the bridegroom; but the friend of the bridegroom, which standeth and heareth him, rejoiceth greatly because of the bridegroom's voice: this my joy therefore is fulfilled. He must increase, but I must decrease." "He would be a false friend who tried to win the bride for himself, but all John's joy was summed up in this, that the bridegroom was going to have his bride." He was very different from Samson's friend, for we read that "Samson's wife was given to his companion, whom he had used as his friend." Had John been grieved when his disciples left him, it would have been disloyalty to the bridegroom.   To keep the sheep instead of restoring it to the good Shepherd would be dishonesty.

The passage in Deuteronomy says that the sheep thus found is to be kept "until thy brother seek after it."   The parable in Luke tells us that the good Shepherd begins to seek directly He misses it, and goes after it "until He find it."   He often does this through the instrumentality of others.

The following verse (Deut. xxii. 4) also reminds us of another gospel simile, "Thou shalt not see thy brother's ass or his ox fall down by the way, and hide thyself from them : thou shalt surely help him to lift them up again."   The Lord used this same illustration when answering the lawyers and Pharisees about healing on the Sabbath day.   "Which of you shall have an ass or an ox fallen into a pit, and will not straightway pull him out on the sabbath day?" His application shows what was meant by lifting up the animal that was fallen down ; to succour those who had need of Him, to heal them as no one else could, this was like raising the helpless animal out of the pit.

The command in Deuteronomy teaches that we are to be on the look-out for such in their need.   We may be quite sure that Moses did not refer merely to these animals, for as the apostle said in 1 Cor. ix. 7–10, commenting on Deut. xxv. 4 : "Doth God take care for oxen ? or saith He it altogether for our sakes ? For our sakes, no doubt."   We are not strong enough to raise the fallen, any more than we are wise enough to find the lost, but He condescends to allow us to help Him.   Three times over in these verses the command is repeated, "Thou shalt not (or mayest not) hide thyself" (verses 1, 3, 4).   "Thou shalt in any case bring them again to thy brother."   Must we not all plead guilty to having disobeyed this word, for have we not often seen the sheep going astray, or the animal stumbling in the road, and done nothing to bring it back, or to raise it up again ? It would indeed be an unbrotherly act to see those belonging to One so near of kin in such need, and deliberately to hide ourselves from them instead of coming forward to help. The right thing is always to go at once to Him whose they are, and tell Him of their straying or their falling, and He will show us what we can do for Him.

Immediately preceding the directions about the lost sheep there is the law concerning *the rebellious son* (Deut. xxi. 18–21). It is in striking contrast to the parable of the prodigal, and well illustrates the difference between law and grace. The law sentenced such an one to stripes, and finally to stoning. How different to the reception of the prodigal, the " much " kissing of the father, the ring, the shoes, and the best robe.

III.—Old Testament Illustrations [1]

We are reminded of many parable scenes as we study the Old Testament pictures, some of which are indeed typical of the parables.

In the life of *Joseph* there are two or three such incidents. The treatment he received from his brethren, and their jealousy when he related his dreams, remind us of the citizens in Luke xix. who said, " We will not have this man to reign over us." The very words they uttered are almost identical, " Shalt thou indeed reign over us ? or shalt thou indeed have dominion over us ? and they hated him yet the more for his dreams and for his words." Of the nobleman in Luke we read also, " His citizens hated him." Stephen in his address showed how the

---

[1] See also Appendix III., " Isaiah liii. illustrated by the Parables."

rejection of Joseph was a type of the rejection of the
Lord, but just as the former was at last acknowledged
by Israel to be their deliverer, so the city that once
hated Him will by-and-by welcome the despised One
as their Saviour and King.

We are also reminded of the parable of the wicked
husbandmen where we read of Jacob sending his well-
beloved son to seek his brethren. " I will send thee
unto them." So the father in the parable said, "What
shall I do? I will send my beloved son." Their
reception was the same in both cases. Joseph's
brethren " conspired against him to slay him ;" they
said one to another, " Come now, therefore, and let
us slay him." Envy at the father's love, and the
thought of his future exaltation, made them wish to
take his life. There was one in the little group who
hindered them from shedding Joseph's blood, but in
the parable, as in the sadder reality, there was none
to pity. The husbandmen not only said, " This is the
heir : come, let us kill him, that the inheritance may
be ours," but actually carried out their purpose, " So
they cast him out of the vineyard, and killed him."
How little the husbandmen thought that the one
whom they thus slew would come into his inheritance
in spite of them. They thought to wrest it from Him,
but it was by His death that He gained His glorious
inheritance in the saints, and added to the riches
which belonged to Him as the Father's Son. The
treatment which Joseph received at the hands of his
brethren, instead of frustrating the fulfilment of his
dreams, was the very means by which they came
to pass.

The use of *double symbolism* was strikingly explained
by Joseph when he stood before Pharaoh, showing
that it was a Divine plan, by which to emphasise the
facts represented. The principle is the same whether
it occurs in visions or in parables. Joseph was

interpreting Pharaoh's two dreams, and said, "The dream of Pharaoh is one : God hath showed Pharaoh what He is about to do. . . . And for that the dream was doubled unto Pharaoh twice, it is because the thing is established by God, and God will shortly bring it to pass" (Gen. xli. 25–32). The teaching was the same in both, but the symbolism in one case was taken from the animal kingdom, in the other from the vegetable kingdom. There are two other pairs of dreams in Joseph's history ; the first two are those which he himself dreamed, where also the same revelation was doubled under different symbolism. The sheaves in the first, and the sun, moon, and stars in the second, bowed down to Joseph's sheaf or star. In one the figure used is earthly, and in the other it is heavenly. We often find these two linked together in Scripture, *e.g.*, in the promise to Abraham, where his seed is compared to the sand of the seashore, and to the stars of heaven. In this double picture, according to the rule Joseph gave, the certainty of its fulfilment is emphasised, and the twofold nature of Abraham's seed is indicated, namely, the earthly people—his children after the flesh, and the heavenly—his children by faith.

The symbolism of these two dreams—which were in themselves parables in vision, reminds us of the double symbolism at the close of the parable of the tares. In the interpretation, the Lord having explained the gathering out of the tares, and the harvesting of the wheat, changes the simile, and adds, "Then shall the righteous shine forth as the sun in the kingdom of their Father." He turns from sheaves to shining— from earthly fruit-bearing to heavenly glory. The same change of simile from fruit-bearing to shining[1] is to be found in Mark and Luke, where the parable of the sower is immediately followed by the lesson from the

---

[1] In both cases the shining is in an earthly sphere.

candle, and we also find both figures in the golden candlestick in the Tabernacle. The pattern represented fruit-bearing, for the branches of the lampstand were formed of buds and blossoms and almonds; while its object was shining.

The other pair of dreams did not prophesy the same events under different symbolism, but must be contrasted the one with the other. The dreams of Joseph's two fellow-prisoners foretold the different destiny which awaited each, shame and death in one case, restoration and honour in the other. These three pairs of dreams well illustrate the different kinds of double parables, which are considered in chaps. xviii. and xix. First, those where the teaching is the same, but the symbolism different; second, those which also supplement one another; third, those which give opposite pictures. We may be sure from Joseph's statement to Pharaoh that the Lord had the same reason for repeating the lesson under different figures. We might use Joseph's words, and say, " For that the (parable) was doubled unto (us) twice ; it is because the thing is established by God, and God will shortly bring it to pass."

One more incident in the life of Joseph illustrates a parable story. When his brethren came into Egypt to buy corn, " Joseph said to the ruler of his house, Bring these men home." Three times over we are told that he brought them into Joseph's house (Gen. xliii. 17, 18, 24). He might have said like the servant in Luke xiv., " Lord, it is done as Thou hast commanded." Though they were reluctant and fearful, yet he compelled them to come in, and Joseph's feast was furnished with guests. They did not treat the invitation like those which were bidden in the parable.

The story of Joash is a wonderful picture of a kingdom in mystery. It is a very complete type, a prophetic picture, and we have New Testament warrant for thus making use of it. The wicked Athaliah, the daughter of Jezebel, had tried to kill all the seed royal, and thought that she had succeeded, but one "from among the . . . slain" was "hid in the house of the Lord." It was still the kingdom of David, though a usurper reigned, and though the people chose "a murderer" (Acts iii. 14), as they had done when they proclaimed Absalom king. God's promise to David was not broken, but the kingdom was in mystery. The king was hidden and only a few knew that he lived. The picture is a very striking one with its many accurate typical details. The high priest (for the true kingly power is in abeyance) lets certain of the people into the secret, and tells them that "the king's son shall reign, as the Lord hath said." He also "shewed them the king's son." He might have said, "It is given unto you to know the mysteries of the kingdom of David, but to the rest of the people it is not given."

Those who were the recipients of the secret were the priests and Levites, who had access to the temple, the place where the king was hidden. The high priest instructed them as to their various duties in connection with the king's proclamation and coronation, for though he was the rightful king he had not yet been crowned. Their attitude was to be one of waiting and watching till he should receive the kingdom. Several groups of faithful ones are described, and the different places allotted to them. The priests and Levites only were permitted inside the temple, and they were summoned to take their places by the side of the king when the time came for him to be proclaimed—a beautiful type of those who have the right of access now, and who are waiting for the rallying cry. "Be ye with the King when he cometh in, and when he goeth out," was the

word to the Levites when they were thus summoned,
just as the apostle says concerning those who are to
be caught up to meet the Lord in the air, " So shall
we ever be with the Lord."

"A third part" were to be at "the thresholds
(*marg.*), a third part at the king's house, and a third
part at the gate of the foundation ; and all the people
shall be in the courts of the house of the Lord." Of
all these groups none would see the king till he was
actually proclaimed, but the Levites were to come
out with him. A most remarkable picture even in
its details of the two stages of the Lord's return, and
the " crowning day that's coming by-and-by."   Then,
too, we notice that it was only in the seventh year,
just before the king was to be proclaimed, that the
high priest made it clearly understood that he was
soon to be crowned.   Before this, there had probably been rumours about the one that was hidden
in the temple, but few knew for certain of his presence there.   How the fact must have changed their
lives when Jehoiada "showed them the king's son !"

The state of Israel during that interval was typical
of the mysteries of the kingdom ; the kingdom in
abeyance, a usurper reigning, but the king's son
hidden, and secret followers waiting and watching
for the crowning day.   The parables concerning the
mysteries of the kingdom of heaven do not, like this
marvellous type,[1] reveal the first event in the coronation ceremonies, represented by the summoning of
the tribe and family of the high priest to take their
places by the side of the king's son.   This was
reserved for the apostle Paul, who received it as the
direct revelation from the High Priest himself.

We have New Testament warrant for taking this
picture as typical.   In Rev. ii., in the epistle to the
Church in Thyatira, we read of Jezebel and her

[1] See " The Priests and Levites, a Type of the Church."

children who try to seduce the Church. The words were addressed to a Church that was to last till the coming of the Lord, "Hold fast till I come," and we may, therefore, look upon the period of Athaliah's reign as a type of the days when the kingdom is in mystery.

The story of *Naboth's vineyard* reminds us of the vineyard in the parable of the wicked husbandmen. At the instigation of Jezebel, the plot was made to kill Naboth that the vineyard might belong to Ahab. The husbandmen in the parable coveted the vineyard for themselves. They had already acted as though it were theirs, for they had refused to give the fruit to the rightful owner, "Those husbandmen said among themselves, This is the heir : come, let us kill him, and the inheritance shall be ours. And they took him, and killed him, and cast him out of the vineyard." We read of Naboth that "they carried him forth out of the city, and stoned him with stones, that he died." Jezebel's plot, by which she got rid of the one who stood in her way, was almost the same as that carried out by "the chief priests and elders and all the council" in fulfilling the prophecy of the parable. They sought false witness, and at "last came two false witnesses," who testified against Him, so that "the high priest rent his clothes, saying, He hath spoken blasphemy : what further need have we of witnesses ? Behold, now ye have heard His blasphemy. What think ye ? They answered, and said, He is guilty of death." This had been Jezebel's plan. She wrote to the elders and nobles, and told them to "set two men, sons of Belial, before him, to bear witness against him, saying, Thou didst blaspheme God and the king : and then carry him out, and stone him, that he may die." When the Jewish rulers "killed the Prince of Life," did they remember that they were following the example of

Jezebel, and using the same means to make the innocent appear guilty? Had they thought of this they might also have known that the inheritance thus seized would bring no blessing, but that their wicked deed would be as surely punished as that of Jezebel; and that in the very place where the innocent blood had been shed, there the judgment would fall. They adopted the same plan when they wanted to rid themselves of Stephen (Acts vi. 11–14).

The parable of the unjust judge, and *the widow's cry*, "Avenge me of mine adversary," is illustrated by two Old Testament stories. In 2 Kings viii. 3 we read that when the woman of Shunem had returned out of the land of the Philistines, whither she had gone to escape the famine of which Elisha had warned her, she "went forth to cry unto the king for her house and for her land." The story suggests what was the nature of the vengeance which the widow in the parable required. It was the restoration of her property that she wanted, and she obtained justice from the king at once, for he "appointed unto her a certain officer, saying, Restore all that was hers, and all the fruits of the field since the day that she left the land, even until now."

There is another widow who needed help to regain her property. The story of Ruth tells how she came to the kinsman Boaz, and how he redeemed all that belonged to her. The elect of God who cry day and night to Him, appeal to a King, a Kinsman and a Judge, and their prayer will surely be heard.

There is in Jer. xxxii. a very interesting incident, the record of *the purchase of a field*, which was intended at the time it occurred to be an acted parable to the people of Jerusalem.

It illustrates and illuminates the parable of the hidden treasure in Matt. xiii.

The imprisoned prophet was told by Jehovah that

he was about to receive a visit from his cousin Hanameel, who would come begging him to buy his field in Anathoth. According to the word of the Lord, Hanameel came and made his request, saying to Jeremiah, " Buy my field, I pray thee, . . . for the right of inheritance is thine, and the redemption is thine; buy it for thyself." Knowing it was of the Lord, Jeremiah complied, and the transaction was completed.

After he had bought the field, instructed by the Lord he charged Baruch, saying, " Take these evidences, this evidence of the purchase, both which is sealed, and this evidence which is open, and put them in an earthen vessel, that they may continue many days : for thus saith the Lord of Hosts, the God of Israel, Houses and fields and vineyards shall be possessed again in this land."

It seemed a foolish thing to buy a field when the oppressor held possession of the country, but Jeremiah was commanded to do it as a prophecy, and a promise that the land would one day be owned once more by Israel. Jeremiah was the only one who had a right to buy the field, but he could not enter into his property till the enemy had restored it.

The little parable in Matt. xiii. does not give us so complete a picture of the transaction, but we know that He who is there represented as buying the field was the only One to whom it might be said, " The right of inheritance is Thine, and the redemption is Thine : buy it for Thyself." The invader knew nothing about any treasure that might lie hidden beneath the soil, and he who purchased it could not publicly take possession till the usurper had been expelled.

In Jeremiah's case the evidence was hidden securely till that day should come. In the parable it is the treasure that is buried. The evidence of the Lord's

purchase is written in living epistles which are sealed
by the witness, "that Holy Spirit of promise, which is
the earnest of our inheritance, until the redemption
of the purchased possession" (Eph. i. 13, 14). The
witnessing and sealing of Jeremiah's document were a
promise that a day was coming when the purchased
possession would come into the hands of its owner.
The sealing of the Spirit is the testimony to the
transaction, and He Himself is the earnest. In the
day of the redemption of the purchased possession,
when the usurper will no longer hold sway over the
land, the treasure will not any more remain hidden.
Meanwhile the evidence of the purchase is put in
"earthen vessels," "that they may continue many
days."

In looking at the parables which naturally link
themselves together, we notice those in which a
similar expression is used (pp. 322–328). In the same
way there is an Old Testament vision and a New
Testament parable which both tell of a servant
who said to his master, it is "done as thou hast
commanded." The parallel is very striking in many
ways.

In the well-known parable of Luke xiv. the servant
is sent forth into the streets and lanes of the city,
and told to bring in to the great supper "the poor,
and the maimed, and the halt, and the blind," and
returns with the words, "Lord, it is done as thou hast
commanded, and yet there is room." The parable is
recorded immediately after the Lord had been mourning over Jerusalem in those wonderful words, "O
Jerusalem, Jerusalem, which killest the prophets, and
stonest them that are sent unto thee; how often
would I have gathered thy children together, as a hen
doth gather her brood under her wings, and ye would
not! Behold, your house is left unto you desolate:
and verily I say unto you, Ye shall not see Me, until

the time come when ye shall say, Blessed is He that cometh in the Name of the Lord" (Luke xiii. 34, 35).

In Ezek. viii. the prophet is permitted to see the abominations which are practised by Israel in its apostasy, the seventy of the ancients of the house of Israel offering incense to idols, saying, "The Lord seeth us not: the Lord hath forsaken the earth;" and twenty-five men[1] at the door of the temple all worshipping the sun. In chap. ix., before the judgment is poured out, the man clothed with linen which had the writer's ink-horn by his side is called; "And the Lord said unto him, Go through the midst of the city, through the midst of Jerusalem, and set a mark upon the foreheads of the men that sigh, and that cry, for all the abominations that be done in the midst thereof." He was to be immediately followed by other servants who were to execute judgment, and their instructions were, "Begin at My sanctuary." The chapter concludes with the words of the man clothed with linen which had the ink-horn by his side, who "reported the matter, saying, I have done as Thou hast commanded me." The rulers in Israel who in the vision are seen to commit such abominations are, in the parable, represented by those that were bidden. In both pictures there is a second class with whom the servant has specially to do: in the one those that sighed and cried for all that was done in the city; and in the other those who were helpless and needy, but willing to be brought to the feast. The ones marked by the man clothed with linen were not the rulers, those who came to the feast were not those bidden. In both cases the servant was sent on his errand through the streets of the city. He was able in the one case to mark all them that sighed over the sad condition of Jerusalem, showing that He could read their hearts, and in the other He had power to

---

[1] These probably represent the twenty-four elders and the high priest.

bring in the guests, leading the blind, and supporting the maimed and the halt. Thus, by the way in which He accomplished His errand, and by the fact that in both He reports that the work commanded was fully done, we may gather that the same Person is represented — the Holy Spirit Himself. He is the only One who can undertake such errands, and say that He has done as was commanded. He alone can put the seal upon the forehead. It is noteworthy that He is sent forth in the prophecy just as "the glory" is preparing to leave the city, and that the parable is spoken immediately after our Lord's solemn words, " Behold, your house is left unto you desolate."

The prophet had already seen that "the glory of the God of Israel was gone up from the cherub, whereupon He was, to the threshold of the house," and it was not until this had taken place, and until all the mourners in Israel were sealed, that the judgment was poured out. It was because of the rejection by the nation that the Lord said, " None of these men which were bidden shall taste of My supper."

In Esther vi. 14, we have an example of the sending of a messenger when the feast is ready to bring them that are bidden. "The king's chamberlains hasted to bring Haman unto the banquet that Esther had prepared." He had received the invitation before, but they came to tell him that all things were ready. It is interesting to notice that this was evidently the eastern custom referred to in the parable of the wedding feast.

There is a link in Ezek. xiii. with the story of the houses built on the rock and on the sand. The Lord God there compares the false prophets to those who built a wall and daubed it with untempered mortar. They professed to bring a message from God, but it was a vain vision, a lying divination, " Whereas ye

say, the Lord saith it; albeit I have not spoken."
The wall thus reared would fall, and, as in the case
of the house built on the sand, its destruction would
be due to the storm. The passage in Ezekiel defines
what this is. "Therefore thus saith the Lord God,
I will even rend it with a stormy wind in My fury;
and there shall be an overflowing shower in Mine
anger, and great hailstones, in My fury, to consume
it." This is the storm which the house without a
foundation cannot meet. The untempered mortar
with which the wall was daubed was a plaster of lies.
What a contrast to the rock of the parable, the
sayings of Him who said, "I am the *truth!*" The
house founded on His Word has no need to fear
the storm.

The clothing of Joshua, the high priest, in Zech. iii.
reminds us of the story of the prodigal. One scene
represents man at his best, for the high priest would
naturally take the highest place in the nation for
holiness; the other pictures man at his worst, and
tells of one who has been down into the depths of
sin. God's grace is needed for the first, but it reaches
to the last. Joshua in his filthy garments teaches that
"All our righteousnesses are as filthy rags," and it is
harder to believe this than that all our sins are as
filthy rags. It was when he stood before the angel of
Jehovah that this was revealed, and he was speechless,
like the prodigal, while the change of raiment was put
upon him.

Zechariah's vision of the ephah corresponds in
many ways with the parable of the leaven.

The Jews who listened to the parable must have been
familiar with the prophecy, and this is an additional
proof that they would have had no hesitation in
understanding the leaven to signify something evil.
The ephah of the vision would contain the same
quantity as the three measures spoken of in the

parable. Mention is made in both of a woman, and of something cast into the ephah. In the vision it is distinctly stated that this represented wickedness. The two women who fly with it to the land of Shinar have been taken to signify the great double-sided system of Rev. xvii. and xviii., called Mystery Babylon —false religion on the one hand, and civilisation and mercantile power on the other. The women are possessed of wings like the wings of a stork, an unclean bird, and thus there is a connection with the birds of the air which in the parables stand for Satan's power. We know that he will be the great mover in the building up of the colossal and double-sided Babylon of Revelation.

The ephah of Zechariah is to be set up in the land of Shinar, and this also clearly points to Babylon. It is thus a prophecy of the rebuilding of the literal city which is to become the centre of apostate religion and worldly power.

The vision in Zechariah represents the end of apostate Christendom, and the parable of Matt. xiii. the beginning of corrupt Christendom. The leaven of Matthew prepares for the "wickedness" of Zechariah, for the evil which permeates the kingdom of heaven in its earthward aspect makes possible, and leads up to, the seeming triumph of Satan's counterfeit kingdom.

IV. OLD TESTAMENT CHARACTERS

The stories of the Old Testament shepherds beautifully illustrate the parables of the good Shepherd, and other characters may be grouped together in the same way.

We have an example of a shepherd's *leading* in the story of Moses, who first led the flocks of his father-in-law to Horeb, and afterwards guided the children of Israel as a flock to the same mountain (Isa. lxiii. 11 ; Ps. lxxvii. 20). In John x. we have the good Shepherd *leading* His sheep.

This passage also tells us how He *delivers* them, and mentions the enemies of the sheep which He must encounter; and this is illustrated by David's history. He conquered the lion and the bear, while John x. speaks of the wolf, and contrasts the true Shepherd and the hireling who careth not for the sheep. We are reminded of the latter in the prophecy of Zech. xi. 17, "Woe to the idol (or worthless) shepherd that leaveth the flock ! "

Zechariah was told to take the instruments of a foolish shepherd, and in an acted parable to represent the coming of the one thus prophesied and described : " For, lo, I will raise up a shepherd in the land, which shall not visit those that be cut off, neither shall seek those that be scattered, nor heal that that is broken, neither shall he feed that which is sound, but he shall eat the flesh of the fat, and shall tear their hoofs in pieces " (verse 16, R.V.). This is the picture of one who will pretend to be a shepherd, but who proves that he cares nothing for the sheep. He does not even miss the wanderer, much less go "after that which is lost, until he find it," like Him who is so beautifully pictured in the parable in Luke xv.

Jacob was very different from this, for he showed the responsibility felt by a faithful shepherd, and is thus a beautiful type of Him who says in John x., "My sheep . . . shall never perish." If anything happened to the least of the flock Jacob was responsible. "That which was torn of beasts I brought not unto thee ; I bare the loss of it ; of my hand didst thou require it, whether stolen by day, or stolen by night." Probably such things often happened to some of Laban's flock in spite of Jacob's care, but the sheep of the good Shepherd are absolutely safe in His hand.

Jacob speaks also of the suffering which this constant watchfulness entailed. "Thus I was : in the day the drought consumed me, and the frost by night; and my sleep departed from mine eyes" (Gen. xxxi. 39, 40); but the suffering was nothing to that incurred by Him who laid down His life. Jacob might endure hardships, David might face dangers, but neither of them had to give his life for the sheep.

In David we have a picture of a shepherd who reigns and shepherds at the same time. This reminds us of the scene in Matt. xxv. when as the great Shepherd the king at His coming will divide the sheep from the goats, and then lead the sheep so that "they shall hunger no more, neither thirst any more."

In Ezek. xxxiv. there is a wonderful description of the two kinds of shepherds, those who think only of themselves instead of the sheep, and the Lord Himself as the good Shepherd. This chapter is a picture of Israel's history. There is a sevenfold description of their condition under their unfaithful shepherds. They had become diseased, sick, broken, driven away, lost, scattered, and wandering (verses 4–6). When the Lord Jesus was on earth He was filled with compassion when He beheld them "as sheep having no shepherd," but the chapter in Ezekiel looks forward to the time when Israel will once more be seen to be "the sheep of His pasture." Then He will search and seek them out, deliver them, bring them out and gather them, feed them, cause them to lie down, bind up and strengthen that which was sick (verses 11–16). The following verse reminds us of the dividing of the sheep and goats in Matt. xxv.

V.—THE PSALMS

Like all other portions of the Word, the Psalms of David are full of symbolism ; and seeing in his songs foreshadowings of our Lord's parables, we may link them together, and read into them all we know concerning the same subject from the New Testament. Unconsciously we all do this. For instance, in reading the words of the twenty-third Psalm, we naturally and rightly give them the New Testament interpretation which is found in Luke xv. and John x. Not only do these passages add to the meaning of the Psalm, but the utterance of the Psalmist, "The Lord is my Shepherd," gives a deeper meaning to the words of our Lord when He said, "I am the good Shepherd." David said that Jehovah was the Shepherd ; the Lord Jesus claimed that He was, and therefore it was but another way of saying that they were one, as He expressed it in the same chapter (John x. 30), "I and My Father are one." The Jehovah of the Old Testament reveals Himself as the Lord Jesus Christ in the New.

We have already noticed that the utterance of the parables foretold in Ps. lxxviii. 2 (see Matt. xiii. 34, 35), made it necessary that they should be spoken : "That it might be fulfilled which was spoken by the prophet, saying, I will open My mouth in parables." Without this quotation we should not have read the Psalm as a prophecy of these wonderful discourses, and should not have been sure that the speaker in the Psalm was the Messiah Himself.

The teaching of the *first* Psalm reminds us of the two kinds of servants depicted in Matt. xxiv. 45–51. The wise servant in the parable is like the man who is accounted happy in the Psalm, "Blessed is the man that walketh not in the counsel of the ungodly, nor standeth in the way of sinners, nor sitteth in the seat of the scornful." The evil servant does all these three things, even eating and drinking with the drunken. The "faithful and wise servant, whom his lord hath made ruler over his household," gives those under his charge their "meat *in due season.*" Feeding on the Word himself (Ps. cxlv. 15), he has always something ready for the needs of others, for he is like the man in the Psalm whose "delight is in the law of the Lord; and in His law doth he meditate day and night. And he shall be like a tree planted by the rivers of water, that bringeth forth his fruit *in his season.*"

We might apply to him who is accounted blessed in the Psalm the words spoken by the Lord in the parable : " Blessed is that servant, whom his lord, when he cometh, shall find so doing."

The evil servant in the parable is very unlike this, and it is true of him as of those described in the Psalm : "The ungodly are not so . . . Therefore the ungodly shall not stand in the judgment." The evil servant who said in his heart, "My lord delayeth his coming," will not be able to stand before him, but will, at his return, be cast out of the house, and his lord "shall appoint him his portion with the hypocrites"—those with whom he had walked, stood, and sat when his lord was absent.

The *second* Psalm is that of the wicked husbandmen, and takes us a step further than the parable. It tells us that though they conspired against the well-beloved Son, and their conspiracy seemed to succeed, they did not really prevent His coming into His inheritance. Their treatment of Him might postpone the day, but in spite of all, though they knew it not, God had said, "Yet have I set My King upon My holy hill of Zion."

The parable shows only the husbandmen as guilty ;

the Psalm condemns the whole world.   The Gentiles, "the kings of the earth," and "the rulers" of the nation, all were concerned in the great conspiracy "against the Lord, and against His anointed."   Israel was most guilty; but they were not alone, as we see by the prayer of the disciples in the Acts when they quoted this Psalm : "For of a truth, against Thy holy child Jesus, whom Thou hast anointed, both Herod and Pontius Pilate, with the Gentiles and the people of Israel, were gathered together" (Acts iv. 25, 27). The husbandmen had said : "This is the heir ; come, let us kill him, and the inheritance shall be ours." This was the "vain thing" which they imagined, but they could do nothing but "whatsoever Thy hand and Thy counsel determined before to be done" (Acts iv. 28).   Those who listened to His parables were angry because "they perceived that He spake of *them*"; yet they were not repentant, for they saw not that He spake of *Him* of whom the Psalm prophesied. Had they really known Him they would never have carried out the plot.   "They that dwell at Jerusalem, and their rulers, because they knew Him not, nor yet the voices of the prophets, which are read every sabbath day, they have fulfilled them in condemning Him."   Thus Paul well describes the husbandmen and their deed.   Both Psalm and parable describe the vengeance which would fall on the conspirators.

The closing verse of the Psalm reminds us of the exhortation: "Agree with thine adversary quickly, whiles thou are in the way with him."   "Kiss the Son, lest He be angry, and ye perish from the way."

It is well to link these two passages together ; for while the Lord enjoined His hearers to agree with the adversary quickly while in the way with him, the Psalm shows the only manner in which the two parties can come to an agreement.   Homage must be paid to the Son, and then the other adversary, the law,[1] will at once relax his hold. For "Christ is the end of the law for righteousness to every one that believeth."

Both passages describe travellers on the way. In the Gospel the debtor is being haled to the judge; in the Psalm the Lord Jesus is introduced, who alone can deliver from the adversary and from the judge. He has taken the debt upon Himself, and the payment which He has made is sufficient for all debtors, and efficient for all who will believe in Him. So the Psalm closes: "Blessed are all they that put their trust in Him;" they are no longer travelling under charge of the adversary, and drawing nearer and nearer to the court-house, where they will hear their doom pronounced; but are journeying in company with the Son to the Father's house and the many mansions, knowing that "There is, therefore, now no condemnation (or judgment) to them which are in Christ Jesus." "Who is He that condemneth? It is Christ that died."

Many of the Psalms by their symbolism link themselves with the parables. We have already noticed the "Shepherd Psalm," and the closing verse of the hundred and nineteenth is the cry of the lost sheep: "I have gone astray like a lost sheep, seek Thy servant." The eightieth tells of the Shepherd of Israel and of the vine.

The marriage song is in the forty-fifth Psalm, and tells much of the King Himself, while the parable of the marriage feast speaks chiefly of the guests. The Psalm also describes the bride and her beautiful apparel. She is not mentioned at all in the parables, and the reason for this may be that the revelation of the bride dispensationally follows the coming of the Lord. From Rev. xix. we learn that it was not till "after these things," after the judgments had been

[1] See pages 317, 318.

poured out, and after John had heard " as it were the voice of a great multitude and as the voice of many waters, and as the voice of mighty thunderings, saying, Alleluia ; for the Lord God omnipotent reigneth," that he also heard the call, " Let us be glad and rejoice, and give honour to Him : for the marriage of the Lamb is come, and His wife hath made herself ready."

In Psalm xix. the rising of the sun is compared to " a bridegroom coming out of his chamber, and rejoiceth as a strong man to run a race." John the Baptist spoke of our Lord as the bridegroom at His first coming. In His reply to John's disciples, He Himself adopted the simile, and in His parables and the Revelation He pictured Himself thus at His return. Many passages speak of His coming as the sunrise, but this verse links the two figures. There is a beautiful passage in Ps. cxxx. in connection with the night season parables,[1] " My soul waiteth for the Lord more than they that watch for the morning ; I say, more than they that watch for the morning."

There are many Psalms which refer to the Lord as the Rock, *e.g.*, Ps. xviii. 2, 46 ; xxvii. 5 ; lxi. 2 ; lxii. 2, 6, 7, &c. Ps. xlvi. 1, 2, might be called the song of the house on the rock, which has no fear, even when the storm comes.

VI.—SOLOMON'S PARABLES

It was an acknowledged fact amongst the Jews that Solomon wrote in parables. In the Apocrypha we read of him, " Thy soul covered the whole earth, and thou filledst it with dark parables. Thy name went far unto the islands ; and for thy peace thou wast beloved. The countries marvelled at thee for thy songs, and proverbs, and parables, and interpreta-

[1] See Appendix I.

tions" (Ecclesiasticus xlvii. 15, 17). In the light of the New Testament some of his parables are no longer dark, for we can see in them prophecies of the greater than Solomon.

Perhaps the most beautiful of all is the parable of the little city in Eccles. ix. 13–17 ; a picture of the world, attacked by Satan, but delivered by the Lord Jesus. "There came a great king against it, and besieged it, and built great bulwarks against it. Now there was found in it a poor wise man, and he by his wisdom delivered the city."

Every word in these verses is full of meaning. What hope was there for the little city with the few men to garrison it, when the great king determined to capture it ? The contrast between the two forces is very marked, and again between the "great king" and the "poor wise man." Who would think that such a monarch would be defeated by any one so insignificant, but though the king was strong the poor man was stronger than he. His wisdom devised the plan which delivered that city. "Wisdom is better than strength" (verse 16). The wisdom of the Lord Jesus is better than all the strength of Satan. Well may we say with Solomon, "This wisdom have I seen also . . . and it seemed great unto me" (verse 13).

Solomon does not tell us what the scheme was, for he did not know the wonders of the plan of salvation. In order to save the "few" men, the Lord had to lay down His own life. The description of the treatment of the poor wise man was also prophetic—his "wisdom despised, and his words not heard." We read in Isaiah liii. the confession of Israel in future days, when they shall have looked upon Him whom they have pierced. They will mourn over their long rejection, and remember how He was treated by their nation. "He was despised, and we esteemed Him not." How sad is the account of the city's ingratitude, "Yet no man remembered that same poor man." Having done so much, but forgotten ! Alas ! that this should have been true of Him who became poor in order to save. Here again Solomon's picture is very beautiful ; he does not represent the saviour of the city as a great man or a rich man, but as one of the humblest of the citizens, poor and obscure, making no great noise in the place, and never causing his voice to be heard in the streets in loud demonstrations. " The words' of wise men are heard in quiet " (verse 17). If we are quiet we shall hear Him, and as Solomon tells us elsewhere (Prov. i. 33), if we hear, we shall be quiet ; we shall not be afraid of the great king when we have listened to the wisdom of the poor wise man. " Whoso hearkeneth unto Me shall dwell safely, and shall be quiet from fear of evil." Those who have learnt to know what He has done for the city are not those by whom He is forgotten. He longs to be thought of with gratitude, as Joseph did ; " Think on me . . . show kindness, I pray thee, unto me ; and make mention of me," was his request, but we read, " Yet did not the chief butler remember Joseph, but forgat him." The Lord Jesus made one request to His own before He left the little city, when He ordained the feast of remembrance, " This do in remembrance of Me," showing how He still values the loving thoughts of His people.

There is another parable about the poor wise man in Eccles. iv. 13–16, which is not so plain. The Revised Version makes it clearer than the Authorised Version. The poor wise youth is evidently the Lord Himself, and the old and foolish king represents Solomon. " Better is a poor and wise youth than an old and foolish king . . . For out of prison he cometh to reign," or " came forth to be king." Surely this looks forward to the greater than Solomon. " Yea, even in His kingdom He was born poor." Solomon considers the kingdom of the second, that is to " stand up in his stead." He contemplates the number of his subjects, "There was no end of all the people, even of all them over whom he was ; yet they that come after shall not rejoice in him." Is this a prophecy of our Lord's rejection, a hint of the long centuries after His incarnation, when men shall not have learnt to rejoice in Him ? The king adds, " Surely this is vanity and vexation of spirit," but this sad picture is not the end. The seventy-second Psalm, Solomon's own, either written by him or specially for him by David, tells of that glad day when all nations shall call Him blessed, and " Blessed be His glorious Name for ever ; and let the whole earth be filled with His glory."

In the same book of Ecclesiastes, we have a striking parable about eating and drinking (chap. v. 18–20). We may be quite sure that there is a deeper meaning in it than that which refers merely to natural food, and need not hesitate to apply it to the spiritual food which is so absolutely necessary. Every word is suggestive.

"Behold that which I have seen : it is good and comely for one to eat and to drink . . . Every man also to whom God hath given riches and wealth, and hath given him power to eat thereof, and to take his portion, and to rejoice in his labour ; this is the gift of God." A good appetite is the gift of God, whether it is a natural appetite, or a spiritual one. In both cases it denotes health, and promotes health. There is no spiritual vigour if our appetite for the Word of God be poor. He has indeed given to us riches and wealth in this inexhaustible mine, but we need to receive from Him also the "power to eat thereof." As new-born babes, we should desire "the sincere milk of the Word." Even the tiny infant, if healthy, has power to enjoy its food, but as it grows older the child learns to help itself ; it can take its portion without needing to be fed, and the young man can

rejoice in the labour, by which he obtains the food
itself.   This suggests a growth of experience in
feeding on the Word.   We are not always to
remain babes, requiring the food to be put into
our mouths.   We must learn to study the Word for
ourselves, and even to labour diligently, that our
appetites may be satisfied.   The more we know of
this, the more we shall rejoice in our labour, but
unless we have this gift of God, a good appetite for
the Word, the labour will be a burden instead of a
joy—we shall not care to take our portion, and shall
have no power to eat thereof.   The next verse
applies specially to feeding on the Word of God, for
it says of the one who has been described as rejoicing in this gift of God, " God answereth him in the
joy of his heart " (verse 20).   The word " answereth "
is the same as that used in Deut. viii. 2, 3, 16, " He
humbled thee, and suffered thee to hunger," and in
Dan. x. 12, " to *chasten* thyself before thy God."   The
first passage refers to the eating of manna, as given
for a type of feeding on every word that proceedeth
out of the mouth of God, proving the natural
food to be a type of the spiritual.   The effect
of thus feeding on God's Word is to humble the
soul in His presence, and that was the result which
the study of the books had upon Daniel, so that he
poured out his heart in the wonderful confession in
Daniel ix. ;   and in chap. x., having had a revelation
from God, was prostrate before Him.   " Fear not,
Daniel ; for from the first day that thou didst set
thine heart to understand, and to chasten thyself
before thy God, thy words were heard, and I am
come for thy words."   Daniel had this gift of God,
a good appetite, and having rejoiced in his labour,
God answered him, first by thus humbling him, and
then by giving a literal answer to his prayer.
Solomon's parable is continued in the opening

verses of the next chapter (Eccles. vi. 1–2), where he
shows that loss of appetite is an evil disease. "There
is an evil which I have seen under the sun, and it is
common among men. A man to whom God hath
given riches, wealth, and honour, so that he wanteth
nothing for his soul of all that he desireth, yet God
giveth him not power to eat thereof, but a stranger
eateth it; this is vanity, and it is an evil disease."
The inability to take food, whether for the body or
soul, is the beginning of very many evil diseases, and
alas! we must acknowledge with Solomon that "it
is common among men." To starve in the midst
of plenty is sad indeed, and how can the Christian
be strong if he has no appetite for the Word of God ?
The riches, wealth, and honour are all there, but the
fault is in himself, he has lost his power to eat thereof.
What is he to do in such a case ? Solomon tells us
that this is "an evil disease," and the best thing we
can do if we have only the first symptom, is to go to
the great Physician who, when He was here, healed
"all manner of sickness, and all manner of disease."
Loss of appetite comes from many causes, want of
fresh air, too little exercise, a life of idleness, feeding
on sweetmeats, or injurious food, etc., and all these
things have their counterparts in the spiritual life.

Many other passages from the writings of Solomon
may be linked to this parable; for instance, he tells
us in Eccles. ix. 11, that "the race is not to the swift
. . . neither yet bread to the wise." It is not by our
wisdom that we can find food in the Word of God.
The less we depend on ourselves, and on our understanding, and our thoughts, the more shall we expect
from Him.

It is interesting to note in the books of Proverbs
and Ecclesiastes many verses which contain the same
symbolical language as the parables of our Lord.

Thus we are reminded of the parable of the

houses with and without foundation in Prov. xxiv.
3, "Through wisdom is an house builded, and by
understanding it is established; and by knowledge
shall all the chambers be filled with all precious and
pleasant riches."

It is only by heavenly wisdom, understanding
and knowledge that we are enabled to build aright
whether as in Matt. vii. or 1 Cor. iii. Again, in
Prov. xii. 7, we read, "The wicked are overthrown,
and are not; but the house of the righteous shall
stand." And in Prov. xiv. 11, "The house of the
wicked shall be overthrown; but the tabernacle of
the upright shall flourish." The seemingly strong
house of the one is not so secure as the fragile
tent of the other.

But the first of these passages speaks to us also of
the wisdom of the Lord Himself, by which He is
building His own temple. In this same chapter there
is a beautiful little parable, showing how He in His
wisdom carries on the work. Solomon says, "Prepare thy work without, and make it fit for thyself
in the field; and afterwards build thine house (xxiv.
27). We may be sure that he was not merely referring to the building of a man's own dwelling. It was
the principle on which he himself built the temple
of Jehovah. "The house, when it was building, was
built of stone made ready before it was brought
thither; so that there was neither hammer, nor axe,
nor any tool of iron, heard in the house while it was
in building" (1 Kings vi. 7). In this he furnished a
beautiful type of the way in which God Himself first
prepares His stones in the field of the world, makes
each one fit for Himself, and afterwards builds His
house. The living stones are being prepared and
the temple is being built.

There is another building referred to in Prov. ix. 1,
"Wisdom hath builded her house, she hath hewn out

her seven pillars." It is wisdom's banqueting house, the place where she receives her guests, for the passage continues, " She (wisdom) hath killed her beasts ; she hath mingled her wine ; she hath also furnished her table ; she hath sent forth her maidens ; she crieth upon the highest places of the city, Whoso is simple, let him turn in hither ; as for him that wanteth understanding, she saith to him, Come, eat of my bread, and drink of the wine which I have mingled." Thus we are reminded of the parables of the feasts, and as in the Gospel they who accepted the invitation were the poor who could not provide a feast for themselves, so wisdom invites those who need her most. It is the simple who have no wisdom, it is the hungry that need food. The simple, despised by the world, are they who receive the invitation, and are sure of the blessing. It is well to take our place as simple ones, for the promise is given to them who lack wisdom (Ps. xix. 7 ; cxvi. 6). Wisdom's feast in chap. ix. is contrasted with folly's banquet at the close of the chapter.

The solemn passage in Prov. i. 24, 27, reminds us of those who refused the invitation to the feast by making light of it, or by inventing excuses. " Because I have called, and ye refused ; I have stretched out My hand, and no man regarded ; but ye have set at nought all My counsel, and would none of My reproof ; I also will laugh at your calamity ; I will mock when your fear cometh ; when your fear cometh as desolation, and your destruction cometh as a whirlwind ; when distress and anguish cometh upon you." The parable in Matthew, which tells of the lavish provision for the guests, and of the grace that made them welcome, describes also the vengeance taken by the king upon those that were bidden, who refused his invitation. " When the king heard thereof, he was wroth ; and he sent forth his armies, and destroyed those murderers, and burned up their city."

Prov. xxv. 6, 7, is almost identical with the words used in Luke xiv., when the Lord spake to those who chose out the chief rooms, "Better it is that it be said unto thee, Come up hither, than that thou shouldest be put lower in the presence of the prince whom thine eyes have seen." The Lord in the parable tells us that the places of the guests will be re-adjusted, when "He that bade thee cometh." It will surely cause shame in the presence of the Prince if those who have assumed high places have to take lower ones (comp. 1 John ii. 28).

Prov. xx. 8.—"A king that sitteth in the throne of judgment scattereth away all evil with his eyes." So will it be when He sets up His throne as in Matt. xxv. A look from the king's son was sufficient to make the man speechless who had not on the wedding garment.

Prov. xiv. 35.—"The king's favour is toward a wise servant," and in the parables the servants show their wisdom by faithfulness in trading, diligence in serving, constancy in watching. In Prov. viii. 34 the Lord Himself is speaking about the watching ones just as He did in the Gospels, "Blessed is the man that heareth Me, watching daily at My gates, waiting at the posts of My doors."

The closing verses in the fourth of Proverbs remind us of several of the Lord's parables, especially of that in which He taught the disciples that defilement arises, not from what goes *into* the mouth as food, but from what comes *out* of the heart and mouth in speech. The importance of keeping the heart with all diligence is the central thought in Solomon's sevenfold chain of precepts. They divide themselves into two groups, the first three showing how the Word reaches the *heart* through the *ear* and *eye,* and then four teaching that the heart governs the walk.   He speaks of hearing the Word (verse 20), studying it, and keeping it in the heart (verse 21) ; then the preacher begins again with the *heart* (verse 23), and goes on to speak of *mouth* (verse 24), *eyes* (verse 25), and *feet* (verses 26, 27).   If the heart is "kept with all diligence," the mouth will not be "froward," for as the Lord teaches us, "Out of the abundance of the heart the mouth speaketh."   If the heart and mouth are kept from evil the eyes will be able to "look right on" and the eyelids "straight before" us to the bright hope of His coming, and this will ensure the feet running the race set before us.   But the first link in this sevenfold chain has to do with the ear, "Take heed how ye hear," "Take heed what ye hear." This is the first step towards avoiding the defilement which comes out of the mouth, and the first step towards being like the good man who "out of the good treasure of the heart bringeth forth good things."

There are many passages amongst the words of Solomon which speak of sowing and reaping.   In Eccles. xi. 6 he urges the necessity of sowing at all times, evening as well as morning, for "thou knowest not whether shall prosper either this or that, or whether they both shall be alike good."   How well we might apply these words to the parable of the sower who, as he scatters his seed upon the surface of the earth, can hardly tell where it may fall.   The words of the preacher in Prov. xi. 24, "There is that scattereth, and yet increaseth," agree with the words of the apostle in 2 Cor. ix. 6, "He which soweth sparingly shall reap also sparingly."   We are all familiar with Solomon's little parable of the field of the slothful man (Prov. xxiv. 30).

Prov. xi. 18, and xxii. 8, remind us of Gal. vi. 7, "Whatsoever a man soweth, that shall he also reap."

The first sentence of Prov. xi. 4, "Riches profit not in the day of wrath," and verse 28, "He that trusteth in his riches shall fall," are illustrated by the parable of the rich man in Luke xvi.

The close of this verse, "The righteous shall flourish as a branch," and chap. xii. 12, "The root of the righteous yieldeth fruit," have fresh meaning when we link them with John xv.

Prov. xxviii. 19, "He that followeth after vain persons shall have poverty enough," sums up the experience of the prodigal.

Prov. xiii. 7 describes Him who sold all that He had that He might purchase the field and the pearl, "There is that maketh himself poor, yet hath great riches."

CHAPTER XIV

THE MIRACLES AND THE PARABLES

THE Lord taught both by miracles and by parables. A parable sufficed when the needed lesson could be conveyed by some simple stories of everyday occurrence, gathered from town and country life, from the roadside or the house, from the palace or the farm. But there were other lessons that could only be taught by means of a miracle, and yet a parable was often latent in the miracle. "Without a parable spake He not unto them," and we know that "without a parable" He worked not a miracle, for He spake by His acts as well as by His words. The miracles were "signs." They were no mere displays of power, but were as full of spiritual meanings as the parables themselves.

The connection between the two may be viewed in several aspects—(i.) The miracles as acted parables; (ii.) Those which called forth parables; (iii.) Those which were explained by parables or linked with them by some word or expression; (iv.) Those which represent night scenes; (v.) Those which are linked with Old Testament typology; and (vi.) Those which have a dispensational meaning.

I. We might look upon all His miracles as *acted parables*, but the fact that they had a spiritual meaning is specially clear in connection with the miracles of healing. We have indeed one little parable which embraces them all. "He said unto them, They that be whole need not a physician, but they that are sick. . . . I am not come to call the righteous, but sinners to repentance" (Matt. ix. 12, 13). The healing of the body therefore is a picture of the healing of the soul. The results of sickness and disease upon the human frame typify the effects of sin upon the life, character, and history of a man. The forgiveness of sin and the healing of the body were thus shown to be typical the one of the other. In the healing of the paralytic (Mark ii. and Luke v.), the Lord performed the miracle in order that they might know that He had "power on earth to forgive sins." In the case of the man at the pool of Bethesda, not only was the disease from which he suffered a judgment upon his sin; but it was emblematic of the way in which sin disables, and its removal was a picture of the change that comes into the life by the knowledge of sin forgiven. We may thus group together all the various miracles of healing which our Lord performed, and see in them different aspects of the ruin wrought by sin and Satan, showing how Christ is able to overcome their power and undo their work. To quote from a former Bible study, "Three times He raised the dead, as a sign that His voice could reach those who were dead in trespasses and sin; natural death was but a picture of spiritual death. Palsy might be taken to represent the enfeeblement of sin; fever the restlessness and contagion of sin; blindness, the ignorance of sin; demoniacal possession the enmity of sin; deafness, inability to hear; and dumbness, inability to testify. In the man with the withered hand we see inability to work; in the impotent man, inability to walk; in the woman bowed down with the spirit of infirmity the degrading and depressing tendency of sin. Many of these are negative in character, but leprosy represents the corruption of sin and speaks to us of its activity and progress." [1]

But besides this large group of miracles there

[1] "The Study of the Types," p. 79.
Kregel Publications

are several others which link themselves with the
parables in such a way as to show that they were
acted parables.

The two occasions on which He gave a miraculous
draught of fishes naturally remind us of the parable
of the net. He who knows "all the fowls of the
mountains" knows all the fish in the waters, and
can direct His servants, whether in miracle or parable,
to cast the net in the right place. He explained the
parable, by showing that the fish represented men ;
He spiritualised the miracle by giving Peter his commission, " I will make you fishers of men."

It is interesting to compare the two miraculous
draughts of fishes, the one when Peter received his
call to discipleship and service, the other, the resurrection scene, when after his fall he was again
sent forth. Both took place on the sea of Galilee ;
were preceded by a night of fruitless toil ; were
followed by a commission to Peter ; brought Peter
to the feet of Jesus ; proved to Peter that the Lord
knew more about fishing than he did ; and both
brought deep conviction to his heart, in the first case
of his sinfulness, in the second of his want of love.

In the First	*In the Second*
The Lord Jesus was in the ship.	He was on the shore.
He said, " Launch out into the deep."	" Cast the net on the right side of the ship."
The net brake.	The net was not broken.
Peter was made a fisher of men.	A shepherd of the sheep.
He was convicted of sinfulness.	Of want of love.
The number of fishes was not given.	There were a hundred and fifty and three great fishes.
The ship began to sink.	The net was dragged to land.
It was at the beginning of Christ's ministry.	After the resurrection.

Viewed in connection with the parables of the fig-
tree, the miracle following the cursing of the literal

fig-tree is very evidently an acted parable. It stands out as the only one which was a miracle of judgment. Almost all were deeds of mercy and compassion, signs truly of His power, but the time was not yet come for His hand to be stretched forth in wrath. We have seen that the two parables about the fig-tree in the history of Israel form a pair (pp. 153, 163), and this miracle must chronologically be placed between the two. The unfruitfulness is described in the first parable, the curse which caused it to wither away is pronounced in the miracle, and the budding again is foretold in His prophetic discourse.

The doom of the fruitless tree did not fall on it as a hasty judgment ; the curse was not uttered in sudden anger, but the Lord shows to His disciples by His comment and explanation that it was an act of faith. Faith must have something to rest upon. He was in communication with His Father about it, and knew that it was in accordance with His will ; and so He uses this solemn incident to teach the power and conditions of prayer.

II. We also find a connection between miracles and parables when the miracle was *followed* by a parable, and called it forth.

This is specially clear in the parable of the strong man (Matt. xii.), for just before it was spoken, there "was brought unto Him one possessed with a devil, blind and dumb ; and He healed him, insomuch that the blind and dumb both spake and saw." The parable which followed was in answer to the accusation of the Pharisees, that He cast out devils, "by Beelzebub, the prince of the devils," and it explained that the Lord had, by healing the poor devil-possessed man, entered into the house of the strong man and spoiled his goods.

When the Lord healed the man with the withered

hand, in the synagogue on the sabbath day, His answer to those who found fault with Him was a parable as well as an illustration. "What man shall there be among you that shall have one sheep, and if it fall into a pit on the sabbath day, will he not lay hold on it, and lift it out? How much then is a man better than a sheep?" (Matt. xii. 11, 12). Here we have Him as the good Shepherd lifting one of the sheep out of the pit, while in Luke xv. and Matt. xviii. we have Him seeking for it when it was lost.

The parable in Luke commences in the same way, "What man of you, having an hundred sheep, if he lose one of them, doth not leave the ninety and nine in the wilderness, and go after that which is lost until he find it?" The question, "How much then is a man better than a sheep?" applies to both parables. Both were spoken in answer to the murmurings of the Pharisees, the one when they complained that He healed on the sabbath day, the other when they scornfully charged Him with receiving sinners.

The sequel to the opening of the eyes of the blind in John ix. is, as we have seen, the key to John x.

III. There are some miracles which are linked with parables by means of a word, a name, or an expression.

We have already noticed an instance of this when comparing the request of the Syrophœnician woman, and the desire of Lazarus at the rich man's gate. The crumb in the one case suggests a meaning for the crumb in the other.

Might there not also be an incidental connection between the raising of Lazarus and this last parable? The beggar is named Lazarus, and this could not have been without intention. The rich man asks that Lazarus may be sent back to his father's house to testify to his five brethren, for he says, "If one went unto them from the dead, they will repent;" but Abraham replies, "If they hear not Moses and the prophets, neither will they be persuaded though one rose from the dead." Another Lazarus *was* allowed to return, but the result was that the chief priests consulted that they might put Lazarus to death. They were no more ready to believe in the Lord Jesus Christ than they had been before.

The parable of the Pharisee and the publican in Luke xviii., and the cleansing of the lepers in Luke xvii., are linked together by the little word "far off" which describes the position of the publican in the parable and the lepers in the miracle (see p. 52). Both were unclean—both knew it, and felt that they were unfit to approach; and a sense of need made them both cry for mercy, "Jesus, Master, have mercy on us;" "God be merciful to me a sinner." The prayer was heard; the lepers were cleansed, the publican was justified. Was he like the leper who returned to give thanks, or like the nine who returned not? We cannot tell, unless the parable of the eighteenth of Luke was a glimpse into the heart experience of the publican whose history is given in the following chapter. Zaccheus, the publican, who sought to see Jesus, and who was known by the crowds to be a sinner, was he the one who had with deep contrition owned his sinfulness to God? Did the man who went down to his house, justified in Luke xviii., go down to his house in Luke xix. accompanied by the Lord Himself, who was thus a "guest with a man that is a sinner?" The publican of Luke xviii. knew himself to be a sinner, but he was a justified sinner. The Lord who could see the one standing afar off not daring to lift up his eyes, could also discern him who was hidden amongst the leaves of the sycamore tree. Whether they were the same or not the parable and the story of Zaccheus are beautifully linked together.

The parable is linked on the other side with the miracle of the cleansing of the lepers.

The rites enjoined in Lev. xiv. for the cleansed leper were divided into two stages : the offering of the birds, and the touching of the members with the blood and the oil. The ceremonial did not take away the plague of leprosy, but took place after it had been removed, and thus the chapter seems to teach that God not only puts away sin but justifies and sanctifies the sinner.

The cleansed leper was presented "before the Lord" (the expression is nine times repeated in Lev. xiv.), and thus access was granted to him who had before been "without the camp"; and by the blood and oil, it was shown that his life was claimed for God. The lepers who stood "afar off" in Luke xvii. were first healed by the Lord, and when they showed themselves to the priest, as commanded, they would be permitted to bring their offerings as people of God, and their restored lives would in type be sanctified to Him. The publican in the parable was by the Lord's own verdict justified; this was typified by the first portion of the ceremonial. The publican of Luke xix., after receiving the Lord joyfully, at once recognised His claim upon his life, and desired to dedicate his substance to Him; this represented the second part.

Who would venture to change the order of the chapters ? According to a so-called "harmony" the story of the lepers should be placed much earlier, but the perfect chain would then be broken.

Two of the parables teach that spiritual bankruptcy, when acknowledged, is the first step towards blessing. The prodigal when he had *spent all*, and began to be in want, came to himself, and then came to his father. He never thought of leaving the far country whilst his funds lasted. The debtors who had *nothing to pay* were freely forgiven, and we are reminded of these parables when we read of the woman with the issue of blood, who came in the crowd, and touched the hem of His garment. We are told that she had *spent all* her living upon physicians, neither could be healed of any. If she had had something left, she might have gone elsewhere, but having nothing wherewith to pay her fee, she went to the great Physician who alone could cure her. It is only when we have come to the end of our resources that He can help us. "When the poor and needy seek water, and there is none, and their tongue faileth for thirst, I the Lord will hear them." We are often told of the rich ones of earth who started almost penniless to make their fortunes, but the wealthy ones of heaven (and we may all be spiritual millionaires) began by being burdened with an enormous debt. Not one will ever claim to be self-made, for the grace that forgave the debt also gives the wealth.

IV. The parables which describe *night scenes* emphasise the thought that they relate to the time of His absence. There are certain miraculous incidents which naturally seem to be connected with these parables. This is especially the case with the beautiful story of the disciples in the ship tossing on the lake, while the Lord Himself is alone on the mountain praying, yet watching them all the time. This wonderful picture is in itself a lovely little parable. The dark stormy night without Him, ending in the bright morning when He joined them; for "in the fourth watch of the night (the morning) He cometh unto them" (Mark vi. 48). What a change then takes place; instead of trouble "good cheer" (verse 50); instead of contrary winds "the wind ceased" (verses 48, 51); instead of "in the midst of the sea" (verse 47), "immediately the ship was at land whither they went"

(John vi. 21). Just as great will be the change for the Church between the night of His absence and the morning of His return. Like so many of the parables, this is also a picture of the future experiences of the Jewish remnant.

V. There are other miracles which are closely associated with Old Testament *typology*. None of His miracles were without deep spiritual teaching; but when they are explained by the types we may feel doubly sure of this.

The feeding of the five thousand is, in John vi., compared and contrasted with the giving of the manna in the wilderness. The manna only *sustained* life, but "the bread of God is He which cometh down from heaven, and *giveth* life unto the world." The manna could not do this. The New Testament substance far transcends the Old Testament shadow, and the feeding of the multitude, like a parable, embodied many of the lessons which the type foreshadowed. The Lord's own commentary explains the two, as He said to them, "Labour not for the meat which perisheth, but for that meat which endureth unto everlasting life, which the Son of Man shall give unto you." He further explained how they were to labour for that bread : "This is the work of God, that ye believe on Him whom He hath sent." To feed on the bread was to believe on Himself.

VI. Like the spoken parables, some at least of the miracles seem to have a *dispensational* character. This we have already noticed in the cursing of the fig-tree, the crumb granted to the Syrophœnician woman, and the storm scene on the lake. The first miracle, the water turned into wine, has evidently a far deeper meaning than that of merely providing a luxury for a marriage feast. It links itself with the symbolism of the parables, where the new dispensation is compared to the new wine. The first

miraculous act in His ministry was to provide a new
wine which, on the authority of the governor of the
feast, was better than their best.

It is suggestive that the waterpots were those prepared for the purification of the Jews. The miracle
represented the changing of the old ceremonial into
the new wine of the new dispensation.

The second miraculous draught of fishes in resurrection power seems also to suggest the new dispensation. "The miracle which had already shadowed
the work of the fishers of men is repeated, but with
altered circumstances, typical of the change which
was at hand. For now the Lord is no longer with
them in the ship, but stands dimly seen upon the
shore, yet from thence issues His directions, and
shows the presence of His power working with them
in their seemingly lonely toil." [1]

The healing of Mary Magdalene out of whom He
cast seven demons links itself with the parable of the
unclean spirit; we have seen how this represented
the condition of the nation in their rejection of Himself. The reformation after the captivity, and again
under John the Baptist's teaching, had been like the
sweeping and garnishing of the house, but the unclean
spirit returned with seven others worse than himself,
and "the last state of that man is worse than the first.
Even so shall it be also unto this wicked generation,"
but this will not be for ever ; the evil spirits will be
cast out, even as they were out of Mary Magdalene.
Thus the promise will be fulfilled, "I will cause . . .
the unclean spirit to pass out of the land" (Zech.
xiii. 2).

In the same way, since in this parable He Himself likened the apostate nation to a devil-possessed
man, we may take the healing of the demoniac as
another picture of the restoration of Israel. What

[1] Canon Bernard, "Progress of Doctrine in New Testament."

a changed picture it presents—seated at the feet of Jesus, clothed, and in his right mind, and sent forth to tell what great things the Lord had done for him. The people of the district had besought the Lord that He would leave them, and their prayer was answered ; they did not want Him, and so He went away for a time.   This is a picture of the way in which the world treated Him ; but when He returned to the same place what a different reception ! Possibly the preaching of the healed man had made the difference.   "They knew Him, and ran through that whole region round about, and began to carry about in beds those that were sick, where they heard He was.   And whithersoever He entered, into villages, or cities, or country, they laid the sick in the streets, and besought Him that they might touch, if it were but the border of His garment ; and as many as touched Him were made whole."   They had also heard probably of the miracle He had wrought after He had left their shores, and so wished to imitate the woman who had touched the hem of His garment.   When He comes back again to the world that has rejected Him, the preaching of the remnant (Rev. vii.) will have prepared the way for the great ingathering, and a multitude whom no man can number will be the sheep on His right hand.

CHAPTER XV

THE PARABLES AND THE EPISTLES

IT is very important that the parables should be studied in the light of the epistles, for there are many links between them, and it is equally important that the epistles should be read as sequels to the parables. Neither portion of God's Word can be really understood without the other.

I. In the first place the parables *explain* the writing of the epistles. They tell us how it was that Greeks and Romans were now addressed instead of only Jews. It is true that the parables do not fully reveal the position of the Church in this dispensation, but they explain the causes which brought about a condition of privilege for the Gentiles; trace the steps which led up to it; and prepare the way for the revelation made to the apostle Paul.

The Church epistles are but the result of the broadcast scattering of the seed, foretold in the parable of the sower; and of the universal invitation sent out into the highways and hedges of Gentile peoples. The parables explain that this was a consequence of Israel's rejection. The turning from Israel which was foretold in them was fully accomplished in the period covered by the Acts of the Apostles; and thus the parables are the bridge which join the two dispensations.

II. We also see that the epistles are the *sequels* or supplements of the parables. The Lord told His disciples that He had yet many things to say unto them, but they were not able to bear them.   Some of these He was able to teach them in the days of resurrection intercourse, but much still remained which the Spirit of truth revealed to the apostle Paul, and through him to the Church.   Because we do not find all this in the parables we must not conclude that there is no connection, but must rather study them in the fuller light of the mystery made known to the apostle of the Gentiles.   In many cases, as we shall see, the apostle used the same symbolism to teach further lessons.

III. Besides this the parables are *explained by* the epistles.   Many of those which were recorded by Matthew, who was formerly a publican, are expounded by Paul, who was once a Pharisee.   For instance, twice over, Paul says, " A little leaven leaveneth the whole lump."   In 1 Cor. v. he refers thus to evil walk, and in Gal. v. to evil doctrine which had crept into the Church.   Contrary to nature,[1] he commands the purging out of the leaven.   This is not possible in actual fact, but in spiritual things the only way of preventing the leaven from spreading is to remove it.   By these two allusions to leaven he explains the parable in Matt. xiii., and shows that he at least understood it to be typical of evil, as he knew that the Corinthians and Galatians would also do.   At the feast of unleavened bread to which he refers, not only were the children of Israel forbidden to eat of leaven, but it was to be put right out of their houses.   "There shall be no leavened bread seen with thee in all thy coast seven days." Until the leaven had been purged out it was impossible for the Church in Corinth to keep the feast with the unleavened bread of sincerity and truth.   The man that had sinned must be put away that the leaven

---

[1] In his parable in Rom. xi. the symbolism is "contrary to nature," for the wild olive is grafted into the good tree instead of the good graft being inserted into the wild plant.

might not spread. The same was to be the treatment of the unsound doctrine; but in the present day a false charity is preached (as well as the false doctrine) which allows the leaven to spread as rapidly as it will.

Paul's double use of these words, " A little leaven leaveneth the whole lump," suggests an interpretation for the meal in the parable (see page 133). But in the parable there is no suggestion that the leaven could possibly be separated from the meal after it has once been introduced.

IV. Another important fact, to be learned especially from the epistles, is that Israel's history is *typical*. It is very interesting to apply this to the parables, for it opens up to us a large field of study. It is Paul who so clearly explains the typical character of Israel's history. It is he who shows that the story of Hagar and Ishmael was allegorical, and affirms that all the events of wilderness journeyings happened to the people for types, and were written for our admonition. We may be equally sure that this is true of the Jewish parables. Paul made the statement concerning the events recorded in the Pentateuch.[1] The same principle doubtless applies to events preserved in the historical books, and we need not limit it to their past history. We may see spiritual meaning in the prophetic books without robbing Israel of their literal fulfilment. There are many who have been so accustomed to spiritualise the Old Testament prophecies that they have lost sight of the fact that these are promises of blessing to Israel, and are still unfulfilled. The headings of our Bible are very misleading in this direction, as they claim for the Church what belongs to Israel.

---

[1] That these Old Testament Scriptures were written with a view to New Testament readers is clearly proved by the apostle's threefold assertion— that Genesis was "for us" (Rom. iv. 23, 24); Deuteronomy "for our sakes" (1 Cor. ix. 9, 10); Exodus and Numbers "for our admonition" (1 Cor. x. 11).

But having acknowledged to the full this literal future fulfilment, the epistles teach us that we may go a step further, and claim for ourselves the typical interpretation. We thus learn that the " I will "s of Ezekiel are as full of spiritual teaching for us to-day as the " I will "s and " I have "s of Exodus.

From the Gospels we see that passages relating primarily to Israel are not merely applied to the Lord Jesus, but were fulfilled in Him. It is very striking to notice this in connection with the words from Hosea, " Out of Egypt have I called My Son," and to mark the manner in which they are quoted in Matt. ii. 15. Read with their context it is evident that the prophet was speaking of the nation, but the Evangelist prefaces them with the words, " That it might be fulfilled which was spoken of the Lord by the prophet."

From the epistles we learn something else as to the Old Testament prophecies, for again and again Paul quotes them in reference to the Church. Although in their original setting they are evidently promises of millennial blessing to Israel, he claims them for the present dispensation also. To mention only one example—in addressing the Corinthians He says, " For ye are the temple of the living God ; as God hath said, I will dwell in them, and walk in them ; and I will be their God, and they shall be My people." This was the promise to Israel, but Paul claims it for the Church, and we may be quite sure that he was right.[1] It is very important to recognise this principle in our study of the parables, so that while acknowledging that many of them refer to Israel, we may not miss the teaching that they contain for ourselves.

V. The apostle leads us a step further, for he

[1] See also Hosea i. 10, quoted in Romans ix. 24–26 ; Isa. xxviii. 16 ; and Joel ii. 32, in Rom. x. 11 ; Isa. liii. 1, in verse 16 ; Isa. lii. 11, in 2 Cor. vi. ; Isa. lx. 1, in Eph. v. 14 ; and Isa. liv. 1, in Gal. iv. 27.

shows us in his epistles that the Old Testament symbolism which was so largely made use of in the parables, has to a certain extent changed its meaning in the present dispensation. Many figures which represented Israel in the olden days, and which will do so again, are taken during this parenthesis to refer to Jew and Gentile. Paul shows that though a figure refers to Israel in the Old Testament, it may be used now concerning the Church. The fact that it was Jewish once is no proof that it is not ours now. For instance, he uses a very familiar symbol of Israel in the eleventh of Romans, and describes the change of dispensation under the figure of breaking off the natural branches of the olive tree, and the grafting in of the Gentiles. This engrafting has brought us into possession of many of the blessings and privileges of Israel, including their responsibilities as witness-bearers, and thus the olive of the Old Testament changes to the olive of the New.

We have already seen how Israel is often symbolised in the Old Testament by the vine. In the fifteenth of John, the Lord shows that the true vine is Himself and those united to Him. He says, "My Father is the Husbandman," and the apostle, proving that this is not merely Jewish, says, "Ye are God's husbandry." He asks the Corinthians, "Who planteth a vineyard, and eateth not of the fruit thereof?" thus comparing work for God now to labouring in a vineyard, and reminding us of several of the parables.

This suggests to us that many of the parables which from their symbolism evidently refer to Israel, may possibly also have a meaning for the present dispensation. Such is the marvellous fulness of God's Word that we must not think we have exhausted its meaning when we have understood one interpretation.

There are many other Old Testament symbols of Israel which are applied to believers now. For instance, the Shepherd and the sheep, the temple, the priesthood, &c.

In Old Testament days the children of Israel were the sheep of His pasture. The vine and the flock were two of the most frequent figures under which they were represented, and sometimes occur together. For example, in the eightieth Psalm, at the beginning the Psalmist calls upon the Shepherd of Israel, and later he prays Him to look upon the vine which He brought out of Egypt. The same pair of figures is familiar to us in John x. and xv. In the former, in the picture of the good Shepherd and His flock, the Lord describes the change of dispensation, the leading out of His own from the fold of Judaism, and the uniting to them of the other sheep which were not of that fold.[1]

In this passage also the two figures are linked together. "Who planteth a vineyard, and eateth not of the fruit thereof? or who feedeth a flock, and eateth not of the milk of the flock?" (1 Cor. ix.).

VI. This brings us to another lesson which is to be gathered from the epistles, viz., that much which the Lord stated concerning Himself in the parables is now true of His people, many of the similes used of Him being applied to His servants also. He is the dresser of the vine, His Father is the Husbandman, and His servants are labourers together with Him; He is the Shepherd, they are the under-shepherds; He is the builder of the temple, His church (Matt. xvi.); they too

---

[1] If the writings of the apostle John were of later date than those of the other writers of the New Testament his Gospel must have been written after the revelation of the mystery to Paul. At the very commencement he speaks of the rejection by Israel as an accomplished fact. "He came unto His own, and His own received Him not:" and we see that in all the chief symbolic utterances there is a suggestion of the change of dispensation. All believers, not merely Israel, are included under the figures of the sheep, the harvest from the corn of wheat, and the branches of the vine.

are builders (1 Cor. iii.), and must see to it that they do not introduce the wrong materials. The Lord is the Sower, His servants are also sent forth with the seed. In the parables we have this double use of some of these figures, but the apostle carries them further. He shows by his quotations from the Old Testament that some of the prophecies concerning our Lord include His Church. He was the herald whose coming was foretold in Isaiah lii. 7, "How beautiful upon the mountains are the feet of *Him* that bringeth good tidings, that publisheth peace." But He has delivered His message and has returned to the glory, leaving His followers to publish the glad news. The apostle therefore quotes the words, "How beautiful are the feet of *them* that preach the gospel of peace."

The promise to the Lord, "I will give Thee for a light to the Gentiles," was claimed by Paul as his commission (Acts xiii. 46, 47). "Lo, we turn to the Gentiles, for so hath the Lord commanded *us*, saying, I have set thee to be a light of the Gentiles, that thou shouldest be for salvation unto the ends of the earth."

The fact that the servants represent their Master is foretold in Mark xiii. 34. "For the Son of Man is as a man taking a far journey; who left his house, and gave *authority* to his servants." In His absence they are to take His place.

The symbolism of the epistles may be divided into two kinds—*First*, that which links itself with the parables of our Lord, and *second*, that which suggests new parables. There are very many passages which belong to the first class.

2 *Cor. ix.* 6, 10.—We are reminded here of the parable of the sower, "Now he that ministereth seed to the sower, both minister bread for your food, and multiply your seed sown." There is a reference in the passage to the receiving and giving of temporal

things, but it may also be taken in connection with the receiving and sowing of the Word. We must sow that which has already fed our own souls; and the harvest will be in proportion to the amount of seed sown. "He which soweth bountifully shall reap also bountifully" (verse 6).

Gal. vi. 7–9.—We learn from Gal. vi. that the harvest will not only depend on the quantity but on the quality of the seed. "Whatsoever a man soweth, that shall he also reap. For he that soweth to his flesh, shall of the flesh reap corruption; but he that soweth to the Spirit, shall of the Spirit reap life ever-lasting. And let us not be weary in well-doing; for in due season we shall reap, if we faint not." This reminds us of the parable of the tares. Useless or harmful weeds, as well as good seed, may be sown in the field of an individual life as in the field of the world of which our Lord spoke, and in both cases the reaping will be according to the sowing. This passage is often rightly used as a solemn warning, but it is also a sure promise of a precious harvest to be reaped even now by those who sow to the Spirit. The reaping begins in this life as in the parable of the sower, though the harvest will not be fully gathered till "the end of the age," as in that of the tares.

1 *Cor. xv.* 35–38.—The apostle also uses the figure of sowing and reaping in his great resurrection chapter. "That which thou sowest, thou sowest not that body that shall be, but bare grain, it may chance of wheat, or of some other grain; but God giveth it a body as it hath pleased Him, and to every seed his own body" (verses 37, 38). It is like the seed described by our Lord in His parable in Mark iv. When the harvest is come, the seed will be found to have grown, we know not how.

Gal. v. 22, 23.—Fruit-bearing is more clearly defined in Paul's epistles than anywhere else. The whole cluster of precious fruit is here enumerated, and the apostle shows that it consists of *being* rather than *doing*. It is not the same as service, though service is often depicted as fruit-bearing; the two should always go together, for we are to be "fruitful in every good work." As the poet has beautifully expressed it, "They also serve who only stand and wait," but we generally think of service as active, while fruit-bearing may be passive. God's children are called to doing and suffering, and while the doing is active service, the suffering may be passive fruit-bearing. It does not cease when activity ceases, and this is a very comforting thought when called aside from service, or placed in circumstances where we are, as we think, unable to work for God.

2 *Tim. ii.* 6.—"The husbandman that laboureth must be first partaker of the fruits." This may bear a twofold application, but by looking at the connection it seems especially to refer to the Lord Himself. The exhortation in verse 8, "Remember Jesus Christ," is a key to the whole chapter. In the fight the soldier must remember Him who hath chosen him to be a soldier (verse 4); in the games the wrestler is to remember Him who is to award the prizes (verse 5); the workman is to study to show himself approved unto God (verse 15), the servant to aim at being "a vessel unto honour, sanctified, and meet for the Master's use" (verse 21), and he that beareth fruit should remember that it is for the refreshment of the Husbandman (verse 6). He must be first. In John xv. the Lord not only says, "My Father is the Husbandman," but, "Herein is My Father glorified that ye bear much fruit." This is also true in connection with Gal. v. 22, He is the first to enjoy the fruit of the Spirit in the lives of His own; others may be refreshed with the sweet cluster of love, joy, peace, but it is primarily for Him.

Heb. vi. 7, 8.—" The earth which drinketh in the rain that cometh oft upon it, and bringeth forth herbs meet for them by whom it is dressed, receiveth blessing from God : but that which beareth thorns and briars is rejected, and is nigh unto cursing : whose end is to be burned." In this passage we have the threefold secret of fruit-bearing ; drinking in the rain, being dressed and tended, and receiving blessing from God. Here again the herbs of grace in the garden of the Lord are for them who dress and tend the soil ; the owner must have the largest share, and there is a portion for the labourers with Him. It reminds us of the words of the song, " My vineyard, which is mine, is before me : thou, O Solomon, must have a thousand, and those that keep the fruit thereof two hundred." He claims a fivefold portion. The first of these conditions, the need of the rain, reminds us of Gal. v. 22, for the rain is a frequent simile of the Holy Spirit ; the third requisite, receiving blessing from God, takes us to 1 Cor. iii., where we learn that though Paul and Apollos may labour, fruit is produced only when God giveth the increase. The herbs of grace and the fruit of the Spirit must be brought forth in the same way.

James v. 7, 8.—" Be patient, therefore, brethren, unto the coming of the Lord. Behold, the husbandman waiteth for the precious fruit of the earth, and hath long patience for it, until he receive the early and latter rain. Be ye also patient ; stablish your hearts ; for the coming of the Lord draweth nigh." Here also it is not certain whether the apostle James refers to the Lord Himself as the husbandman or to the labourers with Him. It is certainly true of Him. It is He who at His coming will gather the " Harvest Home." There is an ingathering which is present, but that to which reference is here made is future. It is the reaping which will take place in connection with His return. For this He is patiently waiting, longing for the gladsome day when He will gather His wheat into His garner. The patience of Christ (2 Thess. iii. 5) is like that of a husbandman waiting for the harvest. The Epistle of James is addressed to the twelve tribes scattered abroad, and has a special bearing on Israel's history in the last days. The last chapter is full of meaning when we see in it an exhortation to the believing remnant during the time of Jacob's trouble. Surely it is not by accident that there is a reference to the three and a half years of drought in Elijah's days, the exact period of the Great Tribulation. At the close of that time, when the apostasy of Israel had been purged on Carmel, Elijah prayed again, and "the heaven gave rain" (1 Kings xviii. 45 ; James v. 18). The latter rain is constantly mentioned in connection with the renewed blessing on Israel, when the Spirit is poured out upon the nation at the Lord's return. "I will pour upon the house of David, and upon the inhabitants of Jerusalem, the Spirit of grace and of supplications, and they shall look upon Me whom they have pierced" (Zech. xii. 10). Is not this the latter rain referred to in James v. 7, for which the husbandman has long patience ?

To return, however, to the writings of the apostle Paul. We find that he often links together plants and buildings as similes of believers.

Col. ii. 7.—"Rooted and built up in Him." *Eph. iii.* 17, "Rooted and grounded in love." 1 *Cor. iii.* 9, "Ye are God's husbandry, ye are God's building." This last verse comes in the centre of the passage. The verses immediately preceding it speak of the husbandry, those which follow of the building.

In coupling these similes the apostle was following the example of the great Teacher, who interwove the two in His parable of the husbandmen. They who rejected the Beloved Son as the messenger of the Father rejected the stone. The leaders of Israel were

thus compared to husbandmen and to builders. We
need not therefore be surprised that the apostle makes
use of the same double symbolism. In 1 Cor. iii.
God is the Husbandman, God is the Builder, but in
both respects the apostle says, "We are labourers
together with God." He compares himself, as we
have seen, to a husbandman in planting and watering
(verse 6), and to a master-builder who lays a foundation
for another to build thereon (verse 10). This parable
links itself with the builders on the rock and on the
sand. There are two classes of builders in each, and
they are tested by the flood or the fire, and in each
the work of one class of builders is destroyed. The
question in the Lord's parable is as to the foundation,
and both saved and lost are represented ; but in Paul's
parable the builders are all saved ones, are all on the
foundation, and the question is asked as to the "sort"
of materials of which the house is built. The gold,
silver, and precious stones, which alone can stand the
fire, speak of God Himself. The same figures are used
elsewhere as similes of Him, and here, as in Rev. iii. 18,
we have the Trinity. The gold signifies the Divine
(Job xxii. 25, *marg.*), the silver the redemption of the
Lord Jesus Christ, the precious stones the beauty and
grace of the Holy Spirit; or we may take them all
three as figures of the Lord Jesus, who as wisdom is
thus symbolised (Prov. iii. 14, 15 ; viii. 10, 11 ; see
also Job xxviii. 12–20).

2 *Tim. ii.* 19.—"Nevertheless the foundation of
God standeth sure, having this seal, The Lord knoweth
them that are His. And, Let every one that nameth
the name of Christ depart from iniquity." There is a
seal upon the stone to make it sure. Before the door
of the garden tomb they rolled a great stone, and the
chief priests and Pharisees came to Pilate and asked
him to "command that the sepulchre be made sure."
He said to them, "Go your way, make it as *sure as ye*

can." So they went and made the sepulchre sure, sealing the stone. But how "vain the stone, the watch, the seal" before the angel of the Lord. When man seals a stone God can easily break the seal, but when God seals a stone neither man nor devil can shake it, much less remove it.

The figure of believers as a temple of the Holy Spirit is often used by both Peter and Paul, for it was this figure which must have been in the mind of our Lord when He said, "Upon this rock I will build My Church." In 1 Cor. iii. 11, 17; Eph. ii. 20, 21, and 1 Peter ii. 4–8, we have references to Christ, the foundation on which the temple is being built. In other passages individual believers (1 Cor. vi. 19), or the whole Church (2 Cor. vi. 16), are compared to a temple. We have both the individual and collective aspect.

In contrast to these we have the two aspects of Satan's dwelling-place in the parables. The individual dwelling is in the parable of the strong man armed, who is overcome by the stronger than he. According to Paul's epistle, the Holy Ghost comes to dwell in the captured stronghold, and makes that which was a "palace" of Satan a palace for Himself (comp. 1 Chron. xxix. 1). The temple in its collective aspect is in striking contrast to the parable of the evil spirit which returns with *seven* others worse than himself to the dwelling that has been swept and garnished. We are told that this refers to the unbelieving nation who, in their rejection of Christ, become a dwelling-place for Satan (Matt. xii. 45).[1]

2 *Tim. ii.* 20, 21.—Paul here refers to the great house in connection with its furniture. It is not the same as the temple, for there is a difference between the Church which is His body and the household.

---

[1] It is suggestive that in contrast to this the plenitude of the Spirit is spoken of in Revelation as "the *seven* Spirits of God."

The vessels to dishonour may be useful to the servants in the house, but only the vessels unto honour will be fit for Himself. "All King Solomon's drinking vessels were of gold" (1 Kings x. 21).

1 *Thess. v.* 1-10.—Night watching is another link with the parables. We are not to sleep like those who belong to the night season, but should be on the outlook for His return. Verses 6 and 10 may be linked together, "Let us not sleep as do others ; but let us watch and be sober." He "died for us that whether we watch or sleep, we should live together with Him." The words are the same, and our being caught up to meet the Lord in the air does not depend on our attitude, but on our being "Christ's at His coming." If we sleep, as even the wise virgins did at first, we are not living *like* them that wait for their Lord, and we shall miss the blessing He bestows on them who at His coming He finds so doing.

Rom. xiii. 11-14.—"Knowing the time, that now it is high time to awake out of sleep : . . . The night is far spent, the day is at hand : let us therefore cast off the works of darkness, and let us put on the armour of light. . . . But put ye on the Lord Jesus Christ." The parable of the night season is presented here in another form, there has been sleep as in the case of the virgins, but it is high time to awake : not in this case because of the midnight cry, but because the day dawn is near. Cast off the garments of the night, "the works of darkness," the lusts of the flesh ; dress for the day. "Put on the armour of light, . . . put ye on the Lord Jesus Christ."

2 *Cor. v.* 20.—"Now then, we are ambassadors for Christ." This passage reminds us of the messengers sent forth in the parables : in that of the husbandman their message is a demand for fruit, in the marriage supper it is an invitation to the feast. Perhaps the apostle Paul was also thinking of the two kings in

Luke xiv; if so, there is a beautiful contrast illustrating the difference between man's thoughts and
God's thoughts. The rebel king finds out that his
case is desperate, and he feels that his only chance is
to send an embassage desiring conditions of peace;
but Paul tells us of one that comes in the opposite
direction, "as though God did beseech you by us:
we pray you in Christ's stead, be ye reconciled to God."
Oh, the grace of His conditions! He against whom
man has rebelled, needs not to be entreated, but Himself beseeches.

1 *Cor. iv.*—"Let a man so account of us, as of the
ministers of Christ, and stewards of the mysteries of
God." The apostle takes up the Lord's simile of the
steward, and seems specially to refer to the eighth
parable in the thirteenth of Matthew, of the scribe
instructed in the mysteries of the kingdom. In other
parables stewards are mentioned. It was Paul's ambition to be judged faithful, not by his fellow-servants,
but by his Master. The parable in Matt. xiii. shows
that a faithful steward is one who uses his master's
goods aright; the unjust steward in Luke xvi. is one
who wastes his master's goods.

1 *Cor. ix.* 9, 10.—"It is written in the law of Moses,
Thou shalt not muzzle the mouth of the ox that
treadeth out the corn. Doth God take care for
oxen? Or saith He it altogether for our sakes?
For our sakes, no doubt, this is written; that he that
ploweth should plow in hope, and that he that
thresheth in hope should be partaker of his hope."
The Lord refers both to plowing and to oxen, and
this symbolism must have been specially precious
to the apostle, for it was revealed to him in the
"heavenly vision" on the road to Damascus; the
voice from heaven spoke to him under the same
figure, "It is hard for thee to kick against the pricks."
He re is a picture of the ox that would not submit

to the light yoke, but rebelled against the goad. The Lord Jesus wanted the service of Paul of Tarsus; He was about to send him forth to labour in His field, and this revelation from heaven brought in response the question, "Lord, what wilt Thou have me to do?" The rebellion was over, and he henceforth gladly took his place at plowing or threshing.

Two leaders stand out prominently in the early history of the children of Israel, and the same thing repeats itself at the beginning of Church history. Peter and Paul in many ways resemble Moses and Joshua. Although their work and message were very different, yet both couples were raised up of God for their great mission, Moses to head the exodus from Egypt, the apostle Peter from a dead Judaism; Joshua to lead the people into the land itself, Paul to guide to the inheritance of faith. It has often been pointed out that Peter views the Church in its wilderness journey, and speaks of "strangers and pilgrims," while in the Epistle to the Ephesians, Paul brings before us our position in the "heavenlies," the antitype of the land. To both Moses and Peter the shepherding of God's flock was entrusted. God "made His own people to go forth like sheep, and guided them in the wilderness like a flock" (Psa. lxxviii. 52). Moses was put in charge of them (Psa. lxxvii. 20), and the Lord said to Peter, "Feed My sheep." Before receiving the commision, both were impetuous in the use of the sword. Moses slew the Egyptian who was smiting one of his brethren, Peter drew his sword in the garden of Gethsemane, and cut off the ear of Malchus. The great sin of each was, that they "spake unadvisedly" with their lips. The leadership of both was accredited by signs and miracles, though in one case they were plagues of judgment, and in the other, with one exception, miracles of healing. Even in their last words there was a similarity, for they both urged upon their hearers the importance of remembering the past. How often Moses in the Book of Deuteronomy repeats the injunction, "Thou shalt remember"; while Peter in his second epistle several times tells them that he is writing in order to bring important truths to their remembrance. Had these exhortations been heeded, how much sorrow would have been averted, but alike in Israel and in the Church the memories of God's people have failed, and the past has been too often forgotten.

We think of Joshua and Paul as warriors rather than as shepherds. Joshua made "war a long time" (chap. xi. 18), and Paul too fought the good fight. A wondrous vision was given to each. Joshua in the plains of Jericho, and Paul on the road to Damascus, met with the Lord Himself; the one saw the Captain of the Lord's host on earth, the other heard the voice from heaven, "I am Jesus, whom thou persecutest," and from henceforth he recognised Him as the Head of the body. We hear Joshua inquiring, "Art Thou for us, or for our adversaries?" and the apostle asks, "Who art Thou, Lord?" Their question answered, their attitude is still the same. Joshua asks, "What saith my Lord unto His servant?" and Paul, "What wilt Thou have me to do?" Both are alike commissioned and encouraged by God to "be strong," and assured of His presence with them.

The symbolism of the epistles of Peter and Paul is in keeping with this contrast between the apostles themselves. The former, remembering his Lord's last commission, refers to the chief Shepherd (1 Pet. v. 4), to the under-shepherds, and to the flock (1 Pet. v. 2 ; ii. 25); and thus we are reminded of the parables about the good Shepherd.[1] The apostle Paul introduces a

_____
[1] See Appendix IV. "Peter and the Parables."

new set of similes in keeping with his character as the leader of the host of the Lord, in their conquest of the land of promise. We can better understand Eph. vi. if we imagine him contrasting the position of the Church and Israel; *they* fought against heathen nations who would prevent their taking possession, but, the apostle writes, "We wrestle not against flesh and blood, but against principalities, against powers, against the rulers of the darkness of this world, against spiritual wickedness in heavenly places." The literal typified the spiritual, the land was a type of the heavenlies, the nations of Canaan of the enemies of our faith.

The figure of the soldier in his complete armour (Eph. vi.), though not in parable form, is prominent amongst the similes used by the apostle Paul. He again refers to the soldier when addressing Timothy (2 Tim. ii. 3, 4; iv. 7). If Paul wrote the Epistle to the Hebrews, it would accord with his character as the Joshua of the Church for him to speak of the Lord as the "Captain of their Salvation" (Heb. ii. 10).

But there is another reason why the apostle Paul, though often referring to the parables of our Lord, uses such an entirely different class of figures in his epistles. He was writing to Romans and Greeks, and therefore took many of his symbols from customs and laws with which they were familiar. These were not the subjects of the Lord's parables, for they would not have been so appropriate to His audience; but to those whom Paul addressed they were very familiar figures. Thus he refers to the victor's triumph when he led captives in his train (2 Cor. x. 5; and ii. 14), also to the famous Isthmian games, and other contests which were so popular with Grecian athletes and Grecian crowds. The races and the wrestling matches had also become common throughout the Roman Empire; for Nero himself in his craving for applause figured in the arena, and was proud of being crowned with the wreath.

1 *Cor. ix.* 24–27 ; 2 *Tim. ii.* 5, *iv.* 7.—Paul's allusions to these contests, therefore, would be well understood, especially in Corinth, as, for example, to the fight of the gladiator, the training of the athlete, the necessity of adhering to the rules of the races, the need of looking to the goal, the crowns that were awarded to the victors, and the "bema" on which the adjudicator sat, from which the prizes were distributed. He constantly drew lessons from these familiar scenes, but he pointed out the contrasts as well as the similarities between the earthly and heavenly races. In the Greek competition only one could gain a reward, but in the spiritual all may win the prize. *They* strove for a fading or corruptible wreath or crown, *we* for an incorruptible.

Heb. xii. 1–3.—In the Epistle to the Hebrews we are exhorted to run the race "looking unto Jesus." His race is over, and now He sits at the right hand of the throne of God. We, who are still on the course, are told to consider Him and the race He won, lest we be wearied and faint in our minds.

There are two or three words used by the apostle, which contain in themselves a little parable, when we understand the law or custom to which they refer. This is especially the case in connection with the passage in Gal. iii. and iv., about the different stages in the life of a Roman citizen's son. It is impossible to understand the force of the illustration in either chapter unless we know what the apostle meant by the two words "schoolmaster" and "adoption"; they both referred to epochs in the life of a Roman youth ; our word schoolmaster or tutor gives us quite another idea from that which it would convey to the Galatians. "Children . . . from the age of six to fourteen used to be consigned by their father to the care of a slave called a 'pædagogus,' who was neither qualified nor allowed to teach them anything, but whose office it was to conduct them to school. So brought to the school of Christ, where learning comes by faith (such is his argument), let men beware how they revert to the carnal ordinances of the Jewish law." [1]

The other word, "adoption," is used four times by Paul (Gal. iv. 5 ; Rom. viii. 15, 23 ; Eph. i. 5), and was much fuller in meaning than the word we use. When we speak of adoption we imply that a child of other parents has been taken into a family, and given the place of a son or daughter of the house. We are not thus adopted into God's family ; we must be born into it : " Behold what manner of love the Father hath bestowed upon us, that we should be called children of God : and such we are " (1 John iii. 1, R.V.). Mephibosheth was like an adopted son to David, for he was "as one of the king's sons " ; but we are God's own children. The adoption of sons meant something very different to the Roman ; and as we notice this in connection with Paul's use of the word, the passages have a new meaning, beautifully consistent with the fact that we are children by birth, and not merely by adoption in the ordinary sense of the word.

Dr. Pierson writes : " In the Latin the word adoption referred to the declaration of a son's majority. When the young man attained the legal age his father took him into the Forum, and from the bema or platform said to the citizens, 'This is my son, he has now come to full age, he inherits my name, my property, my social position.' Then he took off the toga prætexta, the boy toga or coat, and put on the toga virilis, the manly toga. He invested him in the presence of the citizens with the sign of full manhood, and said,

[1] Dean Burgon.

'This is my son.' In your minority you are but children, when you come to your majority you are full-grown sons. There is a day of manifestation coming when God shall take you as His child and set you on the Forum of the universe, and He shall before that universe say, ' Be witness this is My son in Christ, he is the joint-heir of My name, of My nature, of My possessions, of My throne.' And then we shall lay aside the body of our humiliation, the toga that we wore when we were minors, and put on the body of our glory, which is the garment we shall wear when we get to our majority ; and this new investment of the redeemed sons of God in the presence of the universe is adoption."

Thus we see that the first part of Paul's little parable or allegory in Gal. iii. depicts Israel under the law ; the second (Gal. iv.) speaks of the glorious portion of the Church at the coming of the Lord. The two figures, symbolical of the two dispensations, are contrasted—under the pedagogue, or waiting for the adoption—and the lesson is that we are not under the law, but are looking forward to soon entering upon our inheritance.

The pictures though similar are distinct. The children of Gal. iii. do not grow up into those of Gal. iv. In the first part of the passage the apostle is speaking of the seed of Abraham, in the second of the children of God by new birth. As he shows in the same verse, " Abba Father " is the first cry of the new-born infant, adoption the coming of age of the full-grown son. But the same Spirit inspires the cry of the babe and the hope of the young man, and the cry is the earnest of the "adoption." " As sleeps the oak within the acorn, so slumbereth heaven within the first cry of Abba Father."

CHAPTER XVI

THE PARABLES AND THE APOCALYPSE

BEFORE closing our study of the parables there is one more book in the Bible to which brief reference must be made, that entitled "The Revelation of Jesus Christ, which God gave unto Him, to show unto His servants things which must shortly come to pass." This preface at once establishes a link between the Apocalypse and the parables, for they too were a revelation first from God Himself to the Lord Jesus Christ, and then from the Lord to His servants, of things which would shortly come to pass. The Evangelist Matthew was not the composer of the parables recorded by him, and the apostle John did not originate the visions which he thus described. The Lord Himself being the Author alike of Apocalypse and parable, we shall expect to find the same symbolism in both. He represents Himself in the Revelation as in the parables as King, Master, Owner of a vineyard, Husbandman, Shepherd, Conqueror, and Judge ; while men are spoken of as subjects, sheep, fruit of the earth, virgins, and corporately under the figure of a woman and a bride. The visions which the apostle saw were in many cases the continuation of the picture stories which he had heard from the lips of Him on whose bosom he had loved to lean. He now saw in the glory Him whom he had before known in humiliation, but the voice was the same. "The hearing ear" listened to the parables, and "the seeing eye" gazed on the visions. There is a special blessing pronounced on those who read and study the last book in the Bible ; and there was a special blessing for those who heard and understood the parables (comp. Rev. i. 3 ; Matt. xiii. 11–17). The expression " He that hath ears to hear let him hear " occurs in connection with the words spoken by the Lord Jesus and with " what the Spirit saith unto the Churches " (Matt. xiii. 9, 43 ; Mark iv. 9, 23 ; vii. 16 ; Luke viii. 8 ; xiv. 35 ; Rev. ii. 7, 11, 17, 29 ; iii. 6, 13, 22 ; xiii. 9). It has been pointed out that these words precede the promise to the overcomers in the first four epistles, and follow them in the last three as though to mark the increasing failure of the testimony. What is addressed at first to the whole Church can at last be spoken only to individuals.

The connection between the epistles to the seven churches and the seven important parables in the thirteenth of Matthew has often been noted. In many ways they are similar. The same controversies have been held over them, and interpretations given by Bible students to the one chapter correspond very much with their method of explaining the others. Those who believe that the thirteenth of Matthew has nothing to do with the present dispensation, think the same of Rev. ii. and iii.; and those who find in the parables a chronological description of the time of His absence see a similar panorama in the seven epistles. We may, however, adopt a more comprehensive view of the former, believing the parables in that chapter, especially the first four, to have been true in the past, in the present, and in the future. It seems most probable that the epistles to the seven churches have in the same way several applications.

1. The fact that they were in the first place addressed to actual churches would not interfere with their interpretation, any more than the knowledge that the events of the exodus were real incidents in the lives of the children of Israel prevents their being full

of typical teaching for us.   When speaking the words, "Behold, a sower went forth to sow," or "The kingdom of heaven is like unto a net," the Lord may have pointed from the boat to a sower in the field, or to a fisherman on the shore ; but such illustrations would not have interfered with the interpretation of His parables ; and no one doubts that the Pauline epistles were addressed to literal churches.

There may have been a real seat of Satan alluded to in the epistle to Pergamos.   The great altar discovered some years ago suggests that it was actually a centre of wickedness and devil-worship.   A real Polycarp was a bishop of Smyrna, and may have been specially included in the address ; but facts such as these do not lessen their deep importance for present or future days.   (See Appendix V.)

2. For there is a much more important interpretation than that which refers to the actual assemblies that may have existed in the time that the apostle wrote.   In a very striking manner the epistles to the seven churches give a chronological panorama of church history, delineating with a few touches the leading feature of each era.   Ephesus tells of the days immediately succeeding apostolic times when early love began to wax cold ; Smyrna, of the persecutions which followed ; Pergamos, of increasing error ; Thyatira, of the rise of Roman Catholicism, the period of Latin Christianity, followed by the Reformation ; Sardis, of Protestantism soon becoming a dead system ; Philadelphia, of revival and brotherly love ; and Laodicea, of popular religion.   But it is very important to notice that the last four stages continue to the end. Though thus viewed each belongs specially to a different period of church history, they are also synchronous, for they are to exist side by side till He come (see chapters ii. 25 ; iii. 3, 11, 16).   This is what we see around us to-day. Papacy, Protest-

antism, a revival of spirituality and service, and an increase of popular, political religion. Thus the seven addresses to the churches in Asia give a faithful prophecy of the condition of things during the time of the Lord's absence—"the mysteries of the kingdom."

3. But from another point of view we may give a present interpretation to all the seven addresses, as we do to the parables. We cannot afford to relegate such words as those addressed to the church in Ephesus to past days. If they had a meaning for the church in existence when John wrote, and for the period immediately following, they are equally important now. Israel's past is typical of the present, and the Church's past is also full of warnings.

4. It is very evident that there are individual lessons of warning and encouragement in each epistle.

5. There are some Bible students who see in the seven letters a special application to days to come after the Church has been taken away, and this seems most probable, but when they add that this is the *only* interpretation they limit the meaning of these wonderful chapters. It would need many volumes to exhaust their fulness. If they contain prophecies of days to come we may be quite certain that they were intended "for our admonition" also.

These four or five methods of interpretation are all possible. There is nothing at all contradictory in them, and remembering that the words are the last messages of our Lord from the glory, that they are essentially divine, we may be quite sure that there is a fulness of meaning in them which far surpasses that which would be contained in merely human writings.

Both the parables in Matthew and the epistles in Revelation demand therefore successive and manifold interpretations, and are full of individual and collective teaching.

6. It has been pointed out that the promises to the overcomers cover all the dispensations in their symbolic references. (i.) The first one refers to eating the tree of life in Paradise, the last ends with the throne, and between these two we are reminded of (ii.) Noah saved from death, (iii.) wilderness days when the manna was given, and the stones on the high-priest's shoulder and on the breast-plate were inscribed with Israel's names, or, as some take it, the stones engraven with the law. (iv.) There is the kingly dispensation, (v.) the prophets "separated from the world and confessing the truth in an apostate age," (vi.) "the dispensation of the Son and close identification with Him," and (vii.) "the dispensation to come when a suffering people on earth shall pass right from suffering to the throne." It is not by accident that such wonderful sequence exists in these promises, though there may be differences of opinion as to the periods to which reference is made.

7. There are in several of these addresses to the seven churches striking parallels with Matt. xiii.

(i.) In the words to Ephesus there is a reference to patience, and in the sower there is bearing fruit with patience.

(ii.) In Smyrna there are those "which say they are Jews, and are not, but are the synagogue of Satan" (ii. 9), like the darnel of the parable.

(iii.) The church in Pergamos dwelt "where Satan's seat is" (verse 13), and verse 14 enumerates some of the errors which like birds of the air had come to shelter in the branches of the mustard tree.

(iv.) In Thyatira the woman Jezebel "which calleth herself a prophetess" is seen teaching and seducing the Church (chap. ii. 20), reminding us very forcibly of the woman in the parable who is introducing the leaven.

(v.) In Sardis, in the midst of the church which

had a name to live and was dead, the Lord said He had His special treasure, "a few names even in Sardis," which were by-and-by to be confessed before His Father (chap. iii. 4, 5), just as the treasure at present hidden in the field will one day be displayed. The parable is not to be limited in any way to the Sardis period, but both teach the same truth.

(vi.) In Philadelphia the promise to the overcomers speaks of the time coming when all will know, as the Lord says, "that I have loved thee" (ver. 9). They were to Him as the pearl of great price. In this epistle, too, we can only say that there is an illustration of the truth taught in the sixth parable in Matt. xiii., for the pearl does not refer merely to Philadelphian overcomers, though they be included in it.

(vii.) In the words addressed to Laodicea there is a solemn warning of the separation that will take place when mere professing Christendom is spued out of His mouth, reminding us of the division which will be made when the good are gathered into vessels and the bad are cast away.

In Revelation v. we have the sequel to the parable of the treasure hid in the field. The sealed roll has been variously explained; some have thought it represented the Scriptures, others that it was a book of judgment. The most satisfactory interpretation seems to be that which takes it to represent the title-deeds of the Redeemer to "the purchased possession," which could not be opened till the seven seals of judgment had been broken. If we consider the scene in connection with the parable we see in it the claiming of the field by the One who paid such a price to obtain it, "The Lion of the tribe of Judah, the Root of David hath prevailed to open the book" (verse 5).

"It was Christ's death that gave Him title to claim the throne of the kingdom of heaven upon earth."

This was faintly symbolised in the parable by the man selling all that he had in order to buy the field. When the day comes for Him to open the title-deeds and claim the purchased possession, the treasure will no longer remain hidden. The object of the purchase will be revealed as it is embodied in the new song. They sang a new song, saying, "Worthy art Thou to take the book, and to open the seals thereof : for Thou wast slain, and didst purchase unto God with Thy blood of every tribe and tongue, and people, and nation" (R.V.). Is not this a description of the treasure ? We have no space to dwell on the beauties of the chapter, or to touch upon the various ascriptions of praise from the ever-widening circles around the throne, but in the words that sound forth from the many angels ("the number of them was ten thousand times ten thousand, and thousands of thousands") we have a beautiful link with the parable. They cry "with a loud voice, Worthy is the Lamb that was slain to receive power, and riches, and wisdom, and strength, and honour, and glory, and blessing." What a contrast !   He sold all that He had, and this is His reward.   "Ye know the grace of our Lord Jesus Christ, that though He was rich, yet for your sakes He became poor, that *ye* through His poverty might be rich," and that *He* also might become rich.   He receives His riches back again and the treasure too.   He impoverished Himself that He might be enriched, for the riches of His grace to sinners now will add to the riches of His glory to all eternity (Eph. i. 18).

Reference has already been made to Rev. vii. as containing the key to the closing scene in Matt. xxv. The chapter first contains the account of the sealing of the 144,000. Like those in Ezek. ix., upon whom the man clothed with linen set a mark (pp. 200, 202), the seal was in the forehead in contrast to the mark of the beast in the foreheads of those who worshipped him (Rev. xiii. 16).

After these sons of Israel had been sealed, the seer beholds the multitude whom no man can number, who have passed through the Great Tribulation. The first company probably represents the "brethren" mentioned in Matt. xxv.; the second the "sheep" who have believed their message, and who when the witnesses are persecuted by Antichrist risk their lives by proving their friendship. The thirteenth of Revelation shows what it would cost to take such a stand, and thus we learn the real significance of showing sympathy with His "brethren" in that day. The chapter closes with the same figure as that used in Matt. xxv., the Shepherd and His sheep. "The Lamb which is in the midst of the throne shall be their Shepherd, and shall guide them unto fountains of waters of life, and God shall wipe away every tear from their eyes" (verse 17, R.V.). Their experience as they came through the Great Tribulation had been very different (verse 14). They had shared with His "brethren" hunger, thirst, homelessness, nakedness, sickness, and imprisonment, but now "they shall hunger no more, neither thirst any more; neither shall the sun light on them, nor any heat."

Rev. xii. may be linked with the parable of the widow who cried continually to the judge, "Avenge me of mine adversary." It tells us who the adversary is who has been behind all the other enemies of Israel, shows something of the way in which he persecutes her, and describes in symbolic language the last attempt that he will make. Then, indeed, the elect will cry "day and night," and God will avenge them speedily.

In Rev. xiv. the numbered company who stand with the Lamb on Mount Zion, having His Father's Name written in their foreheads, are called "the first-fruits unto God and to the Lamb." They are evidently the Pentecostal first-fruits typified in Lev. xxiii. 17, not the sheaf of the first-fruits mentioned in verse 10.

There is a *double harvest* spoken of at the close of Rev. xiv. The first reminds us of that prefigured in the parable of the tares, the division between the wheat and the darnel, and the binding up of the latter ready for the fire. The vintage of the earth in the following verses speaks only of judgment, and corresponds with the picture in Isa. lxiii. of the time when He who is now mighty to save will prove Himself mighty to execute judgment. The wine-press is the same in both passages. These harvests seem to be prophesied in Joel iii. 12, 13, in connection with the Lord's return to earth, "Let the nations bestir themselves, and come up to the valley of Jehoshaphat: for there will I sit to judge all the nations round about. Put ye in the sickle; for the harvest is ripe: come, tread ye, for the wine-press is full, the vats overflow; for their wickedness is great" (R.V.).

We learn from the parables that Satan tries to spoil the work of God by corrupting it, as in the parable of the leaven; and by *counterfeiting* it, as in the parable of the tares. Other parables show us that Satan has his dwelling-place in individual souls, and in a people or nation, just as God Himself has His temple in the heart of the believer, or in the midst of His Church.

The apostle Paul tells us that Satan transforms himself into an angel of light in order to deceive men, and ever since the earth became man's realm, and has been the field of battle in the great war of the centuries, Satan has tried to defeat God's purposes by counterfeiting His plans, or corrupting His work. Justin Martyr (about the middle of the second century) explained heathen mythology in this way, believing that it was part of Satan's plan of campaign, when God gave a prophecy, or promise, to substitute his imitation, and thus, as Paul said, men worshipped demons. In these wonderful days of progress, the astonishing discovery has been made that the true was copied from the false, the pure Jewish religion evolved from Babylonian corruption. Such theories are very much like suggesting that the coin of the realm which comes from the Mint and the Bank of England is an imitation of counterfeit coin. Satan is the very prince of forgers, and many of his counterfeits are represented in the Book of Revelation, which also shows the ultimate issue of the great struggle.

One of the Lord's sweetest titles in Revelation is that of the "Morning Star," and this, strange as it may seem, was once a name given to Satan. "How art thou fallen from heaven, O Lucifer (*marg.* day-star), son of the morning!" How different his position now!

The apostate woman stands in contrast to the Bride of the Lamb. Antichrist, to whom the devil gives his power, puts his mark on the foreheads of his worshippers, while the true witnesses for God are sealed in their foreheads (comp. Rev. xiii. 16 with xiv. 1). The mark in each case is a name, the name of Antichrist (chap. xiv. 11), or the Father's name (verse 1).

The beast, as he is called, "had two horns like a lamb, and he spake as a dragon" (chap. xiii. 11). He will be an Antichrist in a double sense, opposed *to* Christ, and trying to pass *instead of* God's own Anointed One. But he cannot disguise the voice, "He spake as a dragon," and it will not deceive the sheep of the good Shepherd, who know His voice.

Satan now appears as a roaring lion seeking whom he may devour, but the Lord Jesus, the Lion of the tribe of Judah, will prevail, and prove Himself stronger than he.

We read in Rev. xviii. 16 of a gilded city, but the city of Rev. xxi. 21 is of pure gold ; the former was only decked with gold, the inhabitants were clothed in fine linen, but it was not the fine linen spoken of in Rev. xix. 8.

This gilded city with all its luxury is the seat of the great apostasy, which in the preceding chapter is called Mystery Babylon. Like the two women in Zech. v. who bare the ephah to the land of Shinar, we have a twofold aspect of the colossal system— its religious and its civil power. In the thirteenth of Matthew the Lord reveals to us the mysteries of the kingdom, here He reveals a mystery which is intimately connected with them, and might be said to be included in the history of the tares, the mustard-seed and the leaven. The mysteries of Scripture are secrets which can only be revealed by God. His estimate is not the same as man's ; the tares are mistaken for the wheat ; and the religion of Mystery Babylon becomes the religion of the professing Church, first, in the days of Latin Christianity, and again in the apostasy at the end.

There is evidently first an allusion to Rome, and the appropriateness of the title Babylon, as applied to it, has often been pointed out. The earliest apostasy of Old Testament days had its seat in ancient Babylon; the great papal apostasy since New Testament times in Rome; but besides this, the latter actually borrowed from the former, and many Romish customs have really a Babylonish origin.[1] But it is thought by many that as there was a literal Babylon and a literal Rome which have given their names to great systems of religion, so in the eighteenth chapter of Revelation there is something more than papal supremacy, viz., an indication of another literal

[1] This is strikingly traced by Rev. A. Hislop in " The Two Babylons."

Babylon which will be the centre of the final apostasy and godless civilisation.

There are many reasons for believing that Babylon will be rebuilt. The vision in Zech. v. foretells it in the setting up of the ephah in the land of Shinar, but there are also several unfulfilled prophecies concerning its destruction which do not apply to the ancient city. Whatever differences of opinion may exist about Rev. xviii. there can be no question about the prophecies in Isaiah and Jeremiah referring to the literal Babylon, for they speak of it in connection with the land of the Chaldeans (Isa. xiii. 19; Jer. l. 35, 45). Its destruction is to be like that of Sodom and Gomorrah as to its suddenness, method, and result (Isa. xiii. 19; Jer. l. 40). No such calamity ever befell the ancient Babylon, and this corresponds with Rev. xviii. 10, 17, 19. It is to be burnt by fire, and that not by accident or incendiarism, as in the case of Rome in the days of Nero, of London in 1666, or of Moscow. When a city is destroyed thus, the fact lives in history; how much more when the fire instantaneously consumes, as in Herculaneum and Pompeii, or recently at St. Pierre? Isa. xiii. 20; Jer. l. 40; and li. 25, 26, have not been fulfilled any more than Rev. xviii. 8, 9, 18.

It was prophesied in Nahum iii. 13, 15, that *Nineveh* should be destroyed by fire; and this was accomplished, as may be seen in the mural sculptures in the Assyrian basement of the British Museum, which have evidently been cracked and blackened by fire.

The result of the devastation of Babylon is to be the same as after the destruction of Sodom and Gomorrah. The place is never to be inhabited again, for after its destruction it is said, "Neither shall the Arabian pitch tent there" (Isa. xiii. 20). There is nothing to prevent the shepherds from doing this among the ruins of ancient Babylon now, and we are told that they constantly do so. Instead of this prophecy therefore being a proof that Babylon cannot be rebuilt, it is a proof that it must be, "For every purpose of the Lord shall be performed against Babylon."

We also read, "They shall not take of thee a stone for a corner, nor a stone for a foundation" (Jer. li. 26). This was not fulfilled after the former destruction, for we are told by explorers that the town of Hillah, near the ruins, is built almost entirely of the stones and bricks of the old city. Many that are engraved or stamped with the name of Nebuchadnezzar can, they say, be seen there, proving two things—first, that his boast was literally true, "Is not this great Babylon that I have built?" and also showing that the prophecy is still unfulfilled.

Babylon, the place of *confusion* (Babel), seems throughout Scripture to be the metropolis of Satan, and in direct antagonism to Jerusalem, God's centre, the place of *peace*. In this sense, as well as that in which the apostle used the words, "God is not the author of confusion, but of peace;" and Babylon must be destroyed before Jerusalem can be made "the joy of the whole earth."

Mystery Babylon is more than papacy, more than Rome, and more than the great city which is to be rebuilt, and to become the centre of a godless civilisation. It seems to include all that is suggested by these two names, Rome and Babylon.

In its last stage it will be worse than papacy. Even that will be too good for the final apostasy. Men will destroy even the vestiges of truth which remain in that system, as they are already beginning to do in their rejection of the Word of God; and Antichrist will deny the Father and the Son as the Romish Church has never done.

The religion of Babylon in Rev. xvii. is that of the Church in Thyatira, which represents the papal era of

Church testimony; that of Rev. xviii. is rather the Laodicean stage where the professing Church thought they were rich and increased in goods when they were really poor, and blind, and naked. But in the epistles in Rev. ii. and iii. the Lord saw His own even amongst this condition of things, and in Rev. xviii. the call is still "Come out of her, My people."

To read Rev. xvii. and xviii. as a sequel to Matt. xiii. is terribly solemn. The double aspect revealed in the former chapters is accounted for and prophesied in Matt. xiii., for it is the outcome of the tares being mixed with the wheat, and the leaven with the meal.

In the next chapter we have the mention of the *marriage supper*, which reminds us of the parables of the marriage feast and the great supper. He that bade them has not yet come to see the guests, or to arrange the seats. Now is the time for the invitation to be given and accepted.

"Let us be glad and rejoice, and give honour to Him : for the marriage of the Lamb is come, and His wife hath made herself ready." The marriage feast in Matthew was prepared for the honour of the Son, and the song of praise here tells us that all the beauties of the bride, all the loveliness of her embroidered dress, are to bring honour to *Him*, and not to her. The garments of fine linen are probably not the same as symbolised by the wedding garment in Matt. xxii., or the best robe of Luke xv. Those seem to speak of the God-given dress which covers the sinner who trusts in the Lord Jesus, as the coats of skins provided by God for the nakedness of Adam and Eve after the fall ; they are Christ Himself. But the "fine linen, clean and white," is interpreted in the passage, "the righteousnesses of saints," wrought by the Spirit in their lives.

"And He saith unto me, Write, Blessed are they which are called unto the marriage supper of the

Lamb." This reminds us of the exclamation of one of the Lord's hearers which called forth the parable of the great supper, "Blessed is he that shall eat bread in the kingdom of God" (Luke xiv. 15).

In the parables there is no mention of the bride ; now, however, she appears. They refer to the period of the King's absence, and especially to the moment of His return, but the revelation of the bride does not take place till after that, and it is not the subject to which He wished to draw attention.

There are various companies in these marriage scenes, and there has been much controversy over the question as to whom they severally represent. In view of the double symbolism of both types and parables (pp. 295, 296), it is quite possible that to a certain extent the faithful servants ; the feasted guests in the Gospels, or those called to the marriage supper in Rev. xix. ; the wise virgins in Matt. xxv. ; and even the bride herself, may include the same groups under different aspects.

What seem to be concentric circles in Scripture do not of necessity represent different companies of people. We see this both in the Old and New Testaments, *e.g.*, the children of Israel, as a whole, typify God's people as to redemption, the Levites typify them in their service, and the priests in their worship ; but the priests and Levites were Israelites as well. So in the New Testament we find gathered around the Person of the Lord, the twelve, the three, and the one who leaned upon His bosom ; and he, the beloved disciple, was one of the three and of the twelve also.

It does not therefore seem wise to attempt to define too accurately, or to draw a line between the different companies represented by these figures.

CHAPTER XVII

PRACTICAL TEACHING

THE parables are so full of practical lessons, and there are so many lines of teaching in them, that it is impossible to do more than suggest methods of study.

By grouping them together in reference to the spiritual lesson which they convey, we find that in this respect, as in others, they supplement one another, and give us complete pictures of Christian life and conduct.

Prayer.—A number of parables illustrate different truths about prayer. Some were uttered, we are told, in order to teach men how to pray, and when to pray; and others give examples of prayer—right prayers and wrong prayers, earnest prayers, and prayers that were too late.

The parable of the importunate widow is introduced with these words, " He spake a parable unto them to this end, that men ought always to pray, and not to faint." Sometimes God allows us to ask again and again for what we desire, that He may test our earnestness and our faith; while at other times He answers at once. Thus in Dan. ix. 21 the answer came as Daniel was praying, "Whiles I was speaking in prayer," but on another occasion, recorded in the next chapter, we read, he "was mourning three full weeks " (verse 2). Again, while sometimes we are led to pray with importunity, at other times, as in the case of Paul, we are taught

to cease praying; God having shown that it is not
His will to grant the request except by the promise
of His all-sufficient grace.

There are two parables which teach the value of
importunate prayer, that of the widow in Luke xviii.,
and of the man who at midnight comes to his neighbour for food for his poor friend. The latter might
be called the parable of the three friends, the hungry
friend, the praying friend, and the wealthy friend. In
both parables the lesson is enforced by a contrast.
An unjust judge is forced to listen to the poor
widow's case, because he is wearied by her constant
appeal; a grudging friend against his will is obliged
to rise in the middle of the night to satisfy the needs
of his troublesome neighbour. If importunity forces
benefits from unwilling men, how much more will
earnest, believing, continual prayer bring down favour
from Him who loves to bless? In these earthly
appeals it succeeded where apparently justice and
friendship failed. The justice of her cause helped the
widow to persist, and the man's faith in the friendship of his wealthy neighbour helped him to go on
knocking.

How great the contrast too in this parable. The
Lord is indeed a Friend that sticketh closer than a
brother, One who neither slumbers nor sleeps. We
need never fear disturbing His rest, nor can we ever
come to Him at an unseasonable hour.

The widow came to lay before the judge her own
case, the man in Luke xi. besought for his friend,
and thus our Lord in the two parables teaches us
to pray for ourselves and for others till the answer
come. The one story illustrates the words, "Ask,
and it shall be given you," the other, "Knock, and
it shall be opened unto you."

Although in the case of one of the three friends,
the lesson is by contrast, the other two which

represent ourselves beautifully picture the two classes.
The one in need was "out of his way" (*marg.*), and
the other had nothing to set before him.   How
utterly unable we are, from our own store, to feed
the hungry ones around us, for no provision of our
own will suffice the needy sinner or the wandering
believer.   But from Him who deigns to be our
Friend we can at all times obtain sufficient.

The other parable which teaches how to pray, immediately follows that of the importunate widow.
The story of the Pharisee and publican describes
two very different sorts of so-called prayer, a prayer
that was no prayer, and the right kind of prayer;
the boast of pride, and the confession of humility.
The Pharisee, though he presumably went to the
temple to pray, came away without having really
uttered one word of true prayer.   He prayed with
himself, and his words were merely words of self-
congratulation.   He asked for nothing, and received
nothing.   He was offering strange incense, and this
was distinctly forbidden (Exod. xxx. 9).

"The Pharisee yonder was *the* saint of his age, but
this publican, who stood afar off from the holy place,
was *the* sinner."   This, though he knew it not, was
the one plea which God could not refuse.   "A broken
and a contrite heart, O God, Thou wilt not despise."
As Mr. Spurgeon quaintly describes it, "When the
messenger of Mercy was travelling through the world,
he asked himself at what inn he should alight and
spend the night.   Lions and eagles were not to his
mind, and he passed by houses wearing such warlike
names, so, too, he passed by places known by the sign
of 'The Waving Plume,' and 'The Conquering Hero,'
for he knew that there was no room for him in these
inns.   He hastened by many a hostelry, and tarried
not, till at last he came to a little inn which bore the
sign of 'The Broken Heart.'   'Here,' said Mercy's

messenger, 'I would fain tarry, for I know by experience that I shall be welcome here.'"

Is there not in the case of the prodigal son a striking example of a prayer that should not have been offered. He "said to his father, Father, give me the portion of goods that falleth to me. And he divided unto them his living. And not many days after, the younger son gathered all together, and took his journey into a far country." The apostle James warns us against such prayer : "Ye ask amiss, that ye may consume it upon your pleasures" (*marg.*). The prodigal's petition was answered, but it brought no blessing. We hear a good deal from some in the present day about *claiming* this and that temporal blessing from God, and that if we have enough faith we can have anything we ask for ; but the promises, upon which such teaching is founded, are conditional on our will being in harmony with the will of God. Even were it possible for us thus to gain what we demand, might it not be, as in the case of the prodigal, the first step into the far country ?

The model prayer is, "Give us this day our daily bread." The prodigal's was exactly the opposite. He wanted to be independent and set up for himself. It would have been much better for him to have allowed his father to give him day by day what he thought best than to have claimed what belonged to him as his heir. We have a similar prayer in the history of Israel. "They lusted exceedingly in the wilderness, and tempted God in the desert. And He gave them their request ; but sent leanness into their soul" (Ps. cvi. 14, 15). Like that of the prodigal, it was prompted by discontent, and the answer brought bitterness.

In the same parable we have another prayer which he planned to utter, but which was never spoken. When he came to himself and thought of the father's house, he resolved to return, and began to plan what he would say; he felt that he could ask for nothing as a son, but would gladly take the place of a servant. He thought that perhaps he might beg for a situation.

In the father's treatment of the returned wanderer we have a beautiful picture of how God gives "exceeding abundantly above all that we ask or think." The son asked for forgiveness; he thought to ask permission to come home as a servant, but he received his answer before he had time to express his thought, and the best robe and the fatted calf were exceeding abundant above either. "Before they call, I will answer; and while they are yet speaking, I will hear."

The elder brother complained that his father, who killed the fatted calf for his brother who was, he thought, in every way so much less worthy than himself, had never given him even a kid. He illustrates that other class of people spoken of by James who do not receive answers to prayer, "Ye have not, because ye ask not;" for the father answered, "All that I have is thine."

In the story of Dives and Lazarus there is a prayer that was too late, when the former begged for relief from his torment, and asked that a warning might be sent to his brethren. He had had plenty of time during his lifetime, but the "good things" had filled his thoughts. If he had prayed before for himself and for others, he would not have prayed in vain when it was too late.

There is the same solemn lesson in Luke xiii. 25, 26, "When once the Master of the house is risen up and hath shut to the door, and ye begin to stand without, and to knock at the door, saying, Lord, Lord, open unto us, and He shall answer and say unto you, I know you not whence ye are." The promise during the day of salvation is, " Ask, and ye shall receive, knock, and the door shall be opened unto you;" but, if delayed too long, the time will come when the knocking will be in vain, as in the case of the foolish virgins, to whom a similar reply is given.

Thus in the parables we have various examples of prayer and no prayer :—

Importunate prayer for one's self	. The widow.
Importunate prayer for others	. The friend.
A prayer that was no prayer	. The Pharisee.
A justifying prayer	. The publican.
Asking amiss	. The prodigal.
A prayer composed but never uttered	. The prodigal.
No prayer	. The elder brother.
Prayers that were too late	. Dives ; false professors ; the foolish virgins.[1]

The intercessory prayer of the Lord is symbolised in the parable of the barren fig-tree. The servants, in two parables, come and tell their Lord about the things that were wrong (see page 277). How much need there is for constant prayer concerning the evils which are around us, in the world and in the Church.

Service.—The group of parables which illustrate Christian service is such a large one, and the lessons inculcated are so varied and comprehensive, that it would need a volume to itself.

They teach that service is to be rendered *in all*

[1] All but the last are in Luke's Gospel.   See also Appendix VI., "The Disciples' Prayer illustrated by the Parables."

places; the sower must sow in all parts of the field; the messengers sent forth with the King's invitation must visit town and country, and bring in guests from the highways and hedges, as well as from the streets and lanes of the city.

It is to *all sorts of people;* travellers and beggars, lame and blind, must be bidden to the feast; the steward must look after the needs of the whole household; the light must shine for those who dwell in the house, for those who visit the house, and for those who see the city from afar.

There must be service *at all times;* the faithful servant must be ever working and watching, day and night, so as to be ready for the Master.

There must be labour at the eleventh hour as well as earlier in the day. Late service is better than no service.

There must be work *with all kinds of gifts* and opportunities. The man with the one talent is just as much expected to double it as those who have five or two entrusted to them.

Each one is to do his own task, not that of another, for the Master has left to every one his work.

The service must be done *to the right Master.* The husbandmen probably did the work of the vineyard well. They were called wicked because they kept the fruit for themselves, not because they neglected the vines.

The immense *diversity* of service is represented by many similes, but though so varied in character, the Master is the same. The servants are not to work for themselves, but their aim and object should be that they may be profitable to the Master.

The sower is to scatter the Master's seed.

The messenger is to carry the Master's invitation or command.

The steward is to look after the Master's property, or feed the Master's household.

The porter is to watch at the Master's gate.

The husbandman is to tend the Master's vine.

The trader is to invest the Master's money.

The reaper is to gather the Master's harvest (John iv. 35, 38).

The field labourer is to plough the Master's field.

The farm labourer is to feed the Master's herds and flocks (Luke xvii. 7–10).

The indoor servant is to serve in the Master's house.

Thus they serve Him in the house and in the field ; in the farm and in the fold ; in the city and in the country ; in the vineyard and in the palace.

The service will all be rewarded according to sovereign grace. The sovereignty is shown in the parable of the labourers in the vineyard, when He gives to all alike, and replies to those who murmur, "Is it not lawful for Me to do what I will with Mine own ?"

The grace is beautifully illustrated by comparing Luke xii. 37 ; and xvii. 7–10. In these two passages He shows that the recompense of the heavenly Master will be very different from that bestowed by an earthly one. In Luke xvii. He proves that our service does not deserve any reward. "Which of you, having a servant plowing, or feeding cattle, will say unto him by-and-by, when he is come from the field, Go, and sit down to meat ? And will not rather say unto him, Make ready wherewith I may sup, and gird thyself and serve me, till I have eaten and drunken ; and afterward thou shalt eat and drink ? Doth he thank that servant because he did the things that were commanded him ? I trow not." If treated like this we should receive neither reward nor thanks ; and at best we are but unprofitable servants ; we cannot even claim to have done those things which were commanded by the Master, and yet,—oh, wonderful grace, He tells us in the other passage that He will do this unheard of thing. He promises in Luke xii., " Blessed are those servants, whom the Lord, when He cometh, shall find watching : verily, I say unto you, that He shall gird Himself, and make them to sit down to meat, and will come forth and serve them." When He returns, His first thought will be for them, and "by-and-by," when they are " come from the field," when field labour is over, or when He returns to the house, He will show His matchless condescension by girding Himself to serve those who have been serving Him.

If He is to do the one unlikely thing mentioned in Luke xvii., of making the servants sit down to meat, will He not also do the other, and thank them for their service ? To receive in that day the thanks of the Master would be a reward indeed.

Twice over in the parables the servants in per-plexity or sorrow come to their Master. In that of the tares, they relate their discovery of the two kinds of grain that are growing in the field. The Master explains how it has happened, then they ask what they are to do, and He tells them to do nothing, for they will do more harm than good by trying to get rid of the tares out of the field of the world. In another parable, that of the debtors, the servants come with sorrow to tell the Master of the evil conduct of the servant who had been forgiven much, but is now ill-treating one who owes him little. It is well in our service to remember the lessons thus taught, to tell the Master about the evils in the world, or in the Church. In neither case could the servants do anything. How often we try to set things right ourselves when prayer is what is needed.

It is stated by Justin Martyr (born about A.D. 114) that the Lord "was in the habit of working as a carpenter when among men, making *ploughs* and *yokes*." We cannot tell whether this tradition is true, but it is certain that He used both these as symbols in connection with service. "Take My yoke upon you," is the command to those who have lost their burden at His feet, and have received rest from Him. First, He gives the rest of forgiveness, then we find the rest of submission. He removes the heavy burden and gives the light one. Reference is evidently here made to the yoke worn by the oxen, and as so often pointed out, it is *His* yoke, borne by Himself as well as by us. The yoke is "the instrument used to connect oxen for work," and from that original meaning it has come into use for "pairing" or "connecting." In service for the Master we are always to be fellow-labourers with Him, there is no independent service.

Reference is made to the plough in another passage. "No man having put his hand to the plough, and looking back, is fit for the kingdom of God" (Luke ix. 61, 62). The incident which called forth this answer and the words themselves remind us of the call of Elisha. We are told that Elijah found him when he "was ploughing with twelve yoke of oxen before him, and he with the twelfth; and Elijah passed by him, and cast his mantle upon him. And he left the oxen, and ran after Elijah, and said, Let me, I pray thee, kiss my father and my mother, and then I will follow thee." Elisha not only left his plough, but he burnt it to make the fire, and from one yoke of oxen made a feast for the people. He thus renounced the old life altogether.

The words of this man's request were almost identical with those of Elisha, and the disciples had just been speaking of Elijah. Had the Lord in passing by thrown His mantle over the man? Had His Spirit gone forth and called him? Doubtless it was so, and the Lord would remind him, before

he really became a disciple, that there must be no
looking back.   How can a man plough a straight
furrow if he is looking behind him ?   " Let thine
eyes look right on, and let thine eyelids look straight
before thee " (Prov. iv. 25).   The difference between
the two incidents is that Elisha left his plough to
follow Elijah, it was the emblem of the old life.   In
the case of the man who would follow the Lord Jesus
the new service was symbolised by the plough.

The Word of God.—There are a great many lessons
taught in the parables about the Word of God.

Almost the first one recorded in Matthew, that of
the builders on the rock and on the sand, teaches the
importance of *doing* as well as hearing.   This was,
indeed, the purpose of the parable.   The Lord pre-
faced it by saying, " Not every one that saith unto
Me, Lord, Lord, shall enter into the kingdom   of
heaven ; but he that doeth the will of My Father
which is in heaven."   And then He continues, " Therefore, whosoever heareth these sayings of Mine, and
doeth them, I will liken him unto a wise man, which
built his house upon a rock."   We have already
noticed the high claim which the Lord here makes
for His sayings, and that none but God Himself
could insist on such a place being given to His Word
(page 24).   In this passage the Lord Jesus makes
His own sayings of equal importance with His
Father's will.   And we know that they are the
same.   The words proclaim the will, and the will is
that the words should be reverenced and obeyed.
In Luke a little expression is added which is not in
Matthew, " Whosoever *cometh* to me and heareth . . .
and doeth ; " we cannot " do " unless we " come."

The parable of the sower pictures the fourfold
measure of reception given to the Word of God.
The interpretation leaves us no doubt as to what
is the significance of the seed.   In Matthew it is

explained to be the Word of the kingdom, but lest
any should say that the parable refers entirely to a
Jewish dispensation, we are told in Mark that the
seed is the Word, and in Luke the Word of God.
It represents the testimony of God in whatever dispensation it is proclaimed.   In this respect it is
helpful in studying the parables, to make use of a
"harmony of the Gospels," as the comparison often
brings out small differences which are most suggestive.   They are not contradictions, but instances of
selection by inspiration, the various Evangelists being
enabled by the Holy Spirit to recall and to record
such words of our Lord's discourses as He meant
them to use, in keeping with the purpose of the
several Gospels.

The parable of the houses built upon the rock and
on the sand proves the importance of hearing and
doing, and following this there is beautiful progress
in the threefold interpretation of the "good ground"
hearers.   In Matt. xiii. 23, they hear the word and
understand it; in Mark iv. 20, they hear the word
and *receive* it; in Luke viii. 15, having heard the
word, they *keep* it.   The wayside hearers are those
who hear and understand not, for there will be no
fruit if the Word is not understood.   The hearing
of the ear is useless unless the Word also sinks into
the heart.   Spiritual growth is suggested in these
three words, understanding, receiving, and keeping.
After understanding there must be submission to
the Word as expressed by receiving, and this is
to be the continual attitude; the Word is to be
kept.   The good fruit can only be borne by
patience.   The same expressions are used by the
Lord in His prayer in John xvii.   He speaks of
His own having received His words, and having
kept them, and He implies that they had understood
them, for they believed surely what the words taught

(verses 6–8). There is in John xiv. a special blessing promised to the one who keeps His sayings. "If a man love Me, he will keep My words ; and My Father will love him, and We will come unto him, and make Our abode with him." He that heareth and *doeth* builds his house upon the rock ; he that heareth and *keepeth* has the Father and the Son to dwell with him in his house. Faith builds, and love receives into its abode. The preacher says concerning the words of the wise, " It is a pleasant thing if thou keep them within thee," pleasant to the Speaker as well as to the hearer. The last book in the Bible opens with a blessing upon those "that hear . . . and keep those things which are written therein."

There are three things which lead to unfruitfulness in the unprepared soil—the birds of the air, the rock and the thorns which, according to our Lord's explanation, correspond with the power of the devil, the flesh, and the world. It has been pointed out that "throughout the New Testament, if the flesh is opposed to the Spirit, and the world to the Father, the devil is the constant enemy of Christ." We have already seen that all the unfruitful soil was unploughed. While the good ground is prepared by the Spirit for the reception of the seed, the enemy does his best to harden the wayside by the tread of the world so as to make it easy for him to catch away the good seed. In the wayside hearers the heart is made hard from without, the rocky ground is hard within.

The fourfold interpretation of the thorns has been already mentioned. They represent cares or carelessness, sorrow or pleasure, poverty or wealth, anything that fills the heart to the exclusion of God's Word. In the language of John's epistle we might sum them up as "all that is in the world, the lust of the flesh, he lust of the eyes, and the pride of life." The soil is not in itself bad, but in this case it is pre-occupied. The ground that can bring forth a luxuriant crop of thorns would be able, were they removed, to produce a good harvest of corn. An energetic worlding will often make an out-and-out Christian.

The Evangelists also mention three different things which act upon the sprouting seed like scorching sunshine on rootless grain—tribulation or affliction (the same word), persecution and temptation, make the buds of early promise wither and die.

The reasons given for this inability to stand the heat are that in the rocky soil there is *no* depth of earth, *no* moisture, and consequently *no* root. The hindrances here are chiefly negative, while in the thorny ground they are positive, though the result is that there is *no* room.

The secret of such different results lies in the position that the seed is allowed to occupy. It has been well and tersely described thus : " In the first, the seed was *on*, but not *in ;* in the second, it was *on*, and *in*, but not *down ;* in the third, it was *on*, and *in*, and *down*, but not *up ;* and in the fourth, it was *on*, and *in*, and *down*, and *up*."

There are three standards of fruit-bearing in the good ground—thirty-fold, sixty-fold, and a hundredfold—which may perhaps be compared to the understanding, receiving and keeping already referred to. A hundred-fold is large increase, but we have one instance in Gen. xxvi. 12 of a similarly plenteous harvest, when " Isaac sowed . . . and received in the same year an hundred-fold, and the Lord blessed him." It is not therefore an impossible yield when God gives the increase either in the natural or spiritual world. This is the first mention in the Bible of the sowing of seed.

It has sometimes been said that the parable teaches that only a quarter of the seed sown was fruitful. This is not so, however, for in the parable it says nothing about the number of handfuls which fell on the wayside, among thorns, or on rocky soil ; the attention of the skilled sower would naturally be directed to the prepared ground, and the harvest alone would show how much of the grain fell upon the land he had so carefully tilled. Some fell on the pathway leading across the field as he, with generous hand, scattered it abroad, but he would not intentionally sow as much amongst the thorns as upon the furrowed field over which the plough had passed.

In the sowing of the heavenly seed, it is not so easy for the sower to tell the nature of the ground. He cannot always see the thorns or the downtrodden path or the rocks, and so he must scatter the seed everywhere, flinging it as far as his arm can reach.

Supposing, however, that he knows of thorns having possession of the soil, and is sure that the ground has been much trodden down, or that there are rocks beneath the thin covering of earth, is he to stay his hand ? What is the best way of getting rid of these things, and of reclaiming the soil ? How can he uproot the thorns and remove the rock ? Here is a strange paradox, not indeed in the parable itself, for no natural seed has such wonderful properties as the Word of God. While the thorns can and do choke the Word, and the rock prevents it from taking root, the Word can kill the weeds, and is the only agency which will break up or destroy the rock, transforming it into fruitful soil.

The Word will lift "the cares of this world" by speaking precious promises to those who are heavy-laden ; the Word will reveal "the deceitfulness of riches" by offering the true riches ; the Word will show the vanity of the "pleasures of this life" which are but "for a season" by telling of the "pleasures for evermore;" and the Word will substitute new desires for "the lusts of other things." If it is the rock that impedes, the Word can break the hardest heart or soften it by conviction; in fact it must be the plough first to make room for itself as the fruit-bearing seed.

There is in Mark iv. 24 the warning, "Take heed *what* ye hear," and in Luke viii. 18, "Take heed *how* ye hear." The "what" will determine the "how." If we listen to other voices we shall not hear clearly His voice, but if we recognise that we are listening to God's Word we shall hear it with reverence, and strive to obey. The attempt to take away its authority by denying the inspiration of Scripture, must of necessity affect the manner in which attention is given to it. The candle gives the thought of testimony, and if this is to be bright we must be careful about both the "how" and the "what." They are as important to our shining as are the wick and the oil to the lamp.

The first and the last of the series in the thirteenth of Matthew alike have to do with the Word of God. The eighth, that of the householder, teaches the way in which all the truths contained in the preceding parables are to be treated, and it applies not only to them but to all God's Word.

The treasure or treasury is the heart. "A good man out of the good treasure of his heart bringeth forth that which is good; . . . for of the abundance of the heart his mouth speaketh" (Luke vi. 45). As Mr. Spurgeon has expressed it, "That which lies in the well of your thought will come up in the bucket of your speech." The householder brings forth both new and old, the right kind of food at the right time, suiting the meals to the eaters, not giving new when he ought to give old, and not giving only new or only old. Variety of diet is essential for sound health of body, and it is the same with believers as to their spiritual food. To feed only on one kind is not conducive to vigorous growth. Food must also be given with regard to the age of the members of the household, the steward must not give meat to babes or only milk to adults.

In Matt. xxiv. 45 we read of the "faithful and wise servant, whom his lord hath made ruler over his household, to give them meat in due season." They must not be starved one day and surfeited the next.

Several of the parables represent a wrong treatment accorded to the Word. The wicked husbandmen refuse to listen to the messengers who bring before them the demands of the owner of the vineyard, even when the messenger is his own son. Thus they illustrate the conduct of those who reject the claims of God made to men through His Word.

The bidden guests in the parables of the marriage feast and the great supper treat His Word in the same way, but while the husbandmen refuse his lawful and just claims, these despise His gracious invitation. The one shows the sin of disobedience to the Word, the other of neglect of the Word. They made excuse; they made light of it. The manner in which the banqueting halls were at last filled with guests suggests to us the thought that with the command there is given power to come. The lame and blind might indeed have made excuse that they could not come; but the one who gave the invitation brought them to the feast, thus teaching something of the effect of the Word in the power of the Holy Spirit.

The two sons (Matt xxi.) both hear the father's command. One refuses to obey but afterwards repents, the other promises obedience but fails to render it. The latter is just as disobedient as if he had refused from the first, and though his promise of doing his father's will might deceive those who heard it and make them think him a dutiful son, the father could not be satisfied with conduct which so entirely contradicted the promise. It is but another picture of the Pharisee and publican.

In several of these parables there is at first a seeming reception of the Word, a partial admission, but no real result. It is even received joyfully for a time by the stony ground hearers, but the shoots wither; those who are bidden accept the invitation in the first instance, but never come; and in this parable there is a promise of obedience, but no performance. Such conduct is, alas! very common in a so-called Christian country, where many profess to be Christians, but neither submit themselves to the commands or claims of God, nor accept His grace.

In the parables which speak of His return, those who watch are those who believe the truth of the Word, "Behold, I come quickly." He has clearly said in the parable that the servants cannot tell whether His return will be at even, or at midnight, or at the cock-crowing, or in the morning; but knowing that He may return at any moment, the faithful ones are on the look-out all night. They have believed His Word, and this has kept them in the right attitude all through the dark hours. There are some who are very busily hurrying through the house to tell all the servants that this is a mistake, that the Master never meant them to be watching all night, that He cannot be here yet, and that before He comes there will be ample warning. Surely such treatment of His Word must be the very opposite of pleasing to the Master. It is the *evil* servant that takes advantage of His absence and saith, "My lord delayeth his coming."

It was unbelief of His Word that allowed the virgins to go to sleep in the first instance, and now that a midnight cry seems to have gone forth, and believers are beginning to awake, it seems sad indeed that any should try to lull them to sleep again by telling them that He cannot be here yet.

It has been suggested that the pound given to each of the servants in the parable in Luke xix. represents the Word of God. It is evidently something for which all alike are responsible, but the way in which they treat it is different. At the reckoning day, those who have traded with it ascribe their success not to their own ability, but to the pound itself. " Thy pound hath gained." The nobleman says to the wicked servant who has merely tied up the pound in a napkin, " Wherefore gavest thou not my money into the bank, and I at my coming should have required it with interest ? " (R.V.) As we have just seen, the heart is compared to a treasury, and it is probable that the bank here has a similar meaning. Money is put into a bank for two purposes—that it may be kept secure, and that it may bring interest. The Word of God treasured in the heart is safe, we cannot lose it, and none can make us give it up. If only in the head it may easily be taken from us. If abiding in the heart it will continue to produce interest for God. What use are we making of this precious capital entrusted to us by God ? Are we investing it, and what profit is it gaining for ourselves in our lives ? Alas ! that many should literally wrap up their Bibles and make no use of them. The condemnation of those who have thus neglected the pound will be terrible indeed.

Several other parables suggest thoughts about the Word of God. The Pharisee boasted of outward conformity to its commands, but had never understood or acknowledged God's claims.

The blind leaders are those who try to lead others though ignorant of the Word themselves.

In John x. we read that the sheep hear the voice of

the good Shepherd. He has two marks upon His sheep, on the ear, and on the foot. They hear His voice and they follow Him. If this is true of the sheep that follow the Shepherd, the opposite must be true of those that go astray according to Luke xv. The sheep who hear His voice follow ; the sheep who do not listen to the Shepherd go astray.

In the simile of the true vine, the Lord shows that His Word has much to do with fruit-bearing. First, it must cleanse, and then abide in us, if we are to bear much fruit (John xv. 3, 7). In this beautiful passage, so familiar and yet so inexhaustible, He makes His Word synonymous with Himself, and how often are the same things true of both the living Word and the written Word ? In verse 4, He says, " Abide in Me, and I in you ; " in verse 7, He says, " If ye abide in Me, and My words abide in you." If the words abide in the heart He is sure to take up His abode there. He comes with them, He is in them, and cannot be separated from them.

Looking at all these parables together, we have a complete picture of the Word under different aspects.

We have it represented as a rock on which to build ; as seed to bear fruit ; as provision on which to feed ourselves and others ; as a light to be displayed ; and as money with which to trade.

It contains commands to be obeyed, claims to be met, invitations to be accepted, messages to be borne, warnings to be attended to, testimony to be given, directions to be carried out, and calls to be followed.

The honest and good heart which receives the Word is compared to good soil, a lamp or candle, a storehouse or treasury, a bank, a vine-branch.

According to these various figures, the voice of a Father, a Master, a King, a Bridegroom, and a Shepherd may be heard in the Word.

We have brought before us the results of hearing

and doing, of hearing and understanding, of hearing and receiving, and of hearing and keeping; and also the judgment upon rejecting, disobeying, neglecting, and making light of the Word.

Joy.—The secret of true joy is revealed to us in the parables, for we learn from them that there is only one kind which really lasts. That joy is the joy of the Lord, first as felt by Himself, then as shared by His own, and experienced in His presence. There is a passing evanescent joy mentioned in connection with the stony ground hearers, where the Word is at first received with gladness; but the seed which springs up withers, and the joy passes away.

The Lord's joy as the Seeker and Finder is described in Matt. xiii. and in Luke xv. In the first, there is His joy over the treasure found and secured at such a cost, reminding us of the words in Heb. xii. 2, "Who, for the joy that was set before Him, endured the cross, despising the shame." In the second, in the threefold parable, there is His joy over the lost ones which He has recovered. The whole of this chapter abounds with joy, a joy which is so great that it must be shared by the finder's friends, neighbours, and servants; those dear to Him and those near to Him, those on earth, and those in heaven.

There is joy over the fruitful branches in John xv. This, too, is shared joy; it belongs not only to the husbandman, but is enjoyed by the fruit-bearers themselves, for the Lord says, "These things have I spoken unto you, that My joy might remain in you, and that your joy might be full."

Sowers and reapers also rejoice together in John iv. 36–38. The first sowers in this place had been those who had taught the woman of Samaria of the Coming One, so that she could say in spite of her sin, "I know that Messias cometh, which is called Christ." Then the Lord must needs go through

Samaria, that He might both sow and reap, and in Acts viii. we find Peter and John in the same district reaping again with great joy that whereon they bestowed no labour. Another—Philip—had laboured, and they had entered into his labour, but even Philip was reaping as well as sowing, for the ground had already been prepared, and the seed scattered by the many Samaritans of that city who believed on Him.

When He was on earth, there was joy at the bridegroom's voice. The friend of the bridegroom rejoiced greatly in His presence.

There is always fulness of joy in His presence, and the highest reward of service is the "Well done, good and faithful servant . . . enter thou into the joy of thy Lord." Many are the passages which describe that future joy, when His own are presented "faultless before the presence of His glory with exceeding joy," and which surpasses the "joy in the presence of the angels" when the lost one is found.

Though we are allowed to rejoice with Him, these parables teach us that whatever our portion may be, His joy is far, far greater, whether it be the joy of finding or of reaping, over the harvest or over the triumph, at His wedding or at His coronation.

The use of riches.—There is much in the parables about the use of riches, both spiritual and temporal, for the one is symbolised by the other.

The two rich men (Luke xii. 16–21 ; xvi. 19–31) did not use their wealth for others. Of the first it was said, "So is he that layeth up treasure for himself, and is not rich toward God." In the explanation of the parable of the sower, the deceitfulness of riches is one species of thorns. "The ground of a certain rich man brought forth plentifully." He had a large harvest, but the only crop his heart produced was an abundance of thorns. The harvest of his field choked the harvest of his life. The first made him rich as to this world, but the lack of the other prevented him from being "rich toward God."

While this rich man hoarded his possessions, the other spent his wealth upon himself, for he was clothed in purple and fine linen, and fared sumptuously every day.

In contrast to their misuse of their riches we have the good man who out of his good treasure brought forth that which is good (Luke vi. 45), and the householder in Matt. xiii. 52. Riches given by God, whether spiritual treasure, or earthly wealth, must be used for Him and not hoarded.

In connection with the parable of the unjust steward, we have a very important statement, " If ye have not been faithful in that which is another man's, who will give you that which is your own ? " This shows a connection between earthly and heavenly things which is often overlooked. We are stewards of the former, they have only been lent to us, but God counts spiritual blessings as our own. If we are unfaithful in our use of the things thus entrusted to us, if we are not putting out to interest for God our money, our time, our health, our abilities, our opportunities, we are impoverishing ourselves as to the spiritual riches which are really our own.

The parables of the talents and the pounds show how God expects His servants to use what He has given to them, that the capital may bring in good interest for Him.

Thus we have in these parables instances of hoarding, squandering, and wasting, and of using and investing riches.

" In the parable of the rich man and Lazarus we see an indication of a change of dispensation from Old Testament conditions. The teaching doubtless is that the outward circumstances of a man *here* and *now* are no proof that he is a righteous man. This was a needful lesson, because in the Old Testament wealth was promised to the righteous. ' The generation of the upright shall be blessed. Wealth and riches shall be in his house ' (Ps. cxii. 2, 3). The Psalmist said he had never seen the righteous begging bread. All this was to be altered ; it was difficult for a rich man to be saved, and many poor were among God's chosen ones."[1]

Not only was the beggar Lazarus poor, but he was suffering ; he neither enjoyed wealth nor health, and yet he was evidently one on whom God's eye rested with favour—one whom He knew by name. In Old Testament days both poverty and sickness were looked upon as judgments for sin, but the teaching of the New Testament shows that it is not necessarily so now. It is important to notice this difference between the dispensations of law and grace. Failing to recognise it many are confused on the subject of health and sickness. Taking Old Testament Scriptures they try to prove from them that sickness is only sent when there has been definite sin or when the soul is wrong with God. It may be sent on this account, but there is no guarantee of health to God's children now, any more than there is a promise of earthly wealth. Under the old dispensation *earthly* prosperity was the reward of obedience to God, in the new dispensation *heavenly* blessings are ours and the earthly circumstances are often used as means of training, opportunities of bringing forth fruit to God. Their position is wholly changed. Instead of health and wealth being the prizes given to those who run well in the way of God's commandments, they are often now withheld that the competitors may be trained for the racecourse. " Prosperity is the blessing of the Old Testament, adversity the blessing of the

[1] Bible Handbook to the New Testament.

New." And this is well exemplified in the story of Lazarus.

Over-anxiety.—The Lord illustrates from the seeds and flowers the uselessness of over-anxiety either as to our service or as to our own needs. In the little parable of the growing seed in Mark iv. 26–29, He shows that the seed springs, the sower not knowing how ; and that he may take his rest, for he can do nothing towards hurrying on the harvest. This is one of the lessons from the parable, and it is equally vain for us to be over-anxious concerning our service for Him.

In teaching His disciples not to be careful about their own needs He used a similar illustration from the lilies of the field.

Consistency.—The importance of consistency is shown in several parables. There must be no contradiction between our words and our actions, our promises and our performance, as in the parable of the two sons ; between the forgiveness we receive and the treatment we bestow, as in that of the debtors ; there must be consistency between our hearing and doing, as in the houses on the rock and on the sand ; between our root and our fruit, as in the parable of the sower, for it is only as we " take root downward " that we can " bear fruit upward " (see 2 Kings xix. 30).

CHAPTER XVIII

DOUBLE PARABLES

AN interesting and important discovery was made in astronomy when the nature of double stars was revealed. Sir Robert Ball tells us that " It had been in the first instance supposed that the proximity of the two stars forming a double was really only accidental. It was thought that amid the vast host of stars in the heavens, it not unfrequently happened that one star was so nearly behind another that when the two were viewed in a telescope they produced the effect of a double star. . . . Herschel's discovery shows that this explanation will not always answer, but that in many cases we really have two stars close together, and physically connected." [1]

So it is with the parables. It is not merely by accident that many are found close together in the Gospel narrative. There are those which are either double in themselves, or seem naturally to be coupled with others. They are actually connected, and just as the double stars affect each other, and are dependent on one another, so the parables in pairs must be looked at conjointly. To measure the movements of one of these distant suns without taking its companion into consideration has been found impossible, and in many of the pairs of parables it is just as important to study the two single stories in connection with one another as well as separately. In innumerable ways they will be found to supplement

[1] Sir R. S. Ball, " The Story of the Heavens."

each other, and many hidden beauties are brought to light when they are thus compared and contrasted.

In studying the Old Testament we see that there are many double types. There are those which, in order to complete the picture, typify the same person or persons in two different ways. For instance, Isaac and the ram both foreshadowed the Lord Jesus in Gen. xxii. The bird that was slain, and the bird that was let fly (Lev. xiv.), were equally types of Him, as also the two goats offered on the day of atonement. But besides these there are many which for various reasons go in pairs—such as the Red Sea and the Jordan, the wilderness and the land, the tabernacle and the temple, &c. In the same way we have both double parables and pairs of parables.

I. There are those which have two parts, differing as to the persons addressed, the symbolism used, or the people described.

1. The parable of the great feast in Luke xiv. is thus divided, or we may say there is an introduction to the chief parable. The first portion was addressed to the guests, teaching them how to choose their places, then the Lord spoke to the host telling him how to choose his guests, and illustrating it by the parable which showed how He Himself acted.

(2) In the parable of the husbandmen the figure changes at the close. After speaking of the messenger whom the husbandmen rejected, He speaks of the stone which the builders refused—the fact was the same and the rejecters were the same; the change of symbolism repeats the lesson and makes it more emphatic.

(3) In the parable in Luke xix. there are two sets of persons described—the citizens who said, "We will not have this man to reign over us," and the servants. The two portions of the parable are interwoven, for

after speaking of the servants, the Lord goes back to the citizens, and says: "But those mine enemies which would not that I should reign over them, bring hither and slay them before me."

(4) In the story of the marriage supper and great feast, we also have two parts—that which deals with the guests who were bidden and their refusal, and that which tells of the broadcast invitation and of those who were brought in. These two portions mark the change of dispensation.

II. There are some which seem to contain double symbolism. We find in the one parable different emblems which represent the same person or class of persons. The picture would not be complete without the two portions.

(1) In connection with the pictures of our Lord Jesus Christ. In the parable of the husbandmen, He is first the well-beloved Son sent by the Father, and slain by the husbandmen, and then He is the Lord of the vineyard, who, when He "cometh," will judge the husbandmen.

(2) In the parable of the sower, the Lord is Himself the first sower ; but He is also the seed, for we cannot separate between the Incarnate Word and the written Word.

(3) In His utterance to the apostle Peter—" Upon this rock I will build My Church," He represents Himself as the Builder and the Rock.

(4) In John x. He says, "I am the Door," and He also says, "I am the good Shepherd."

In several other cases amongst the representations of men, though the double symbolism may not be so plainly taught, the practical lessons which are commonly drawn from them necessitate this twofold application.

(5) In the parable of the sower, we are represented as hearers by the different kinds of soil ; but having

received the seed into prepared ground, we in our turn become sowers.

(6) In the same way, though it is not mentioned in the parable, those who are sent forth into the highways and hedges to invite to the marriage feast, are in the spiritual counterpart those who have themselves accepted the King's invitation.

(7) In the parable of the tares, the good seed represents the children of the kingdom; but is it not probable that the servants, who in perplexity come to their Master, are also the children of the kingdom under a different aspect?

(8) May we not also see a double picture of those saved by grace in the parable of the good Samaritan? The man who fell among thieves having been rescued, is put into the care of one whom the Deliverer can trust, who is instructed to look after him until his return. It is not stated in the parable, but in our spiritual experience each rescued one in his turn is entrusted with the care of others that have just been brought in.

III. A large group of double parables[1] is naturally formed by those which immediately follow one another, supplementing and explaining each other, or giving different aspects of the same truths. This portion of the study will be found of increasing and absorbing interest, for it brings out in a wonderful way their fulness of teaching and perfection of detail.

There are three, if not four, striking pairs of this description in Matthew xiii. (see pp. 124, 128, 136).

(1) The first couple are alike as to the scene depicted, for both represent a field, and a sower scattering grain.

---

[1] In grouping together these parables, there is necessarily some recapitulation of what is contained in other chapters. See Appendix VII. for Table of Double Parables.

(2) In the second pair the pictures are quite different as to the scene and symbolism, but both tell of rapid spread.

(3) The third pair resemble one another in the fact that in each we hear of the exceeding value of a certain object in the eyes of one who is so anxious to obtain it that he sells all. The treasure was buried in the earth, the pearl sunk at the bottom of the ocean.

(4) We may find another of these adjacent pairs in Matt. xiii. by linking the parable of the tares with that of the treasure hid in the field. It is noticeable that the interpretation of the former does not follow the parable itself. It was not until the stories of the mustard-seed and the leaven had been spoken to the multitude that the disciples, alone with the Master, asked for the explanation, and it is immediately followed by another picture of a field. This surely indicates that the two may be coupled together. The contrast is suggestive. The enemy in the one case has succeeded in sowing the weeds with the wheat. He has done his best to spoil the crop, but nevertheless there will be a harvest of precious grain. The Lord will have His garner filled. He turns from this picture of the enemy's seeming success to tell another story of the same field. The usurper may have taken possession of it, but hidden away beneath the soil is the treasure which rightly belongs to Him who once owned the field. He therefore buys it back again that He may have His treasure. In the parable of the tares there is much to discourage, but in the parable of the treasure there is everything to rejoice. The one gives us a picture of a field from which a harvest is reaped, the other of a field from which a treasure is dug.

(5) There are two parables which represent man as a dwelling place of Satan (Matt. xii. 25–30; 43–45; Luke xi. 21–26). In the one he is overcome by the

Stronger than he, who takes possession, and robs him of his spoil. In the other he is only cast out for a time, but returns with seven others worse than himself. Thus evidently the one supplements the other, teaching us that it is not sufficient for Satan to be cast out, another must come in to abide in his place, whether in the individual or in the nation. Reformation will not do, there must be complete subjugation.

(6) When the Lord is telling of the cost of discipleship, He speaks two parables. Three times in Luke xiv. He repeats the words, he "cannot be My disciple." He is emphasising the solemnity of the decision, and showing that it must be no mere empty profession, but something that will influence the heart's affections (verse 26); the life's conduct (verse 27), and the use of personal possessions (verse 33). The disciples of the Lord Jesus may have to bear separation, suffering and loss for His sake. The two parables illustrate two ways of counting the cost. A man building a tower does not begin till he is sure that he can finish, else he is likely to become a laughing-stock to all who behold. So those who would become His disciples must also count the cost. Many have been afraid to follow lest they should be the laughing-stock of their companions, but the Lord tells us that the only laughter that is to be feared, is that which would be well deserved, if there were profession without reality, a setting out, but a turning back. Some of His audience might have said upon hearing this, "If it be so serious a matter I will not attempt it, I will not become His disciple." How often we hear people excusing themselves by saying they do not make any profession, but this does not exonerate them.

The parable immediately following shows that though it be a solemn thing to become His disciple, there is no other course open to us. If we refuse, are we prepared to meet the King against whom we have rebelled ?   Man by nature is like " a king ready to the battle, for he stretcheth out his hand against God, and strengtheneth himself against the Almighty " (Job xv. 24, 25).   If we do not submit, but decide to fight it out, are we prepared for the consequences of meeting One so strong ?   Our only hope is to send an embassage before it is too late desiring conditions of peace, and the sole opportunity for this is when the mighty King is " yet a great way off," when He has but started against the rebel.   While the parable of the tower shows therefore that we must count the cost of *becoming* His disciple, the parable of the two kings shows the importance of counting the cost of *not* becoming His disciple.   If the first make us hesitate, the second shows that we have no choice.   We must be disciples if we would escape His judgment.   The cost of discipleship may be great, but the cost of refusal will be tremendous.   The one may mean loss of much that is precious here, but the other means loss of all things hereafter.   Paul counted the cost and looking at the credit as well as at the debit side, was able to say " I count all things but loss . . . that I may win Christ."

(7) In Luke xv. and xvi. there are two parables which represent men as wasteful.   The prodigal wasted his substance, the unjust steward his master's goods ; the one did so openly in the far country, and the other, secretly in his master's house.

(8) The two parables in the sixteenth of Luke naturally couple themselves together.   Both represent the abuse of wealth, and they are linked together by the words which come between, and which may be referred alike to the parable of the unjust steward, and to the rich man and Lazarus.   The steward who wasted his master's goods, and the rich man who spent all on himself were each unfaithful " in that which was

least " [1]—earthly riches ; both were stewards of that which was "another man's," for wealth is only lent; both took a place "highly esteemed among men," but their life was an "abomination in the sight of God," and both were serving mammon. It is quite evident that the Lord did not mean to imply that it was possible to make friends of the mammon of unrighteousness, in such a way as to provide for eternal welfare. No one by their use of earthly wealth can buy heaven, though it is equally certain that those who abuse wealth will be robbed of spiritual blessings. The unjust steward was applauded by his earthly master for his shrewdness in preparing for the future, but the rich man with all his wealth had made no such provision for his eternal destiny.

(9) There is evidently a connection between the two parables on prayer in Luke xviii., the one taught *when* to pray, the other *how* to pray. The first represented constant pleading, the second contrite pleading.

(10) In speaking of His sudden return, the Lord makes use of two pictures to illustrate the effect on those who are ready, and on those who are not ready. In the one He comes as an expected bridegroom, in the other as an unexpected thief. Both are night scenes, but how different; in one case the house is brilliantly lighted up, the inmates are all ready to open wide the door. No matter how sudden the arrival, they are all on the look-out for Him, and when He comes all is joy and feasting. In the other picture, the house is in darkness, the inmates sleeping, the doors must be broken open, and One enters who is not expected. He goes away again without their finding out that He has been there, and when they discover it, all is terror, dismay, sorrow, and loss.

[1] In verses 10–12 we may link together the words "least," "unrighteous mammon," and "that which is another man's"; and we may connect in another chain the words "much," "true riches," and "your own."

The pictures are all the more vivid from comparison with one another,

(11) In Matt. xxv. we have two very different parables, but apart from their special dispensational meaning, they both teach something about the time of His absence. That of the virgins shows what we are *not* to do—that of the talents teaches what we *are* to do. We are not to sleep, as do others; we are to trade for the Master, redeeming the time, or buying up the opportunities. In both the judgment falls on those who have done nothing; and no special sins are mentioned in either case.

To these we may add other couplets from the shorter utterances of our Lord, where He links together different symbols to teach truths on the same subject.

(12) Thus in Matt. v. we have His words, " Ye are the salt of the earth," " Ye are the light of the world." Salt and light are very different, but both give aspects of witnessing for God. Light dispels darkness—salt prevents corruption. The presence of His own should have this effect in the world as they testify of Him. Darkness and corruption go together, and the double symbolism adds force to this picture of the world's need, and of His disciples' responsibility.

(13) In contrast to the rich man whom He describes in Luke xii., the Lord bids His hearers consider the ravens and the lilies. The rich man built barns in which to bestow his goods — the ravens have " neither storehouse nor barn." The rich man toiled hard to accumulate his wealth—the lilies toil not, neither do they spin. Yet the ravens are well fed, and the lilies are beautifully clothed. One of these illustrations He takes from the animal, the other from the vegetable kingdom. Man in his higher realm of life may learn many lessons from both.

(14) Twice over, when the Pharisees and scribes asked for a sign from heaven, the Lord answered them by two parables from Nature. The one couple is recorded in Luke xii. 54–56, where He referred to the cloud and to the wind. As we have seen, the cloud which brings the refreshing shower is an emblem of Himself ; the wind that brings the heat is a simile of the Holy Spirit. The one speaks of the Incarnation by which was fulfilled the promise that He whose "favour is as a cloud of the latter rain" should come down "as showers upon the grass." The other reminds us of Pentecost when the Spirit came with the sound of the rushing wind.

The Lord describes the cloud as coming from the west, and the wind as blowing from the south ; both therefore represent a coming in blessing — for He speaks of gentle rain and soft wind. There are storms and hurricanes from the north and east, which symbolise judgment, but these are not spoken of here.

(15) The other pair is mentioned in Matt. xvi. 2–4, and describes the different significance of a red sky whether seen in the evening or morning. "When it is evening, ye say, It will be fair weather ; for the sky is red. And in the morning, It will be foul weather to-day ; for the sky is red and lowering." We may be quite sure that there was a hidden meaning in this, for "without a parable spake He not unto them." Comparing it with the wonderful solar parable which runs through the whole Bible, there is a very beautiful but very solemn lesson to be learnt. The redness of the sky at sunset and at sunrise comes from the sun itself. His sunset was at Calvary, when He who was the Light of the world sank beneath earth's horizon. "Lo, He sets in blood no more." We who by faith have seen that crimson sky and have learnt its meaning know that the morrow will usher in a fair day. "We

expect a bright to-morrow," "a morning without clouds."

But to those who have not by faith seen the sunset of Calvary the morning will have no fair promise. The sky will be red and lowering, the weather will be foul indeed for them, for the morning of His coming will bring a storm of judgment. The red sunset tells of blessing in the morning, but the red sunrise of judgment. This little parable is only given in Matthew; but in Mark, where the interview is referred to, we are told that the Lord sighed deeply in His spirit. Was this merely at the unbelief that desired a sign ? Was it not rather at the thought of that red and lowering sky so full of potents of judgment and doom ? This pair of double parables from Nature speaks to us of His incarnation, and of Pentecost, of His death, and of His coming again. The Pharisees could read the weather forecasts, but had no eyes for these hidden meanings or the spiritual signs which told of His presence, any more than they could understand the only sign which He did give them —that of the prophet Jonah, type of His death and resurrection.

(16) In comparing the old and new dispensations He spoke His double parable of the new cloth in an old garment, and the new wine in old bottles. The two should be kept distinct, or the old garment would be rent, and the old bottles burst. The old garment already had a rent in it—the old dispensation was already in the time of our Lord worn out—and the bottles were only fit to hold the dregs of the old wine. To have tried to pour the new wine into them would have been to waste it, for it would inevitably have been spilt.

In Luke there is a striking addition to these parables, " No man also having drunk old wine straightway desireth new; for he saith, The old is better" (Luke v. 39). The Lord does not here say that the old was really better, but that this was the opinion of the Jews, who rejected the new which He offered to them. They had drunk of the old and would not take the new. We are reminded of the marriage in Cana of Galilee. "When the ruler of the feast had tasted the water that was made wine, and knew not whence it was ; (but the servants which drew the water knew), the governor of the feast called the bridegroom, and saith unto him, Every man at the beginning doth set forth good wine ; and when men have well drunk, then that which is worse ; but thou hast kept the good wine until now." The wine which the Lord Jesus provided was better than the best ; and so the scribes would have found had they been willing to taste it, but they did not desire anything but the old of which they had drunk in the past.

In the light of this little parable we see a fresh meaning in the comment of the Evangelist, "This beginning of miracles did Jesus in Cana of Galilee, and manifested forth His glory." The new wine was the revelation of Himself. This gave it the unrivalled flavour, and truly we can say, "Thou hast kept the good wine until now." But even this will grow better and better till He fully manifests forth His glory, in the day when He Himself will drink it new in the kingdom.

IV. There are some parables which are differently paired in different Gospels. This group is very suggestive as giving an indication that the varying order in the Evangelists' narratives is not accidental, but intentional. In the order as well as in the details related, the writers were inspired by the Spirit, and we should miss much if we had only one Gospel.

(1) In Matt. xiii., as we have seen, the two parables of the sower and the tares naturally link themselves together.

There is not only to be the present harvest from individuals, but a future harvest from the whole field. This is consistent with the characteristics of Matthew's Gospel ; it is the *kingdom aspect* of the scene.

(2) In Mark, however, and Luke, the parable of the sower is followed by the words about the candle, thus giving emphasis to *individual responsibility*. We are to take heed *what* we hear (Mark), and *how* we hear (Luke), that we may bear fruit and shine for God. Both depend on the hearing of God's Word. Fruit-bearing and light-giving are but different similes for the same thing, the one suggests the God-ward and the other the man-ward aspect, for the fruit is specially for Him, while the light is for the world ; fruit-bearing and shining are often linked together in Scripture.

(3) The parable of the growing seed in Mark takes the place of the parable of the tares in Matthew, and we may thus link it also with the parable of the sower. It emphasises the lesson that where the seed is good, the soil good, and a good harvest is expected, *time* and *patience* are required before it can be reaped.

(4) The simile of the candle in another discourse is linked with two other of our Lord's utterances, the one recorded by Matthew, the other by Luke. In the former we have the city and the candle (chap. v. 14, 15) ; the city set on the hill, which *cannot* be hid, the candle set in the candlestick, which *must* not be hid. We might alter the old proverb and say, "Take care of the houses, and the city will take care of itself." If every individual light be shining, if every house be illuminated, the city on the hillside will be seen from afar ; but if every house be dark, the city will not shine.

First there must be light in the individual houses, for those who dwell, and for those who enter therein— for the inhabitants and the visitors ; and when the houses are well lit, then the united shining of the city will give light to the world.

(5) In Luke, the collective aspect of the city set on a hill is omitted. The light of the candle (chap. xi. 33, 34) is contrasted with the light of the eye. The former gives light around, the latter gives light within. We cannot shine for God till we are lighted, and to emphasise this the symbolism is changed; the eye must convey the light to the heart, then we can shine as candles. Beholding must precede shining. The light of the body is the eye, the light of the soul is the eye of the heart. By nature this eye is blinded, and if we are to be lights to lighten others, the scales must fall from our eyes, our eyes must be opened. The parable in Luke explains how the candle is lighted. The eye of the heart is a very wonderful thing, for it not only illuminates, but ignites. Its lens is like a burning-glass. Gathering up the rays of the Sun of Righteousness as they fall upon its surface, it focusses them until the heart itself is set on fire, and the whole man becomes " full of light as when the bright shining of a candle doth give thee light." This is the only way in which God's candles are lit. We cannot pass on the flame from one to another, there must be individual beholding before there can be individual shining. Then, too, our Lord tells us that the eye is to be single. Both eyes are to act together as though there were but one, thus producing a single, well-defined image within ; each eye gazing on the same object, not one looking at the world or at self, and the other at Him. It is only when both are fixed upon His face that the rays will be focussed so as to light the heart, and when this has been ignited, and not till then, it will be possible to " shine for those around." First the light for within, and then the light for without.

Jerusalem cannot shine as a city because the houses of Israel have not been lit up ; they are still in darkness, because the veil is upon their eyes ; and the candles cannot be ignited till this is removed. By-and-by they will look on Him whom they have pierced, and that look will set the city ablaze with light, and then indeed the city set on a hill will be seen by all the world. Linking together the double symbolism of Matthew and Luke, we have first the eye lighting the body—the candle ; then the candle lighting the house ; and lastly the city lighting the world.

(6) The simile of the strait gate is recorded in Matthew and Luke, and in both cases it is contrasted with another gate, or door. In Matt. vii. 13, 14, we read, " Enter ye in at the strait gate ; for wide is the gate, and broad is the way, that leadeth to destruction, and many there be which go in thereat ; because strait is the gate, and narrow is the way, which leadeth unto life ; and few there be that find it."

Here the strait gate is the entrance to the narrow way, and it is contrasted with the *wide* gate that leads to the broad road. The fewness of the travellers on the narrow way is due to the fact that the many choose the wide and easy path.

There is no reference to any difficulty connected with entering in. The exhortation or command is simply, " Enter ye in at the strait gate."

(7) In Luke xiii. 24, 25, in answer to the question of a certain man in the crowd (see pp. 40, 41), the Lord says, " Strive to enter in at the strait gate, for many, I say unto you, will seek to enter in, and shall not be able. When once the Master of the house is risen up, and hath shut to the door, and ye begin to stand without, and to knock at the door, saying, ' Lord, Lord, open unto us.' " Emphasis is here laid upon striving to enter—the Greek word is that from which we take our word to agonise.

Thus there are two kinds of striving for entrance, the one referring to the present and the other to the future. The strait gate is not here contrasted with the wide gate as in Matthew, but with the *shut* door.

Those who strive to enter in at the strait gate now will never have to strive to enter in at the shut door hereafter.

In Matthew the two roads are compared, and this is not so in the passage in Luke ; but the broad road of Matthew leads to the shut door of Luke.

V. Another very evident way in which some of the parables couple themselves together is in the cases where the stories are very similar, but where there are differences as to teaching, details, and audience, &c.

The two parables of the feasts, and the two of the trading of the servants come under this head.

(1) The first couple, that of the marriage feast, (Matthew xxii.), and the great supper (Luke xiv.), has already been considered in connection with the work of the servant in Luke, and the servants in Matthew (see page 56). The marriage feast is planned for the honour of the King and His Son ; the great supper is specially for the feeding of the guests. In this respect the one gives the God-ward and the other the man-ward aspect. In the former, those that were bidden made light of the invitation, as it has been well said, "To refuse to go to the marriage of their King's Son was an act of open rebellion for which no excuse could be offered. For this cause, therefore, the guests made no excuse, they simply would not come." In the other, they all with one consent began to make excuse.

(2) The parables of the pounds and talents have often been compared. They are in many respects very similar, and yet they present so many differences that they are clearly separate parables. The one of the talents in Matthew was addressed to the disciples, that of the pounds in Luke was to the multitude. The former was spoken on the Mount of Olives, the latter

at Jericho. The parable of the pounds was evidently delivered just before His triumphal entry into Jerusalem, while that of the talents was spoken afterwards. In one the amount given to the servants is the same, for the pound is given to each of the ten in Luke ; but in Matthew they receive a different number of talents, according to their several abilities. A pound is valued at £3, 2s. 6d., a talent at £342, 3s. 9d. The servant who has five talents gains five, he who has two gains two more, each having doubled the capital entrusted to them ; but in the pounds, in the first case the one pound produces ten, and in another the one pound gains five. All are alike responsible in Luke, but there is a variety of stewardship in Matthew, and this evidently gives us a key to the distinctive teaching. All of us are responsible to God for certain things, which have been committed to each one alike, but there are also varieties of gifts. The number of talents did not represent varying abilities in the sense in which we use the term a "talented person." They were distributed " to every man according to his several ability." They did not cause that ability, but were given because it existed ; so that if a man had five times the capacity he was given five times the talents.

CHAPTER XIX

DOUBLE PARABLES (*continued*)

VI. A LARGE number of parables may be coupled together on account of the same symbolism recurring either in the main subject or in the details.

(1) We have noticed that there are two which represent men as debtors. In the one in Luke vii. 41–43, the leading thought is the freeness of God's forgiveness, and the love which that forgiveness will inevitably beget.

In the other, in Matt. xviii. 23–35, there is again a picture of His compassion in the remission of the debt, but emphasising the effect it should have on our conduct to others, rather than on our love to Him. The five-hundred-pence and the fifty-pence debtors are equally dependent on the mercy of their creditor, for both have "nothing to pay." The one who thinks he has a smaller debt is just as unable to meet it as the one who acknowledges his great liabilities, but their love is in proportion to their appreciation of their debt. The creditor in both cases represents God Himself.

In the parable recorded by Matthew, there is the indebtedness of a man to God, and the indebtedness of his fellow-men to him. Where God is the creditor, the debt is represented by an enormous sum of money, ten thousand *talents*, which would probably equal between £2,000,000 and £3,000,000. When man is the creditor, and a fellow-man the debtor, the sum owed is *pence*, one hundred of which would amount to between £2 and £3. The difference between our currency and that of the Bible narrative makes us lose sight of the immeasurable difference between the two debts. These two parables supplement one another, and together teach us that Divine forgiveness will beget love to God, and compassion to others.

(2) In two parables there are pictures of rich men who had to leave everything behind them—the rich man and his barns (Luke xii. 16–21), and Dives and Lazarus (Luke xvi. 19–31). The one emphasises the thought of what must be left behind, the other, of what lies ahead. The parable in Luke xvi. carries the picture a stage further than the earlier one ; it shows the man's condition after God has said, " Thou fool ! this night thy soul shall be required of thee."

(3) There are two which give us pictures of travellers who found themselves in difficulties. In that of the good Samaritan (Luke x. 30–37), the man who fell among thieves was going away from Jerusalem, the place of blessing, to Jericho, the place of the curse, and fell in with bad company. In the other (Matt. xv. 14), those who were themselves blind, were led by blind guides. The unfortunate travellers in the two stories are described as wounded by the wayside, or blind in the ditch, and both illustrate the condition of man without Christ. In the one, the misfortune was caused by those who pretended to help, who professed to be guides ; in the other, it was brought about by those who intended to injure. The one parable ends by giving a glimpse of the compassion of the good Samaritan, and we know that the One whom he represents also opens the blind eyes. But the blind man here spoken of was evidently Israel, and the blind leaders the scribes and Pharisees (see John ix. 39–41). Some even of these had their eyes opened, notably the Pharisee, Saul of Tarsus, who, when he had received his sight, both physical

and spiritual (Acts ix. 12–17), was sent forth to open
the eyes of others (xxvi. 18).

(4) The household work of a woman is described in
two parables, as a picture of the true Church and the
professing Church. In Luke xv. the former is by the
light of the Spirit doing her divine work of seeking
that which was lost. In Matt. xiii. the woman is
doing a seemingly harmless thing, but one which was
forbidden in connection with God's types. She was
mixing leaven with three measures of meal, and if the
meal was for God, she was making it such that it
could not be offered on His altar.

(5) One of our Lord's parables is very strikingly
supplemented by the symbolism of Paul. In the
parable of the houses on the rock and the sand we
have two classes of builders, one representing the
saved and the other the lost; and in 1 Cor. iii. another
two classes are described, all of whom are saved and
building on the right foundation. The difference
between those in the parable is as to the foundation,
in the Epistle as to the building. In the Gospels
there is sand instead of stone, in the Epistle wood,
hay, and stubble instead of gold, silver, and precious
stones. In both, the work of one class of builder
is destroyed; the house is overthrown by flood, and
the wrong kind of material is consumed by fire.

(6) Twice over we have brought before us the
rock foundation, and in both cases "that rock was
Christ." In each of them His deity is made prominent (pp. 24, 279). In the parable of the builders He
puts His sayings on an equality with His Father's
will. In the other passage, spoken to Peter, He
evidently referred to His deity. "Thou art the
Christ, the Son of the living God." In both pictures
the rock, therefore, is Himself, though the house is
different. In the one the builder is he who heareth
and *doeth* His sayings, and in the other the Lord

Himself is the builder, and the building is composed of those who hear and *confess* Him. In the one, the house is an individual life, in the other, the house is "the Church, which is His body." ₁In the first the only safe way of building is for a man to dig deep, and be quite sure he is resting on God's Word —on the rock Himself, not on the shifting sands of human hopes and speculations, reasonings, and thoughts. In the second the only foundation on which He builds His Church is Himself, a belief and confession of the divinity of His Person and work. How often this has been clearly explained by many writers, and yet there are still those who believe with Rome that Peter was the foundation. Some think that believers are to be "little stones of help," on which Christ is to build ! Such a foundation—mere gravel—would not be any better than the sand. We want the Rock. The apostle Peter had no doubt as to the Lord's meaning ; and does not for a moment appropriate the words, but is very emphatic as to the Lord Himself being the foundation-stone, and all believers the living stones built upon Him. Paul also asserts, "Other foundation can no man lay than that is laid, which is Jesus Christ ; "—not sand, nor shingle, but solid rock.

(7) Not only does Christ our Lord represent Himself as the foundation-stone, but at the close of the parable of the husbandmen and the vineyard He claims by His quotation from Ps. cxviii. to be the head-stone of the corner. It is clear from the Psalm that this looks forward to the time when the builders will acknowledge Him, and when "He shall bring forth the head-stone thereof with shoutings, crying, Grace, grace unto it. The hands (which) have laid the foundations of this house . . . shall also finish it" (Zech. iv. 7, 9). He is Alpha and Omega, the beginning of the building as in the foundation, the completion as

in the top-stone, whether the house represent Israel as in the above prophecy or the Church. He was the foundation at His first coming, He will be seen to be the head-stone of the corner when He comes again.

(8) Amongst the pictures of the shepherd and the sheep there is a double pair of parables, or they may be viewed as a threefold picture. Luke xv. and John x. naturally link themselves, although the scene is very different. In one the good Shepherd goeth *after* the sheep, and in the other He goeth *before* them. If the sheep will not follow Him He must follow them. It is always one or the other, but how different the condition of the sheep ; for in one it is in danger and difficulty, and in the other it is in safety. Thus the two pictures supplement one another. In Luke the shepherd *seeks* the sheep, but in John he *dies* for them.

(9) Besides these two pictures, we have a double description of the need and danger of the sheep that has gone astray. In both Matt. xii. and Luke xv. the sheep has wandered from the shepherd. In one picture it has fallen into a pit, and must be raised up, and in the other it has strayed into the mountains (Matt. xviii.) and needs to be found. The lost sheep is very often represented as straying from the fold *into* the desert. The parable in Luke says that the shepherd left the ninety and nine in the wilderness.

(10) In connection with Israel's history we notice a couple of parables which speak of the nation under the simile of a fig-tree (Luke xiii. 8, 9, and Matt. xxiv. 32, 33). The second is the sequel to the first. When He sought fruit at the time of His first coming, as shown by parable and miracle, He found none ; but when He comes again the buds will give lace to fruit, and He will not be disappointed.

(11) There are two short parables which speak of food for the household, provided by the wise house-holder or the faithful steward, the one in Matt. xiii. 52, the other in Matt. xxiv. 45. In the former the householder brings out of his store-room things new and old ; in the other the steward provides for his fellow-servants' food in due season. There must be food of the right sort, at the right time.

(12) There is a twofold lesson about things new and old. In the parable just mentioned in Matt. xiii. 52, we see that they should be used *in turn*. But in Matt. ix. 16, 17, Luke v. 36, 39, in the similes of the new cloth and the new wine, we are taught that they must be kept *distinct*.

There are some who see only the new in such passages as Matt. xiii. only the position and history of the Church. There are others who see only the old, the kingdom prophesied in the Old Testament. But we must see the old in the light of the new, and the new in the light of the old.

(13) Two parables speak of festal garments. The wedding garment in Matt. xxii. 11, 12, and the best robe in Luke xv. 22, both tell of God's provision for those who sit at His table ; the one was to be worn in the king's palace, the other in the father's house. Each was provided for those who were to sit down at a feast. The wedding garment was refused, but how gladly must the best robe have been accepted. The prodigal knew his rags were unfit for his father's board, but the other probably thought his might pass in the crowd ; his dress was not as bad as the prodi-gal's, and so he would not take what was provided. He was speechless when the king came in, and all eyes were fixed upon his sorry garb ; the prodigal was, probably, also silent when the father said, "Bring forth the best robe," but how different their feelings ! The one was speechless because of

grace rejected, the other because of grace accepted. (Comp. Joshua's attitude in Zech. iii., see p. 203).

(14) There are two parables which speak of an adversary, and beyond this similarity they seem to differ in almost every respect. But though they are so unlike, the contrast is very suggestive.

The first is the exhortation of our Lord, "Agree with thine adversary quickly, whiles thou art in the way with him ; lest at any time the adversary deliver thee to the judge, and the judge deliver thee to the officer, and thou be cast into prison. Verily, I say unto thee, Thou shalt by no means come out thence, till thou hast paid the uttermost farthing" (Matt. v. 25, 26). The other is the story of the importunate widow who day after day cried to the judge, "Avenge me of mine adversary." In the one it is all-important that the defendant should *not* appear before the judge, there is no hope for him if he does. In the other the woman's great desire is that the judge should go into her case.

The scene represented in the one picture has been well explained. "Here the Lord was apparently alluding to Roman law which He thus recognises as supreme in Judæa. . . . By it the creditor had the right of summoning his debtors to follow him to the magistrate's court. But while they were on the way thither, it was still open to them to settle matters amicably between themselves without the interference of the authorities. If, however, they once crossed the threshold of the court, the power of arrangement was taken out of the hands of both parties, and thenceforth the debt was regarded as a crime to be dealt with by the state, and which could neither be condoned nor compromised. Thus when the summons had once been served, the only opportunity left to the debtor for obtaining a favourable settlement was during the short time occupied by the walk to the court. Each of us comes into this world conceived in sin and shapen in iniquity, and consequently the brand of death is at once set upon us by the violated law of God, which thenceforth becomes our adversary, and leads us along the road of life, our debt continually increasing as we go, until we arrive at the judgment court. Yet so long as we are on the way, there is permission at least to settle the debt, and avoid its terrible penalty, if we can find a means to do so. But if we are once made to cross the threshold of the court, which is death, there is then nothing for us but the inexorable Judge, the officer, and the hopeless prison. For 'it is appointed unto men once to die, but after this the judgment.'

"We cannot compromise with our adversary, therefore all that is due to God must be paid to the last mite. An extension of time men have, indeed, often obtained. When they have now come to the gates of death they have earnestly supplicated for a little longer space, and have promised to pay all, if the Lord would but have patience with them. And not seldom their prayer has been graciously heard, they have been brought up again from the very jaws of Hades to the pleasant light of the sun. But the only result was a hopeless increase of the debt, nor was there any deliverance. No, there is but one way in which we can be quit of our inexorable adversary, and that the Lord could not as yet reveal for He had not yet died."[1]

Thus we may take the adversary in this first incident to represent the law. In that of the poor widow the one upon whom she desires vengeance is an enemy of a different kind. He had probably wrested her inheritance from her, preventing her from enjoying what was rightly hers.

There is a very evident dispensational meaning in

[1] G. H. Pember.

this parable, but if the widow represent Israel, there must also be spiritual teaching in her story. In the first instance, they entered not in because of unbelief, then having entered they failed to take full possession because of enemies in the land, and finally on account of unfaithfulness lost their inheritance. We are "blessed with all spiritual blessings in heavenly places in Christ," all the land is ours, but the enemy has prevented us enjoying what rightly belongs to us. We have to war "against principalities, against powers, against the rulers of the darkness of this world, against spiritual wickedness in heavenly places," as Israel did against the Philistines. Satan tries to make us live in poverty when we might be rich. In this sense, therefore, Israel's experience, as depicted in the story of the widow, may be a lesson for us to cry day and night for deliverance from the enemy who would rob us of our inheritance. The first parable may be taken to describe the position of an unconverted soul in relation to the law of God, while the experience of the widow represents that of God's own people as opposed by sin and Satan.

(15) There are two parables which speak of payment being enforced to the uttermost. The one is in the parable about the adversary just mentioned, the other, the parable of the debtors. In the one the debt might be settled on the road, but if this is delayed and put off till too late the man will be cast into prison till he has paid the last farthing or the last mite. We know that once a man is cast into the prison here spoken of there will be no possibility of his paying his debt. There is only one way of ridding himself of his creditor, and that is shown in the parable of the two debtors. His compassion is the debtor's only hope, and this He is willing to bestow. The parable in Matt. xviii. was evidently not intended to teach that the Lord rescinds His

forgiveness; the debt cancelled by Him can never be brought up against us, for He Himself has paid it, and "whatsoever God doeth, it shall be for ever." "Their sins and iniquities will I remember no more." Many other passages teach us this; and the parable evidently does not contradict it any more than the prayer, "Forgive us our debts, as we forgive our debtors," teaches that we can win forgiveness by forgiveness; but both the prayer and the parable show that in His governmental dealings we cannot expect the token of His pardon, the sense of His favour, unless we forgive others. The fullest explanation of the parable of the debtors, as we have seen, is probably to be found in the dispensational application.

(16) In several parables we have a picture of a shut door in connection with the Lord's return. In Luke xii. 36 the Master is outside, and claims admission from His watching servants; in Luke xiii. 25, and also in the parable of the virgins, the Master is inside, and refuses admission to the hypocrites and mere professors.

(17) There are two pictures of a woman's earnestness, that of the woman in Luke xv., who seeks the lost piece of silver "diligently till she find it," and of the widow in Luke xviii. who importunes the judge until he give her the help she craves. These parables represent a twofold picture of the attitude which the Church ought to take, first, by the power of the Holy Spirit earnestly seeking the lost, and secondly, taking no rest until she has fully entered upon the inheritance that belongs to her. How different would have been the history of the past centuries had she not failed in both these respects! But as the years went on instead of seeking the lost, the Church thought only of her own ease; and like the Israelites of old, she has never taken possession of the land

of promise.   The children of Israel, we are told,
never really owned more than one-fiftieth part of
that which was promised to them, and who can say
that the Church has entered even on this portion of
her glorious heritage.   While both pictures represent
a collective action, there is also an example for every
believer individually.   Whenever we want to act upon
the former parable we must act first upon the latter.
The surest way of finding the lost is to be importunate
in prayer for help.

(18) We have a twofold representation of a king taking account of his servants, which is very striking when
the two sides of the picture are compared together.
In the parable of the debtors (Matt. xviii.) there is
a present reckoning for forgiveness, in the talents
(Matt. xxv.) there is a future reckoning for reward.
The one tells of a debt owed *to* God, the other of
interest earned *for* Him ; the first pictures God's losses
through the sinner, the second tells of His gains.
In the one there are those who have nothing to pay ;
in the other, there are those who have something to
pay.   After He has forgiven what we owe, He entrusts
us with capital which is to bring in profits for Himself ; but there can be no trading till the debt has
been acknowledged and cancelled.   The man who did
nothing with his lord's money and was punished,
was one who had never found out that he was deeply
in his lord's debt, and so had never been forgiven.
God's losses through the sinner involved His giving
up His only begotten Son, who undertook the liability
which we had incurred.   It is possible for this to be
cancelled because of the work of the Son *for* us, it is
possible for the interest to be gained because of the
work of the Spirit *in* us, and *through* us.   Surely He,
who has shown such grace to us, deserves that we
should devote our lives to trading for Him.   Both
sides of the picture are beautifully illustrated in what

we might call the parable epistle, the letter from Paul to Philemon. The runaway slave, Onesimus, had robbed his master, but, said the apostle, in the spirit of the Lord Himself, "If he hath wronged thee, or oweth thee aught, put that on mine account; I, Paul, have written it with mine own hand, I will repay it." The old debt having been cancelled he could say of Onesimus, "which in time past was to thee unprofitable, but now profitable to thee and to me."

(19) There are parables which speak of the Lord's two journeys, His earthward and His heavenward journey. (See page 69.) The good Samaritan "as he journeyed" came where the wounded man was, and this, as we have seen, suggests the Lord's incarnation, when He travelled from the glory to the shame. The parable in Mark xiii. and that in Luke xix. speak of the Lord as a man on a far journey. They tell of His ascension; but in both these it is a return journey. The heavenward journey is not the end, for He is coming back again.

(20) There are two pictures of blind men being led. In the reference to the "blind leaders of the blind," their guides can only lead them astray; but in Luke xiv. the servant brings the blind to the feast. What a different condition is thus depicted. There is no mention of the blind in the corresponding story in Matt. xxii., for it would be too difficult for the servants to lead them. When the Lord brings such to His banqueting-house He always opens their eyes before they sit down to the table, as when Elisha had guided the blinded Syrian host to Samaria and prayed, "Lord, open the eyes of these men that they may see. And the Lord opened their eyes, and they saw." After that, at his command, "they prepared great provision for them" (2 Kings vi. 19–23).

VII. There is still another way in which certain of

the parables link themselves together, viz., by the use of the same expression.

(1) We several times hear the Lord saying, "The last shall be first, and the first shall be last." The words were uttered both before and after the parable of the labourers in the vineyard. In Matt. xix. 30, they are in connection with the hundred-fold reward, which they who had given up anything for His Name's sake should receive. Those despised on this account on earth would be honoured in heaven, those poor for His sake in this world would be rich in the next, the last in men's eyes would thus be first in His; whereas those who had been thought great, and rich, and first, would find themselves last of all. When the same words are repeated at the close of the parable in the following chapter they bear another meaning. He was here warning them of thinking too highly of themselves. They were in danger of this from the very fact that they had given up so much, and if first in their own estimation, because of their renunciation, might still be last in His.

The words are again repeated in Luke xii. 30, where we have the solemn picture of those being shut out who expected to be let in. Perhaps they had taken a first place in the religious world, but yet they were not really first, but last. Instead of ranking high they were shut out altogether. Thus, in Matt. xx. 16, we see those who thought they deserved more than others, receiving the same; and in Luke xiii. 30, we have those who expected to be let in being refused admission.

(2) There is another very similar expression which is repeated in connection with two of the parables: "Whosoever exalteth himself shall be abased"; here it is not the first, last, but the highest, lowest, or the nearest, farthest off. We find the words in Luke

xiv. 11 in connection with the placing of the guests
at the feast, and in Luke xviii. 14 in the story of
the Pharisee and the publican. The guests are described as choosing their places according to their
estimate of themselves. " They are permitted to
assign to themselves just the rank they claim. Only
when the King comes in to take His own place
amongst the guests, He takes it at the *opposite* end
of the table from that which they imagined. Then,
of course, 'the first is last, and the last is first'; and
yet their places are decided by their own self-measure-
ment."[1] Thus exalting themselves they are abased.
They thought to take the places nearest their host;
they find themselves furthest off. The places of
honour will be allotted, and the rewards distributed
at the same time. In the parable of the vineyard the
first were discovered to be last, and the last first,
when the owner began to reckon with his servants.
In the parable of the feast the tables are to
be re-arranged when "He that bade" the guests
"cometh." This, therefore, is future; but even now
it is true that "every one that exalteth himself shall
be abased; and he that humbleth himself shall be
exalted." The publican humbled himself before God
and was exalted immediately, for he went down to his
house justified. In the parable in Luke xiv. those
who took the highest place at the *feast* were pictured
as being abased. In Luke xviii. he who took the
lowest place in the *temple* was exalted. Thus the
words refer in the one case to guests, in the other
to worshippers. The expression is also found in
Matt. xxiii. 12, and it there embraces both parables;
for the Lord charges the Pharisees with loving "the
uppermost rooms at feasts," like those whose conduct
He marked in Luke xiv.; also "the chief seats in the
synagogues" (verse 6), and says "all their works

[1] F. W. Grant, "The Numerical Bible."

they do for to be seen of men" (verse 5), and "for a pretence make long prayer," like the Pharisee described in Luke xviii. In verse 11 the Lord shows that taking the place of the servant is even better than choosing the lowest seat at the table : " He that is greatest among you shall be your servant."

(3) In two parables we have the same entreaty and the same response from the Lord. Twice over we read of those who will one day cry " Lord, Lord, open to us." They are the words of the foolish virgins (Matt. xxv. 11, 12), and the false servants (Luke xiii. 25), shut out in the one case by the bridegroom, in the other by the Master. The fact that He replies to each, "I never knew you," or "I know you not," shows that they were not really His own. Their estimate of their lives might be a very high one. In the parallel passage in Matt. vii. 22 the false professors say, we have "In Thy name done many wonderful works," and He says, "Depart from Me, ye that work iniquity." "Wonderful works" in their own sight but "iniquity" in His ! The foolish virgins in the same way probably thought themselves all right ; they even imagined that their lamps were alight when they had no oil at all.

(4) "Yet a great way off." Within a few verses of one another we have these words twice spoken by our Lord ; they occur in Luke xiv. 32, and also in Luke xv. 20 ; and the two scenes are very beautiful when contrasted with one another. Both suggest distance—the rebel king far off from his suzerain, the son from his father. Reconciliation and peace are needed in each case, and the distance must be done away with. The desire in the one instance seems to come from the rebel king, but in the story of the prodigal it is the father that is most eager. The embassage starts when the mighty monarch is "yet a great way off." There is nothing in the parable in

Luke xiv. to suggest how the embassage is received; this is reserved for the beautiful picture in Luke xv., which reveals the matchless grace of the father's heart, and shows how he is looking out for the rebel.

(5) "With what measure ye mete, it shall be measured to you." We find this saying of our Lord's in Mark iv. 24 and Luke vi. 38, and while the simile is the same the lesson is a double one. In the one case we are told that, having received from God, we are to mete good measure to others, and in proportion as we do this shall receive more from Him. If we hoard it for ourselves we shall receive no more from Him. How true it is in our study of the Word, that if we pass on to others what the Lord has taught us, He pours in fresh supplies. When we find nothing fresh in the Word, is it not sometimes because we are not giving good measure to others? The second passage teaches something else, the measure is to be emptied for others; but here it is not merely God who will fill our treasury for us but those around—"Give, and it shall be given unto you; good measure, pressed down, and shaken together, and running over, shall men give into your bosom" —an abundant return. If we would keep our measures full, we must give, and they will thus be replenished to overflowing from God Himself and from our fellow-men. There is a good deal about weights and measures in Scripture; and while "a just weight is His delight" (Prov. xi. 1), He also loves a generous measure (see page 188).

(6) "He that hath, to him shall be given." These words follow those which we have just been considering (Mark iv. 25), and are found in the corresponding passages in Matthew and Luke after the parable of the sower. They are also used at the close of the parables of the talents and of the pounds.

The talent or the pound was taken from the slothful servant who hid his lord's money, and given to the one who had traded most successfully and had gained ten. By comparing the use of the expression in these two connections, it will be seen that they throw light upon each other. "He that hath not" in the one case is he that hears but does not "understand," "receive," or "keep" the Word; while in the other, it is he who is entrusted with a talent or pound, but makes no use of it—he only "seems to have" it. He that "hath" in this parable is he who trades with what is entrusted to him, and in the parable of the sower, he that not only hears the Word but bears fruit with patience. From thus studying the meaning of the expression in the parables about trading, we can better understand the quotation from Isaiah in Matt. xiii., "By hearing ye shall hear, and shall not understand"; because Israel *would* not hear, they *could* not hear. They did not make use of what God had given them, and so the privilege was taken away.

(7) "Many are called, but few are chosen." These words were spoken at the close of two of the parables—that of the marriage supper in Matt. xxii. 14, and that of the labourers in Matt. xx. 16. The application is not the same in the two cases, and the words seem to bear a somewhat different meaning. In Matt. xxii. many are called to the feast, but some do not respond. There is a call of God which the Puritan writers used to call the effectual call, a call which compels, an invitation which draws. But this is not the call here spoken of. It is rather the call of Prov. i. 24, "Because I have called, and ye refused;" while the effectual call is that in Rom. viii. 28, "Called according to His purpose," or in verse 30, "Whom He did predestinate, them He also called." The one was a call that could be rejected, the other is a call

that is the earnest and guarantee of glory ; for " whom He called, them He also justified, and whom He justified, them He also glorified." The chosen ones were in this case those who were thus called and brought in. The banqueting house in the corresponding parable in Luke, was filled with those who needed to be led in or carried, for the guests were blind and lame ; so that the call that was effectual included bringing to the feast as well as inviting. The servant was told to "compel them to come in."

Many are called to the gospel feast, but some refuse —others are called and also brought, and these are the chosen ones, " Chosen in Him before the foundation of the world."

In the other parable where the words occur, it is not a question of salvation, but of service. Many are called to work in His vineyard, but few are chosen, or choice. "Chosen" here does not seem to refer to election or predestination. It rather looks at the character of their service, whether approved or not. David had many followers, but certain men were "chosen," and that because they were valiant and strong, skilful and mighty. There are many who profess to be God's servants, but their service is not acceptable. They are not choice servants. Paul's ambition was, that in all things he might be accepted, or approved.

VIII. There are still some pairs of parables which have not been included. For instance those which give different aspects of the same subject, but with different symbolism. (Many which are mentioned in Part III. might also come under this heading.)

(1) There are the two well-known parables on importunate prayer (see p. 270) which, coupled together, teach us to continue unceasingly in prayer for our-

selves and in intercession for others. They also
suggest the two great subjects for which we need
constantly to pray—victory for ourselves, and food
for others.

(2) Our Lord tells us that there are two ways in
which men treat useless things. In Matt. v. 13 He
speaks of salt, and says that if it has "lost its savour
it is thenceforth good for nothing, but to be cast out,
and to be trodden under foot of *men*." In John xv. 6
we read, "If a man abide not in Me, he is cast
forth as a branch, and is withered ; and *men* gather
them, and cast them into the fire, and they are
burned." Branches are expected to bear fruit, salt
is expected to have savour, therefore fruitless branches
and savourless salt are useless. In the cases of such
branches and such salt, men would naturally cast
the one into a fire and tread the other under foot.
The words about the salt help to remove the difficulty in those concerning the vine. The passage in
John xv. has often been used as an argument that
those who are saved may be lost. We know that
this is quite contrary to the Lord's teaching elsewhere. He did not say here that *He* would cast
branches into the fire, or that *He* would trample
under foot the salt ; but if those who should be fruit-
bearers were fruitless, and those who should be
witnesses bore no testimony : if the branches yielded
no sweetness for Him, if the salt did nothing to stay
the corruption in the world around, neither was
serving its due purpose.

(3) There are two parables in which the Lord
presses home the truth that there must be reconciliation before it is too late ; in Luke xii. 58, 59,
under the figure of the debtor who is about to be
brought before the magistrate ; and in Luke xiv.
31, 32, under that of the rebel king.

IX. In the parables which have been coupled

together in the preceding pages, it is helpful to notice that several pairs give *collective* and *individual* aspects of truth.

(1) In those that speak of the Rock foundation, the building in Matt. xvi. is corporate ; that in Matt. vii. is individual. Double Parables, Part VI. (6).

(2) We have individuals represented as builders in the parables of the houses on rock and sand, and of the tower ; and the national leaders at the close of the parable of the husbandmen. Part VI. (5).

(3) The harvest in the parable of the sower is reaped from the individual believer, that of the following parable is garnered from the whole field. In the first pair of parables in Matt. xiii., both pictures are made up of individuals ; in the second pair, each gives a collective aspect. Part III. (1).

(4) In the two which represent man as a dwelling-place of Satan, one may be a single captive ; the other is the whole nation. Part III. (5).

(5) In connection with light-giving, the city is composed of a number of houses ; the candle is the light in one of them. Part IV. (4).

(6) In the two pictures of importunate prayer, that of the woman represents collective pleading, while that of the man for his friend is individual intercession. In the three parables about a woman, she always denotes a company rather than a single person, though there is of course teaching for us as individuals as well. The woman in Luke xviii. evidently represents Israel, and she may also typify the Church ; the woman in Luke xv. is evidently the Church seeking for the lost in the power of the Holy Spirit ; and the woman in Matt. xiii. in like manner seems to represent the professing Church. Part VIII. (1).

X. So, too, we may notice how *present* and *future* aspects are linked together.

(1) As to harvests in the parables of the sower and the tares. Part III. (1).

(2) As to two kinds of striving to enter. Part IV. (7).

(3) As to the Master's reckoning with His servants. Part VI. (18).

CONCLUSION

WHAT is to be the outcome of our study of the parables ? If it only make us understand their meaning better, it will have done but little for us ; but if it lead us into the immediate presence of the Lord Himself, we shall have gained much by our meditation. There is not a single parable which may not give us subjects for prayer, praise, or confession, and thus draw us into closer communion with Himself.

It is very important to remember that their Author is *still alive*. These gems in the gospel narrative are not merely interesting relics of Hebrew folk-lore, old-world fables long since obsolete, but living words of the living Lord—messages for us to-day, as truly as they were for those who heard them uttered. As we read the words, we may still hold converse with Him who spake them ; we may have fellowship with Him concerning the things which must shortly come to pass ; and when, like Peter and the other disciples, we cannot understand His meaning, we too may ask Him questions about them. May we study the parables in the presence of Him who spake as never man spake, and who is "the same yesterday, and to-day, and for ever."

Many of them will prompt us to prayer for personal blessings, and praise for individual mercies ; and as by means of others we enter into His mind concerning the time of His absence, we shall be moved to confession not only of our own sins, but of the

failures of the whole Church in its fruitlessness and
unfaithfulness.

If we study Israel's history as set forth in the
parables, this should prompt us to intercede for them
also, and to pray that the fig-tree may speedily again
bud and blossom and bear fruit. He who cursed
can also bless. We should pray, too, that the professing Church may be kept from the sins and doom
that have fallen upon Israel.

Time would fail even to name all the subjects
for prayer that are enfolded in the parables, but
if our eyes have in any measure been opened to
see their riches, a further blessing will be received
by again spreading the list before the Lord, and
taking them one by one to Him in prayer and praise.
As we thus hold closer fellowship with Him about
these word-pictures, we shall learn experimentally one
of His purposes in giving them to us.

Take, for instance, the thirteenth chapter of Matthew
and turn it into prayer. The first and the last of the
parables will suggest personal petitions, and subjects
for praise and confession. We think of the good seed
that has been sown in our hearts through years that
are past. Has it been caught away? Has it fallen
into rocky soil, or been choked by thorns? Are we
still bringing forth thorns which are preventing fruitfulness, or are we bearing fruit to His honour and
glory? If we are indeed good-ground hearers, what
patient labour on His part must have prepared our
hearts for the seed. There is no credit due to us;
we were even reluctant to let go the thorns; the
soil by nature is rocky and thorny, and, if uncared
for by Him, would only be trodden down and hard.
Nothing but His grace could have made it even
capable of receiving the seed. Here, then, is a subject for praise and prayer. Are we bringing forth
thirty-fold or sixty-fold or a hundred-fold? Let us

ask continuously for the hundred-fold which, as in Isaac's case, is always, and only, the result of the blessing of the Lord (Gen. xxvi.).

When we look around us on the field and the house, as we study the three parables of the tares, the mustard-seed, and the leaven, how much cause have we for humiliation and prayer? We need to take the place which Daniel took, and make confession that these sad pictures have been increasingly true of the condition of things since the Lord went away. We can look forward with gladness, as He does, to the Harvest Home, but we must grieve with Him over the presence of the tares, the uselessness of the shrub, and the spread of the leaven.

But while these dark pictures move us to shame, confession, and prayer, our hearts break forth into songs of praise over the next two parables. We wonder at the grace of the Lord Jesus Christ, who though He was rich, for our sakes became poor. We marvel that He should have paid such a price for the field, in order that He might possess the treasure; and we cannot understand what moved Him to sell all that He had to buy the pearl. As we realise that we need a special blessing from Himself to enable us in any measure to enter into His thoughts, like Paul we pray "that the God of our Lord Jesus Christ, the Father of glory, may give unto (us) the spirit of wisdom and revelation in the knowledge of Him: the eyes of (our) understanding being enlightened; that (we) may know what is the hope of His calling, and what the riches of the glory of His inheritance in the saints." When we begin our Christian course, our thoughts are centred on what *we* have, but as He leads us on, we learn to rejoice in *His* portion in Israel, in the Church, and in the world.

How shall we turn the parable of the net into prayer? It is difficult to understand it; we may ask for further light on this as on all the obscurities of the parables. We can remind the Lord that the gospel net is now being cast into the sea of the peoples even before this final separation takes place. We can pray that He who once told His disciples to cast the net on the right side of the vessel, and so guided them that their nets enclosed a great draught of fishes, may direct His fishermen still.

As we look forward to His unfulfilled purposes, we may pray, "Thy kingdom come, Thy will be done in earth, as it is in heaven." Sometimes our study of the parables will lead us to worship like David, when he sat before the Lord bewildered and amazed at the unfolding of His plan, and we shall say, like him, "Do as Thou hast said."

When we read of the judgments that are to be poured out, there is surely much cause for earnest prayer. By-and-by we shall learn to praise too, for as the Psalmist says, "I will praise Thee with uprightness of heart, when I shall have learned Thy righteous judgments." The first Hallelujah in the Bible is in connection with this solemn subject (Ps. civ. 35), and the last in Revelation is the same (chap. xix. 3, 4, 6); and when we fully understand, we too shall find, even in this, cause for adoring praise and worship.

The eighth picture in the thirteenth of Matthew, leads once more to personal praise and prayer—praise for the wonderful unfoldings of Himself that He has given; prayer that like well-instructed scribes concerning the things of the kingdom, we may rightly use what He has entrusted to us, and thus be like the generous householder, bringing out of his treasure things new and old, using our Master's goods for His glory.

There is one prayer especially that covers all the parables. "That I may know Him" will more and more be the longing of our hearts. The study of His portrait, and of the revelation which He gave of Himself in these many pictures, will be one means by which the prayer will not only be prompted but answered; and will be instrumental in helping us to obey the exhortation given through the apostle Peter—"Grow in grace, and in the knowledge of our Lord and Saviour Jesus Christ." The practical teaching, if rightly applied to our hearts and lives, will help us to grow in grace; the study of the portrait will enable us to grow in knowledge of Him.

Throughout the parables we hear His voice saying to us again and again, "Behold, I come quickly." Shall our hearts listen unmoved to His voice, or shall they not rather respond again and again, "Even so, come, Lord Jesus"?

May He use our meditations to this end, bringing us more and more into fellowship with Himself, "looking for that blessed hope, and the glorious appearing of the great God and our Saviour Jesus Christ."

APPENDIX

I.—THE PARABLE OF NIGHT AND DAY

THE parable of night and day, darkness and light, runs through the whole Bible from the beginning of Genesis to the end of Revelation, and under very many forms it is introduced again and again in types, symbols, and parables, in Psalms and prophecies, Gospels and Epistles. What a contrast between the total darkness of Gen. i. 2, and the undimmed light at the close of the Revelation! Between the two we have the development of this wonderful parable from nature.

Like the Gospel parables, it may be viewed in several aspects. First we have personal teaching, such as that drawn from Gen. i. by the apostle Paul in 2 Cor. iv. 6. "It is night in one part of the earth turned away from the sun, and day when the sun shines upon it," and this well illustrates the soul's experience, for it is night or day with us according to our attitude towards the Lord Jesus Christ. Very many passages take up this aspect of the subject.

But the solar parable also speaks of the actual appearances of Him who is so often spoken of as the Sun. A night of darkness was upon the earth (Isa. ix. 2), but "His going forth is prepared as the morning," and Zacharias told how, "through the tender mercy of our God . . . the day spring (*marg.* the sun rising) from on high hath visited us." During the short day of His ministry He was the light of the world in a double sense (John viii. 1 2 ; ix. 4, 5 ; xii. 35, 36, 46, &c.).

Then followed the sunset of Calvary when the paschal Lamb was sacrificed "at the going down of the sun"; now it is night, the night of His absence; but we look forward to the morning of His return.

Many of the prophecies which speak of His coming under the figure of the morning may be first applied to His incar-

337

nation and then to His coming in glory, *e.g.*, 2 Sam. xxiii. 4 ; Hos. vi. 3 ; Isa. lx. 1–3.   In the solar parable, therefore, we have a good illustration of manifold interpretations.

II.—DIVISION

On the opening page of the Bible we are told of the division which had to take place before the earth could become the seat of man's dominion.   The first book in the New Testament teaches us that in order to fit the earth to become the kingdom of " the second Man, the Lord from Heaven," there must be just as marked a separation.   The word " divide " occurs several times in connection with the four opening days of creation.   The first is occupied with division between light and darkness.   " God divided the light from the darkness. And God called the light Day, and the darkness He called Night " (verses 4, 5).

On the second day there was a separation between the waters of heaven and earth.   " God made the firmament, and divided the waters which were . . . above the firmament ; and it was so.   And God called the firmament Heaven " (verses 7, 8).

On the third day the seas took their appointed places and the dry land appeared (verses 9, 10).

On the fourth, God said, " Let there be lights in the firmament of the heaven, to divide the day from the night ; . . . to divide the light from the darkness " (verses 14, 18).   Besides being a record of God's handiwork, the chapter is full of typical teaching, as to what He will do when earth is prepared for the kingdom of the Son of Man.   Light will then be divided from darkness ; night will be separated from day ; the heavenly and earthly will take their right places, and the Sun Himself will be seen.

But not only is this great division prophesied in the beginning of the Old and New Testaments, in type in Genesis, in parable in Matthew ; it is also spoken of in the closing chapters of each—in the prophecy of Malachi and the vision of Revelation.   The last verses of Malachi, both in symbolism as well as in subject, are closely allied to the first announcement of this division by John the Baptist (Matt. iii.), and the last chapter of Revelation shows that the separation is final.

III.—ISAIAH LIII. ILLUSTRATED BY THE PARABLES, AND THE PARABLES EXPLAINED BY ISAIAH LIII.

" Who hath believed our report ? "—

    Those who were bidden would not come. (The feasts.)

" When we shall see Him, there is no beauty that we should desire Him "—

    The father had said, " It may be that they will reverence him when they see him. But when the husbandmen saw him, they reasoned among themselves, saying, This is the heir: come, let us kill him." (The husbandmen.)

" He is despised and rejected of men . . . despised, and we esteemed Him not "—

    The stone which the builders refused. (The cornerstone.)

" He was wounded for our transgressions. He was bruised for our iniquities "—

    This was how, when we had nothing to pay, He could freely forgive our debt. (The debtors.)

" The chastisement of our peace was upon Him "—

    And so the great King could make peace with the rebel. (The two kings.)

" All we like sheep have gone astray . . . and the Lord hath laid on Him the iniquity of us all "—

    The lost sheep. Note the conclusion of the sentence, not (as in the parable)—the good shepherd went after the wanderer. The going after the lost sheep involved bearing the sin, and this was why He said, " The good Shepherd giveth His life for the sheep " (Luke xv. and John x.).

" We have turned every one to his own way "—

    Those that were bidden " went their ways." (The feasts.)

" When thou shalt make His soul an offering for sin, He shall see His seed "—

    The harvest from the corn of wheat. In order to bear much fruit the corn must fall into the ground and die. (The corn of wheat.)

"He shall see of the travail of His soul, and shall be
satisfied "—
Satisfied with the treasure and the pearl which He bought
at such a price. (The treasure and the pearl.)
" By His knowledge "—
The wisdom of the " poor wise man " who delivered the
city. (Solomon's parable, Eccles. ix.)
" Shall My righteous Servant justify many, for He shall bear
their iniquities "—
This explains how the publican could be justified when
he cried, " God be merciful to me a sinner." (The
Pharisee and the publican.)
" He shall divide the spoil with the strong "—
When He enters the palace of the strong man armed,
He spoils his house and " divideth his spoils." (The
strong man.)
" He made intercession for the transgressors "—
As the keeper of the vineyard did for the fig-tree. (The
fig-tree.)

IV.—PETER AND THE PARABLES. (An Outline)

(i.) Two questions that were answered by parables :—
(1) " How oft shall my brother sin against me, and I
forgive him ? till seven times ? " (Matt. xviii.
21). Answered by—
The parables of the debtors. A lesson in
forgiveness (23–35).
(2) " Behold, we have forsaken all, and followed
Thee ; what shall we have therefore ? " (Matt.
xix. 27).
The parable of the labourers in the vineyard.
A lesson as to rewards (Matt. xx. 1–16).
(ii.) Two inquiries as to interpretation—
(1) " Lord, speakest Thou this parable unto us, or
even to all ? " (Luke xii. 41). Prompted by—
The parable of the returning Lord (Luke xii.
35–40), followed by that of the faithful and
unfaithful servants (verses 42, 43). A lesson
on watching.

(2) " Declare unto us this parable " (Matt. xv. 15).

The defiled mouth, uprooted plants and blind leaders (verses 10–20). A warning against formalism.

(iii.) Taking note of an acted parable. The Lord's curse remembered.

The withered fig-tree (Mark xi. 20–26), linked with the parables of the fig-tree.

(iv.) A symbolic utterance addressed to him.

" Thou art Peter (a stone), and upon this rock I will build My Church " (Matt. xvi. 18).

(v.) His twofold commission preceded by two acted parables, the two miraculous draughts of fishes, and linked with the parable of the net.

(vi.) A vision with symbolic meaning.

Acts x. The sheet let down from heaven.

(vii.) His epistles and the parables.

(1) The same questions answered by himself.

" How oft shall I forgive ? " Copy the Example, and " have fervent charity, for charity shall cover the multitude of sins " (1 Pet. ii. 21–23 ; iv. 8).

" What shall we have ? " " All things that pertain unto life and godliness . . . exceeding great and precious promises " (2 Pet. i. 3, 4) ; " an inheritance incorruptible, and undefiled " ; " the end of your faith, even the salvation of your souls " (1 Pet. i. 4, 9) ; " a crown of glory " ; " His eternal glory " (1 Pet. v. 4, 10).

(2) The interpretation understood.

Watchfulness (2 Pet. iii. 1–17).

Defilement (1 Pet. ii. 1), false teachers (2 Pet. ii.).

(3) The acted parable recalled, " neither barren nor unfruitful " (2 Pet. i. 8).

(4) The symbolic utterance shared and explained ; first part shared, " living stones " ; second explained, Christ the foundation (1 Pet. ii. 4, 5, 6).

(5) The commission passed on (1 Pet. v. 2, 3).

(6) The vision remembered, its teaching repeated (Acts x. 34, 1 Pet. i. 1, 17); "without respect of persons"; 1 Pet. i. 16 quoted from Lev. xi., the chapter on the unclean animals.

(7) Parables referred to or quoted from—

1. The corner-stone, or stone of stumbling (1 Pet. ii. 7, 8, and Acts iv. 11). The husbandmen and the corner-stone (Matt. xxi. 42–44).

2. "As sheep going astray" (1 Pet. ii. 25); the flock (v. 2, 3); the shepherd (ii. 25); the enemy (v. 8); the lost sheep (Luke xv.); the good Shepherd (John x., &c.).

3. "Good stewards of the manifold grace of God" (1 Pet. iv. 10); the faithful and wise steward (Luke xii. 42–44).

4. "Mist of darkness" (2 Pet. ii. 17); "outer darkness," in the parables of the man without the wedding garment; the foolish virgins; the unprofitable servant.

5. "A light that shineth in a dark place" (2 Pet. 1, 19), the eye and the candle, "as when the bright shining of a candle doth give thee light" (Luke xi. 33–36).

6. "Where is the promise of His coming?" (2 Pet. iii. 4); "My lord delayeth his coming" (Luke xii. 45).

7. "A thief in the night" (2 Pet. iii. 10); the sleeping servants (Matt. xxiv. 43; Luke xii. 39).

V.—THE SEVEN CHURCHES IN ASIA

We know that there was a church at Ephesus in the time of the apostle Paul, and another at Laodicea (Col. iv. 13, 16); and Ephesus itself is specially connected with the closing days of the beloved disciple. It has been thought by some that the so-called epistle to the Ephesians was the one referred to in the above passage as being addressed to Laodicea, and that it belonged also to a group of churches in its vicinity. It is a well-known fact that in the year A.D. 140, Marcion in giving a list of the epistles which he admitted into the canon, mentions "The epistle to the Ephesians" as "The epistle to the Laodiceans." Dr. Godet gives this explanation :—"When Tychicus left Rome for Asia Minor, he had with him three letters, one to the Colossians, one to Philemon, and this which we call the epistle to the Ephesians. . . . Now Tychicus possessed only one copy of this letter. The apostle intended that he should have as many copies made at Ephesus as he would require, in order that each church should have one addressed to itself. The original letter remains in the archives of the church at Ephesus, just as Tychicus brought it, with no indication to whom it was addressed. In the copies, the blank was filled in according to the destination of each. Marcion found at Laodicea that which bore the name of that church, and he therefore, in all good faith, so catalogued it in his canon. But when subsequently the various churches of Christendom were desirous to possess it, they naturally sent to Ephesus, the great seaport and chief city of that region, for copies. Thus the epistle came to be spoken of throughout Christendom as the epistle to the Ephesians, and the words 'at Ephesus' were added to the superscription, though traces still remain of the original blank left to be filled in. In fact, the words are omitted in the two most ancient manuscripts of the New Testament now in our possession, 'The Vaticanus' and 'The Sinaiticus.'[1]

Is it not possible that the group of churches addressed by Paul is the same as the seven for whom the apostle John received the messages? Even in Paul's lifetime a great declension had taken place, so that he wrote to Timothy, "All they which are in Asia be turned away from me" (2 Tim. i. 15).

It has also been pointed out that the churches which receive the greatest praise from the Lord are those of which even still there remains some trace. Dr. Godet calls attention to this. He says, "Ephesus, Sardis, and Laodicea are now nothing but heaps of ruins, while Smyrna is in possession of many churches of all the Christian creeds; Thyatira numbers more than three hundred houses inhabited by

---

[1] "Studies on the Epistles," by Dr. Godet; see also "The Life of St. Paul," by Conybeare and Howson.

Christians; and in Philadelphia Christian worship is celebrated every Sunday (see Keith on the fulfilment of prophecy)."[1]

VI.—THE DISCIPLES' PRAYER ILLUSTRATED BY THE PARABLES

" Our Father which art in heaven "—

    His Father ·and ours—The Father's heart to His well-beloved Son is shown in the parable of the husbandmen, and to wandering sons in that of the prodigal.

" Hallowed be Thy Name "—

    The husbandmen kept for themselves the fruit which belonged to Him. The dying of the corn of wheat, and the harvest it will bring forth has glorified His Name, and will yet glorify it again (see John xii. 24–28).

" Thy kingdom come "—

    When the wheat has been gathered into the garner, " Then shall the righteous shine forth as the sun in the kingdom of their Father."

" Thy will be done in earth as it is in heaven "—

    Sons who pray thus will not act like the two in the parable in Matt. xxi. of whom He asked, " Whether of the twain did the will of his father?" The one who said " I will not; but afterward repented, and went " could not be said to have done it " as it is in heaven."

" Give us this day our daily bread "—

    A daily portion, not " the portion of goods that falleth to me " all at once, as the prodigal demanded.

" And forgive us our debts, as we forgive our debtors "—

    Our forgiveness is not the ground of His, but the result, as we see in the parable of the debtors; but if we do not forgive He may in His governmental dealings visit our transgressions with chastisement.

" And lead us not into temptation "—

    Let us not be thorny ground or rocky ground hearers, keep us from sleeping like the virgins, or wandering like the sheep.

[1] " New Testament Studies," by F. Godet

" But deliver us from evil (or the evil one) "—

Temptation scorches rootless grain, the evil one catches away that which falls by the wayside. Let the seed fall into good soil that the enemy may not seize it. The strong man can be overcome by the stronger than he, the good Samaritan can deliver the man who falls amongst thieves, the Shepherd can rescue the sheep from the lion, the bear, or the wolf.

" For Thine is the kingdom "—

The nobleman went into the far country to receive the kingdom from his father.

" And the power, and the glory, for ever."

And both of these He has put into the hands of His Son as will be seen when the marriage of the Lamb is come, and when at His return He puts forth His power and reigns in glory.

VII.—COUPLINGS

The following lists of some of the Double Parables have been made in order to show at a glance the way in which, by comparison and contrast, they in many cases supplement one another :—

CHAPTER XVIII., PART III.—*Pairs which follow one another.*

| (1) Seed sown in a field. | The sower. | Four kinds of soil. | The Word the 'seed. | Enemy catches away wheat. |
| | The tares. | Two kinds of seed. | Receivers of the Word, seed. | Enemy sows weeds. |

| (2) Extensive development. | Mustard seed. | Rapid growth. | Outward spread. |
| | Leaven. | Wide diffusion. | Inward spread. |

| (3) Great treasure. | Hidden treasure. | Hidden in field. | Made up of many parts. |
| | The pearl. | Sunk in the sea. | One single object. |

| (4) The field. | The tares. | A sad picture. | A harvest reaped. |
| | The treasure. | A glad picture. | A treasure dug up. |

| (5) Satan's dwelling. | The strong man. | A fight. | A conquest. | Subjection. |
| | The evil spirit. | A house cleaning. | A return. | Reformation. |

| (6) Counting the cost. | The tower. | The cost of becoming a disciple. |
| | The two kings. | The cost of *not* becoming a disciple. |

| (7) Wasteful lives. | The prodigal. | Wasted his substance. | Openly in far country. | Result—want. |
| | The steward. | Wasted his master's goods. | Secretly in master's house. | Result—disgrace. |

| (8) Riches abused. | The steward. | Wasted his master's goods. | Made provision for this life. |
| | The rich man. | Spent his own wealth. | Made no provision for eternity. |

| (9) Lessons on prayer. | The unjust judge. | When to pray. | Constantly. |
| | Pharisee and publican. | How to pray. | Contritely. |

| (10) A sudden return. | The bridegroom. | Expected by faithful servants. | Joy and gladness. |
| | A thief in the night. | Unexpected by hypocrites. | Sorrow and loss. |

| (11) His absence. | The virgins. | A wrong occupation. | Sleeping. |
| | The talents. | The right occupation. | Trading. |

| (12) Witness-bearing. | The salt of the earth. | To prevent corruption. |
| | The light of the world. | To dispel darkness. |

| (13) Taking no thought. | The ravens. | Providing no barns. | Well fed. |
| | The lilies. | Toiling not. | Beautifully clothed. |

| (14) Heavenly blessings. | The cloud. | Brings showers. | The King's favour. | Incarnation. |
| | The wind. | Brings heat. | The Spirit's power. | Pentecost. |

| (15) A red sky. | A crimson sunset. | A fair to-morrow. | Blessing through His death. |
| | A red sunrise. | A stormy morning. | Judgment at His coming. |

| (16) Old and new. | Garments. | Not patched with new cloth. |
| | Bottles. | Not filled with new wine. |

IV.—*Different couplings in different Gospels.*

(1) Sower and tares.	{	Matthew.	The enemy's work	Tries to take away seed. Succeeds in sowing darnel.

(2) Sower and candle.	{	Mark and Luke.	Responsibility for hearing.	Fruit-bearing. Light-giving.

(3) Sower and growing seed.	{	Mark.		If a good harvest be expected it requires patience.

(4) City and candle.	{	Matthew.		Light for the world. Light for the house.

(5) Candle and eye.	{	Luke.		Sheds light around, to inmates and visitors. Gives light within, and ignites the heart.

(6) Strait gate and wide gate.	{	Matthew.	Choosing the road.	Narrow way. Broad road.	Leading to life. Leading to destruction.

(7) Strait gate and shut door.	{	Luke.	Striving to enter.	While yet there is time. When too late.	Present. Future.

V.—*Similar stories with different teaching and spoken under different circumstances.*

(1) Banquets.	{	Marriage feast. Great supper.	Many servants to invite. One servant to bring in.	For the honour of King and His Son. For feasting of guests.

(2) Trading of servants.	{	Talents. Pounds.	Variety of gift. Equal responsibility.	Capital, 5, 2, 1. Capital, 1 each.	Result, 10, 4, 1. Result, 10, 5, 1.

VI.—*Similarity of symbolism or detail.*

(1) Two debtors.	{	Two debtors. King and servants.	500 pence and 50 pence. 10,000 talents and 100 pence.	Men debtors to God. Men debtors and creditors.	Result, love to Him. Forgiveness of others.

(2) Rich men who left all behind.

Rich man and barns.	Emphasises what he left.	Hoarded all for self.
Rich man and Lazarus.	Emphasises where he went.	Spent all for self.

(3) Travellers in difficulties.

Good Samaritan.	A dangerous road.	Injured by enemies.	Wounded by wayside.
Blind leaders.	Dangerous guides.	Pretended friends.	Blind in ditch.

(4) A woman's household work.

Lost silver.	Seeking the lost.	A good work.
Leaven.	Mixing the meal.	Forbidden under certain circumstances.

(5) Two classes of builders.

Houses on rock and sand.	Saved or lost.	Two kinds of foundation.	Flood.
Wood, hay, and stubble.	All saved.	Two kinds of material.	Fire.

(6) The Rock foundation.

House on rock.	Individual.	Man builds.	The Rock, Christ's sayings.
Church on rock.	Collective.	Christ builds.	The Rock, Christ's deity.

(7) Christ the Rock or Stone.

Houses on rock.	The foundation.	Alpha.	His first coming.
Stone which builders rejected.	The head-stone.	Omega.	His return.

(8) The good Shepherd.

John x.	Giving life for sheep.	Goeth before.	Sheep follow Shepherd.
Luke xv.	Seeking the lost.	Goeth after.	Shepherd follows sheep.

(9) The wandering sheep.

Matt. xii. 11, 12.	Fallen into pit.	Laid hold on and lifted out.
,, xviii. 12, 13.	Lost on a mountain.	Found and carried.

(10) The fig-tree.

Unfruitful.	The time of His ministry.	Looking for fruit.
Budding again.	The time of His return.	Finding fruit.

(11) Food for the household.

Matt. xiii. 52.	Things new and old.	Of the right sort.
,, xxiv. 45.	In due season.	At the right time.

(12) Things new and old.

The householder.	To be used in turn.
Garments and bottles.	To be kept distinct.

(13) Festal garments.

Prodigal.	Best robe.	Accepted.	Provision for the Father's house.
Marriage feast.	Wedding garment.	Refused.	For the King's table.

(14). Adversaries.	The adversary. The unjust judge.	Defendant anxious to avoid judge. Anxious to gain his ear.	Accused by adversary. Robbed by adversary.	The adversary the law. Sin or Satan.
(15) The debtor's prison.	Debtors. Adversary.	Payment demanded because he did not pardon his creditor. Payment demanded because he did not make terms in time.		
(16) Shut doors.	Luke xii. 36. Luke xiii. 25 (and Matt. xxv.).	Master outside. Master inside.	Claims admission. Refuses admission.	From watching servants. To hypocrites (to foolish virgins).
(17) A woman's earnestness.	The lost silver. The widow.	Seeking lost. Pleading for help.	The Church's work for others. The Church's need for herself.	
(18) The Master's reckoning.	The debtors. The talents.	Present. Future.	For forgiveness or payment. For reward or punishment.	Losses. Gains.
(19) Two journeys.	Good Samaritan. Nobleman.	As he journeyed. A far journey.	Earthward. Heavenward.	Incarnation. Ascension.
(20) Blind men who were led.	Blind leaders of blind. Great supper.	Led astray. Led to feast.	Blind guides. An infallible Guide.	

VII.—*Coupled together by the repetition of similar phrases.*

(1) First last, and last first.

Matt. xix. 30. ,, xx. 16.	Last in earth's eyes, first in heaven's (Mark x. 31). First in the eyes of self, last in His.		
,, xx. 16. Luke xiii. 30.	Labourers. Household.	Those who thought they deserved more, receiving same as others. Those who expected to be let in, shut out.	

(2) "Whosoever exalteth himself shall be abased."

Luke xiv. 11. ,, xviii. 14.	The feast. Pharisee and publican.	The highest lowest. The nearest furthest.	At the table. In the temple.	As guests. As worshippers

(3) "Lord, Lord, open to us . . . I never knew you."

| Luke xiii. 25, and
Matt. vii. 22, 23.
Matt. xxv. 11, 12. | Household.

Virgins. | Entreaty of false
servants.
Entreaty of foolish
virgins. | Master's answer.

Bridegroom's answer. |

(4) " A great way off."

| Luke xiv. 32.
,, xv. 20. | Two kings.
Prodigal. | Rebel from great king.
The son from father. | Embassage from rebel.
Father running to meet
his son. |

(5) "With what measure ye mete."

| Mark iv. 24.
Luke vi. 38. | A good measure brings more from God.
A good measure brings an overflowing return from others. |

(6) " He that hath to him shall be given."

| Matt. xiii. 12.
(Mark and Luke)
Matt. xxv. 29.
Luke xix. 26. | Sower.

Talents.
Pounds. | Fruit-bearers, or more seed to bear fruit
with.
Traders, or more money to trade with. |

(7) "Many are called but few are chosen."

| Matt. xxii. 14.
Matt. xx. 16. | Marriage feast.
Labourers. | Called to the feast.
Called to service. | Chosen as guests
Acceptable as ser-
vants. |

VIII.—*Different aspects of teaching on the same subject with different symbolism.*

| (1) Importunate
prayer. | The unjust judge.

The three friends. | Widow plead-
ing for self.
Man for his
friend. | The Lord contrasted
with unjust judge.
Unwilling friend. |

| (2) What men do with
useless things. | Salt.
Vine. | Savourless salt.
Fruitless branches. | Trodden under foot.
Cast into the fire. |

| (3) Before it
is too late. | Adversary.

Two kings. | Debtor must settle
with creditor.
Rebel with the great
King. | Debt must be cancelled.

Rebellion must cease. |

VIII.—THINGS NOTED AND QUOTED

" In a sword there's hilt, and back, and edge, but only the edge cuts.   In an instrument there's wood, and brass, and belly, and frets, and strings, but only the strings do make the melody.   So there are many passages in parabolic Scriptures subservient to the main scope, which must only be understood with tendency and reference thereunto.   The scope of a parable is the key of a parable."—FRANCIS ROBERTS, 1657.

The Candlestick.—"The brighter the light the less men think of the lamp."

"What hides or chokes the light?   The various things of which our Lord speaks may all be typical.   There is the *bushel* of *business*, worldly wealth or covetousness ; the *bed* of *ease*, sloth or self-indulgence ; the *vessel* of *daily household work*, the *secret place* (cellar R.V.) of *cowardice* which shrinks from an open confession of Christ, or of exclusiveness which seeks to shut out from gospel privileges all who differ from us."—L. M. MOOR.

The House upon the Rock.—" Bind your building to the rock.   A house will not stand merely because it is *on* the rock, you must get its foundation *into* the rock.   The house must take a grip of the rock and the rock must grasp the house."—C. H. SPURGEON.

Thorns.—" Grace is an exotic, thorns are indigenous."— C. H. SPURGEON.

The Labourers and the Prodigal (Matt. xx.).—" There is only One who has really deserved the whole day's pay, and only One therefore who has the right to murmur.   But instead of doing so He came to make it possible for sinners to be saved by grace.   'It is My will to give unto this last even as unto Thee' (verse 14).   God gives to the sinner that believes in Jesus even as to Him.   (Luke xv.) There was only One who could say, 'Neither transgressed I at any time Thy commandment'; and of whom verse 31 was true: 'Son, Thou art ever with Me, and all that I have is Thine'; but so far from murmuring at the reception of the prodigal, He was exposed to their murmuring."—Rev. HENRY BROOKE.

The Marriage Feast.—" All things are ready, come." " It is God's habit to have all things ready. . . . God's thoughts go before man's comings."

" The king's wedding robes were much better than his subjects' best suits. It was a grand sight to see so many all in one royal livery, every guest wearing the uniform of mercy."— C. H. Spurgeon.

The Talents.—" The deposit itself increases by wise use of it ; the sphere of service grows larger as we serve. . . . The man who hides his lord's money in the ground is not the one who has received five talents, or even the man who has received but two. . . . It is the little gift which tends to be despised as little, to the great injury of the people and cause of Christ. For thus the mass of Christians almost drop out of responsibility, drop into inactivity more or less complete. . . . How necessary to remember that ' much more they that are feeble are necessary.' . . . Suppose we have but one talent, every day's believing use of it will carry us on some way towards two. We are not shut up within the limits of God's first gift. We may shut *ourselves* up ; and by hiding our talent in the earth, both lose what we have and the capacity for gaining more."—F. W. Grant.

" Well done, thou good and faithful servant." " Good by the blood of the Lamb, faithful by the Spirit's grace."— W. Lincoln.

" *Ask, and it shall be given you* "—

" We ask for what we wish,
We seek for what we miss,
We knock for that from which we are shut out."

The Good Samaritan—

Luke represents men as		half dead.	Chap. x. 30.
John	„	„	wholly dead.	Chap. v. 25.
Numbers	„	„	dying.	Chap. xxi.
Romans	„	„	living in sin.	Chap. vi.
Ephesians	„	„	dead in sins.	Chap. ii.

Luke xv.—Keywords, *lost and found*—

The Lost Sheep.	*The Lost Silver.*	*The Lost Son.*
One out of a hundred.	One out of ten.	One of two.
Lost foolishly.	Unconsciously.	Deliberately.
Only at a distance	In the dust and dirt.	Actually degraded and debased.

The Prodigal Son.—His career (verse 13); his conduct (verse 13); his condition (verse 14); his conviction (verse 17); his contrition (verse 18); his confession (verse 21); his conversion (verse 23).

Verse 19, " Make me as one of thy hired servants," would have only been " the spirit of bondage again to fear;" verse 24 is " the spirit of adoption."—F. C. BLAND.

Verse 20, " The only time in the whole Bible where God is represented as being in a hurry."—J. N. D.

" Slow are the steps of repentance, but swift are the feet of forgiveness. God can run where we can scarcely limp, and if we are limping towards Him, He will run towards us. These kisses were given in a hurry; the story is narrated in a way that almost makes us realise that such was the case; there is a sense of haste in the very wording of it. His father ' ran, and fell on his neck and kissed him '—kissed him eagerly, he did not delay a moment, for though he was out of breath he was not out of love . . . If you get your Father's many kisses, you will not mind your elder brother being a little hard upon you . . . your Father's kisses will make you forget your brother's frowns."—C. H. SPURGEON.

" Then came his father out and entreated him " (verse 28). " The grace of God for the Pharisee. The Pharisee's opinion of *himself*, " Lo, these many years do I serve thee, neither transgressed I at any time thy commandment " (verse 29)— His opinion of his *father*, " Thou never gavest me a kid," &c. —His opinion of his *brother*, " This thy son."

The Pharisee and the Publican.—" The prayer of the publican is admirable for its fulness of meaning. An expositor calls it *a holy telegram*, and certainly it is so compact and so condensed, so free from superfluous words, that it is

worthy to be called by that name . . . The prayer so pleased
the Lord Jesus Christ, who heard it, that He condescended
to become a portrait painter, and took a sketch of the
petitioner. . . . Luke, who, according to tradition, was
something of an artist as well as a physician, takes great care
to place this picture in the national portrait gallery of men
saved by sovereign grace. . . .

" If you want to know how to behave yourselves as penitents,
be penitents. The best rubrics of worship are those which
are written on broken hearts. . . . Grace in the heart is the
best ' master of the ceremonies.' He who prays with his
heart will not much err with foot, and hand, and head."—
C. H. SPURGEON.

The Pounds.—" I confess I never thoroughly saw the meaning of this parable till I was directed by an eminent expositor
to a passage in Josephus, which, if it be not the key of it, is a
wonderfully close example of a class of facts which, no doubt,
often occurred in the Roman Empire in our Saviour's day.
Herod, you know, was king over Judæa; but he was only a
subordinate king under the Roman Emperor. Cæsar at
Rome made and unmade kings at his pleasure. When Herod
died he was followed by his son Archelaus, of whom we read
in Matthew's account of our Lord's infancy that when Joseph
heard that Archelaus was king in Judæa in the room of his
father Herod, he was afraid to go thither. This Archelaus
had no right to the throne till he obtained the sanction of
Cæsar, and therefore he took ship with certain attendants,
and went to Rome, which in those days was a far country,
that he might receive the kingdom and return. While he was
on the way, his citizens, who hated him, sent an ambassage
after him (so has the Revised Version correctly worded it);
and this ambassage bore this message to Cæsar:—' We will
not that this man reign over us.' The messengers represented
to Cæsar that Archelaus was not fit to be king of the Jews.
Certain of the pleadings are recorded in Josephus, and they
show that barristers nineteen hundred years ago pleaded in
much the same style as their brethren of to-day. The people
were weary of the Herods, and preferred anything to their
cruel rule. They even asked that Judæa might become a
Roman province, and be joined to Syria, rather than they

should remain under the hated yoke of the Idumean tyrants. It is evident that in the case of Archelaus his citizens hated him, and said, ' We will not have this man to reign over us.' It pleased Cæsar to divide the kingdom, and to put Archelaus on the throne as ethnarch, or a ruler with less power than a king. When he returned, he took fierce revenge upon those who had opposed him, and rewarded his faithful adherents most liberally. This story of what had been done thirty years before would, no doubt, rise up in the recollection of the people when Jesus spoke, for Archelaus had built a palace for himself very near to Jericho, and it may be that under the walls of that palace the Saviour used the event as the basis of this parable. Those who lived in our Lord's day must have understood his allusions to current facts much better than we do who live nineteen centuries later. The providence of God provided that observant Jew, Josephus, to store up much valuable information for us. Read the passage in his history, and you will see that even the details tally with this parable."—C. H. SPURGEON.

INDEX TO PARABLES

1. Adversary, The; Israel's opportunity, 152, 153; payment required, 161; compared with Luke xviii., 317–319; with Luke xiv., 329; with Psa. ii., 209, 210.
2. Blind leaders of blind, The; Israel's leaders, 151; doing without the Word, 287; compared with good Samaritan, 312; with great supper, 322.
3. Candle, The; Matthew and Luke compared, 53; following sower, 306; city and candle, 306; candle and eye, 307, 308.
4. Children in market place, The, 66.
5. City set on a hill, The; see above, 3; a figure of Jerusalem, 166.
6. Cloud and wind, The; the Son and Spirit, 61, 62; blindness of Israel, 151; signs from Heaven, 303.
7. Corn of wheat, The; in response to request, 42, 43; His death, 67, 68; the harvest, 127.
8. Corner stone, The; judgment, 95, 161; compared with foundation, 314, 315.
9. Debtors, The; spoken to an individual, 3; at feast, 47; answered a thought, 25, 48; compared with King and Servants, 54, 311, 312; spiritual bankruptcy, 228.
10. Fig-tree, The barren; Father and Son, 57–59; His ministry, 66 unfruitfulness of Israel, 153; intercession, 153, 274; the second offer, 153; tree cut down, 162; compared with budding fig-tree, 315; with cursing of fig-tree, 224, 225 individual and collective lessons, 168.
11. Fig-tree, The budding; see above, 10; Matthew and Luke 52, 53; fresh signs of life, 163, 164.
12. Friends, The three; in answer to request, 41; importunate prayer, 270, 271, 328, 329.
13. Household, The; rewards, 92; joy at Bridegroom's return, 97; two kinds of servants, 207, 208; service, 275; effect of Word, 284, 285; a thief in the night, 83, 84, 301; shut doors, 320; last first, 323; Lord, Lord, open, 325.[1]
14. Householder, The; eighth parable in Matthew xiii., 121, 122, 143, 144; stewards of the mysteries, 247; things new and old, 284, 285, 316.

---

1 Several short parables about the household are here included

15. Houses on rock and sand, The ; Deity claimed, 24, 279; houses, 31, 32; the wall in Ezek. xiii., 202, 203 ; illustrated by Psalms, 211 ; by Proverbs, 217 ; Paul's simile, 243, 244; hearing and doing the Word, 279 ; consistency required, 293 ; the foundation and head-stone, 171, 314, 315.

16. Husbandmen, The ; partially understood, 4, 209; manifold interpretations, 19, 20 ; the Jehovah of the Old Testament, 24; followed question, 37 ; Cæsar's penny, 38, 152 ; far off, 52 ; Father and Son, 57, 58 ; incarnation, 64 ; rejection and death, 67; sending of prophets, 148–150, 155 ; rebels judged, 95, 96; present teaching, 168 ; vine of Old Testament, 171, 172 ; Joseph's history, 192 ; Naboth's vineyard, 197, 198.

17. King and His servants, The ; Israel's jealousy, 159 ; judgment, 161 ; consistency required, 293 ; compared with debtors, 311, 312; with adversary, 319, 320; with talents, 321, 323.

18. Kings, The two; far off, 51 ; ambassadors for Christ, 246, 247 ; compared with tower, 299, 300 ; with adversary, 325, 326.

19. Labourers in field, The, 97, 276, 277.

20. Labourers in the vineyard, The ; in answer to a question, 40 ; rewards, 97 ; covenant of works, 160, 161 ; service, 276; first, last, 324 ; many called, 327, 328.

21. Leaven, The, 119, 120, 130–134 ; compared with mustard seed, 128, 134, 135, 298; with treasure, 145, 146; the ephah in Zech. v., 203, 204 ; explained by Paul, 234, 235 ; compared with lost silver, 313.

22. Luke xv.; the murmuring of the Pharisees, 44, 46 ; the Trinity, 55, 56 ; the Lord's joy, 289.

23. Man on a far journey, The ; the Lord's absence, 70; His return, 83; watching, 211, 219; compared with good Samaritan, 322.

24. Marriage feast, The ; for honour of king's son, 56, 61 ; compared with great supper, 56, 309; division, 85, 88 ; a second invitation, 154 ; destruction of Jerusalem, 155, 161 ; setting aside of Israel, 156 ; the city invited, 166; a bidden guest, 202 ; wisdom's feast, 217, 218 ; the invitation refused, 218 ; the king's eye, 219; the marriage, 210, 211, 267, 268 ; service, 275 ; a seeming reception, 286; double symbolism, 296, 297 ; the wedding garment and best robe, 316 ; many called, 327, 328.

25. Mustard seed, The, 119, 129, 130 ; compared with the leaven, 128, 134, 135, 298 ; with the pearl, 145.

26. Net, The, 141–143 ; separation, 85, 88 ; compared with tares, 144, 145; angels' work, 145, 147 ; draughts of fishes, 224.

27. Old and new cloth and bottles, 304, 305 ; Matthew and Luke, 54 ; things new and old, 316.

28. Pearl of great price, The, 137–139 ; incarnation, 65 ; compared with treasure, 135–137, 141, 298 ; with mustard seed, 145 ; the sea, 146, 147.

29. Pharisee and the publican, The ; the Judge and Justifier, 25 ;

purpose mentioned, 48 ; afar off, 52, 227, 228; Zacchæus, 227, 228 ; prayer, 271 ; outward conformity to Word, 287 ; compared with unjust judge, 301 ; whoso exalteth himself, 323–325.

30. Physician, The, 35 ; an evil disease, 216 ; diseases, 222, 223.

31. Pounds, The ; purpose mentioned, 49 ; far off, 52 ; His ascension, 69; His absence, 70, 74, 75 ; compared with talents, 71, 74–76, 309, 310 ; the message sent after Him, 156, 157 ; rebels slain, 162 ; the city rebelling, 166 ; the pound, a simile of the Word, 287 ; trading with riches, 291 ; two parts, 295, 296 ; he that hath, 326, 327 ; historical incident, 354, 355.

32. Prodigal son, The ; see above, 22 ; a great way off, 51 ; the father's heart, 55 ; jealousy, 160 ; Joshua's clothing, 203 ; spiritual bankruptcy, 228, 229 ; prayer, 272, 273 ; compared with unjust steward, 300 ; best robe and wedding garment, 316.

33. Ravens and lilies, The; following rich man and barns, 42, 302 ; over-anxiety unnecessary, 293.

34. Red skies, 303, 304.

35. Rich man and his barns, The ; see above, 33 ; in response to request, 41, 42 ; compared with rich man in Luke xvi., 290, 291, 312

36. Rich man and Lazarus, The ; see above, 35 ; The derision of the Pharisees, 46, 47 ; Israel's final doom, 162, 163 ; the Syrophœnician woman's crumb, 226 ; Lazarus, 226, 227 ; prayer too late, 273 ; compared with householder, 291 ; change of dispensation, 291, 292.

37. Rock, On this ; the foundation, 171, 211, 243, 245 ; double symbolism, 296 ; compared with corner-stone, 314, 315.

38. Salt and light, 302 ; salt in Old Testament, 176–178 ; savourless salt and fruitless branches, 329.

39. Samaritan, The good ; in answer to question, 36, 37 ; incarnation, 65 ; the Lord's absence, 72, 74 ; double symbolism, 297; compared with blind leaders, 312 ; two journeys, 69, 322.

40. Seed, The growing ; peculiar to Mark, 49 ; His absence, 71 ; the harvest, 97 ; following sower, 306 ; compared with 1 Cor. xv., 240 ; over-anxiety unnecessary, 293.

41. Sheep and the goats, The ; separation, 84–88 ; reward, 93, 94 ; David, the reigning shepherd, 206 ; the key in Rev. vii., 260, 261.

42. Sheep in pit, The ; following miracle, 225, 226 ; compared with lost sheep, 315.

43. Sheep, The lost ; see above, 22 and 42 ; lost sheep in Old Testament, 188–191, 210 ; compared with John x.

44. Shepherd, The good ; the Father and the Son, 60 ; His death, 68 ; following incident of blind man, 44, 226 ; leading out from Judaism, 157–159 ; shepherds in the Old Testament, 204–206; Shepherd Psalms, 207, 210 ; hearing the Shepherd's

voice, 287, 288 ; double symbolism, 296; compared with Luke xv., 315.

45. Silver, The lost piece of, 55 ; compared with the leaven, 313; with unjust judge, 320, 321.

46. Sons, The two ; great profession of Israel, 151 ; two ways of hearing, 285, 286 ; consistency required, 293.

47. Sower, The ; detailed interpretation, 10 ; successive interpretations, 11, 16 ; characteristics of the Gospels, 54, 305, 306 ; His life and ministry, 67, 104 ; key to the change of dispensation, 106, 123 ; compared with the tares, 124, 297 ; with the householder, 121, 144 ; sowing and reaping in the Proverbs, 220 ; in the Epistles, 239–243 ; the Epistles to the seven churches with Matt. xiii., 258, 259 ; service, 275 ; hearing the Word, and its hindrances, 280, 284 ; double symbolism, 296; he that hath, 326, 327.

48. Steward, The ; service, 275 ; compared with householder, 284, 285, 316.

49. Strait Gate, The; in answer to a question, 40, 41 ; Matthew and Luke, 308, 309 ; shut doors, 323.

50. Strong man, The ; an accusation, 43; reception of antichrist accounted for, 161 ; preceded by a miracle, 225 ; compared with unclean spirit, 245, 298, 299.

51. Supper, The great ; see above, 24 ; spoken at a feast, 48 ; His absence, 71, 75 ; a second invitation, 154, 155; setting aside of Israel, 156 ; the servant, 56, 194 ; the man with the inkhorn, 200–202 ; taking a low place, 218 ; service, 275 ; the Word, 285 ; two parts, 295.

52. Talents, The ; see above, 31 ; His absence, 70, 74, 75 ; rewards, 92 ; service, 275 ; compared with ten virgins, 302 ; with king and his servants, 321.

53. Tares, The, 124–128 ; details explained, 10 ; separation, 85–87; harvest, 96 ; compared with sower, 124, 141, 297 ; with net, 144 ; with leaven, 146; the enemy's work, 147 ; angels' work, 147 ; sheaves and shining, 193, 194; double symbolism, 297; with treasure, 298; first-fruits and harvest, 262.

54. Tower, The ; compared with the two kings, 299, 300.

55. Treasure, The hidden; incarnation, 65 ; various views, 140; compared with pearl, 135–137, 141 ; with leaven, 145, 146; with householder, 146; Jeremiah's field, 198–200 ; the opening of the title-deeds, 259, 260; the Lord's joy, 289.

56. Unclean spirit, The ; houses, 31 ; Matthew's addition, 53 ; change of dispensation, 123; reformation under John, 150 ; individual and collective lessons, 168 ; contrasted with God's dwelling-place, 245 ; with the strong man, 298, 299.

57. Uncleanness ; two questions, 36 ; Solomon's parable, 219, 220; remembered by Peter, 341.

58. Unjust judge, The ; spiritual and dispensational teaching intended, 16 ; purpose mentioned, 48 ; Israel's sorrows avenged, 164; the city, 166; a widow's cry, 198; the adversary in Rev., 261; compared with the three friends,

270, 328, 329 ; with the Pharisee and the publican, 301 ; with the adversary, 317–319 ; with the lost silver, 320.

59. Unjust steward, The ; wrong use of riches, 291 ; compared with prodigal, 300 ; with rich man and Lazarus, 300, 301.

60. Vine, The true ; the Father and the Son, 57, 58; with prophecies, 173; clean through the Word, 288 ; the Lord's joy, 289; compared with the savourless salt, 329.

61. Virgins, The ten ; His absence, 73, 74, 75 ; the awakening, 80–82 ; not a divided rapture, 82, 83 ; separation, 85, 89 ; prayer too late, 274; compared with talents, 302 ; oil in the Old Testament, 174, 175 ; shut doors, 320; Lord, Lord, open to us, 325.

INDEX

ACCEPTANCE. Three kinds of, 32.
Acts of the Apostles, The, 153, 233.
Adoption, 252, 253.
Ambassadors for Christ, 246, 247.
Angels' work, 142, 145, 147.
Antichrist, 114, 161, 165, 261.
Appetite, A good, 214–216.
Ascension. *See* Lord Jesus.
Asia, Seven churches in, 255–259, 342–344.
Athaliah, 195, 196.
Attributes, 25, 26.
Author of the parables, 10, 55, 332.

BABYLON, 115, 264–267.
Best robe, 316.
Blind led, 31?, 322.
   „   man cast out, 44, 157, 226.
Blindness of Israel, 3, 4, 151.
Builders and buildings, 31, 32, 217, 218, 243–245.

CANA in Galilee, 230, 231, 305.
Change of dispensation, 100, 102, 104, 105, 123, 124.
   „   of symbolism, 173, 236, 237.
Chronological sequence, 118, 119, 178–180, 256, 257.
City, Israel a, 166, 307, 308.
   „   The guilty, 186, 187.
   „   The little, 212, 213.
Clean and unclean animals, 141, 142, 180–183.
Consistency, 293.

DAVID, the reigning shepherd, 113, 206.
Deity of the Lord Jesus, 8, 10, 23, 25, 279.
Demoniac healed, 231, 232.
Details interpreted by the Lord, 10.
   „   having various meanings, 11.
Devil cast out, 25, 43, 225.
Disease, An evil, 216.
Diseases, 222, 223.
Dispensational meaning of miracles, 230–232.
   „   teaching, 116, 117, 167.
Division between evil and good, 85–91, 338.
Doors in John x., 157–159.
   „   Shut, 320.
Double symbolism, 192, 193, 296, 297.
Dreams, 192–194.

EPHAH, 132.
   „   of Zechariah, 203, 204, 264, 265.
Esther's feast, 202.
Ezekiel's visions, 200–202, 203, 206.

FAITH as mustard seed, 130.
Father and Son, The, 57, 208, 209.
   „   The, as Speaker of the parables, 55.
Father's love, The, 60, 61.
Feasts, Parables spoken at, 47, 48.

Feasts of Lev. xxiii., 134, 178–180.
Field sown and reaped, The, 119, 124, 125, 144.
„ purchased, The, 137, 138, 259, 260.
„ Jeremiah's, 198–200.
Fig-tree cursed, The, 165.
„ in Old Testament, The, 163, 172.
Figures of the Lord, 27, 28.
„ of men, 29, 30.
First-fruits, The, 96, 127, 178, 180, 261, 262.
Fishes, Clean and unclean, 141–143
„ Miraculous draughts of, 224, 231.
Food for the household, 121, 143, 144, 284, 285, 316.
Foundations, 244, 245, 313, 315.
Fruit-bearing, 153, 154, 163–165, 240–242.

GOSPELS compared, 34, 49, 52–54, 305–309.
Greek games, 250–251.

HARVEST, The, 43, 71, 78, 85, 96, 178, 179, 262.
Heaven, The God of, 109.
„ The kingdom of. *See* Kingdom.
Heifer, The, 74–78.

INDIVIDUAL and collective, 168, 243, 330.
Incarnation. *See* Lord Jesus.
Inspiration of Scripture, 8, 9.
Isaac's harvest, 282, 334.
Israel's history typical, 14, 18, 19, 167, 169, 235, 236.
„ past history, 148–150.
„ reformation and profession, 150, 151.
„ fruitlessness, 57, 153, 165, 315.

Israel's rejection, 58, 66, 67, 152, 156, 208, 209.
„ second opportunity, 153, 154.
„ enmity to the messengers, 155.
„ jealousy, 159, 160.
„ judgment, 95, 155, 156, 161, 163, 184–186.
„ restoration, 163–165, 307, 308.

JACOB, the shepherd, 205, 206.
Jealousy of Israel, 159, 160.
Jehovah of the Old Testament, 24.
Jeremiah's field, 198–200.
Jezebel's plot, 197, 198.
Joash's kingdom, 194–197.
Joshua and Paul, 249.
„ the high priest, 203.
Jotham's parable, 130, 173.
Joy, 97, 289, 290.
Judaism, Leading out from, 44, 157–159.
Judgment, 84–96, 335.
„ seat of Christ, 93–95.
„ of living nations, 93–95, 260, 261.
„ at Great White Throne, 93–95.

KING'S rejection in Old Testament, 98, 99.
Kingdom foretold, 98.
„ in mystery, A, 194–197.
„ of God, &c., 102–110.
„ of heaven, 102, 103.
„ „ parables, 105.

LAZARUS of Bethany, 226, 227.
„ of parable, 226, 227.
Leaven, 130, 131, 133, 234, 235.

Leprosy, 177, 178, 183–186, 227, 228.
Lepers cleansed, 227, 228.
Leprous house, 183, 186.
Lord Jesus, Figures of the, 27, 28.
  ,,   the Son, 38, 56–61, 111.
  ,,   the Messiah, 101, 102.
  ,,   the Incarnation, 65, 66.
  ,,   His life and ministry, 66, 67.
  ,,   His rejection and death, 67, 69, 151, 152.
  ,,   His resurrection and ascension, 69, 322.
  ,,   His intercession, 57, 59, 153.
Luke's Gospel, 50, 52–54, 306–309.
  ,,   "Far off" and "near," 51.
  ,,   Prayer and praise in, 50, 51.

MAN, The poor wise, 212, 213.
  ,, with inkhorn, The, 200–202.
Manna, 67, 171, 230.
Marriage Psalm, 210, 211.
  ,,   supper, 267, 268.
Mark's characteristics, 49.
Mary Magdalene, 231.
Matthew and Luke, 52–54.
Measures, 188, 326.
Message sent after Him, 156, 157, 166.
Messengers, Old Testament, 148, 149.
  ,,   New Testament, 155.
Miracles, acted parables, 222–225.
  ,,   of healing, 222, 223.
  ,,   blind man, 44, 226.
  ,,   demoniac, 231, 232.

Miracles, devil cast out, 225.
  ,,   draughts of fishes, 224, 231.
  ,,   feeding of five thousand, 230.
  ,,   fig-tree withered, 165, 224, 225.
  ,,   Lazarus raised, 163, 226, 227.
  ,,   lepers healed, 227, 228.
  ,,   Mary Magdalene, 231.
  ,,   storm on lake, 229.
  ,,   Syrophœnician's daughter, 162, 230.
  ,,   water turned into wine, 230, 231, 305.
  ,,   withered hand, 225, 226.
  ,,   woman with issue of blood, 228, 229.
Moses, 204, 205, 248, 249.
Mysteries of the kingdom, 104–106, 108, 112, 122–124.
  ,,   revealed to Paul, 113–115.
Mystery, A kingdom in, 194–197.
  ,,   Babylon, 115, 264–267.

NEW and old, 121, 122, 316.
Night, 73, 74, 115, 229, 230, 246, 337.
  ,, A thief in the, 83, 84.
Naboth's vineyard, 197, 198.

OIL, 174–176.
Olive, The, 154, 168, 173, 237.
Opening of title-deeds, 259, 260.
Over-anxiety, 293.
Ox, The, 190, 247.

PARABLES. See List.
  ,,   of Solomon, 211, 221.
Parousia, The, 77.
Patristic writings, 11, 12.

Paul's Epistles, 21, 233–253.
„ revelation, 7, 114, 128, 196,
„ symbolism, 248–253.
Payment to the uttermost, 319, 320.
Pedagogue, 251–253.
Peter and Paul, 248, 249.
„ and the parables, 340–342.
Pharisees, 35, 36, 38, 43, 44, 46
Poor wise man, 212, 213.
„ „ youth, 213, 214.
Prayer, 50, 51, 269, 274.
„ Disciples', 344, 345.
„ for understanding, 6, 332.
„ The Lord's, in John xvii., 46, 138, 139.
Present and future, 43, 330, 331.
„ „ „ interpretations, 13, 236.
Progressive revelation, 20, 79, 233, 234.
Prophecy of the parables, 111–113, 207.
„ Typical, 18, 19, 235, 236.
Prophets, 148, 149.
Psalms, 207–211.
Purpose of parables, 3, 48.

QUESTIONS answered, 35–41.
Quotations from prophets applied to Church, 136.

REBELLIOUS son, The, 191.
Reckoning, The master's, 321, 322.
Requests answered by parables, 41, 43.
Rest, 97.
Resurrection, 94, 139, 163, 179.
Revelation, Progressive, 20, 79, 233, 234.
Rewards, 92–95.
Riches, 290–292, 312.
Rock, The, 171, 211.
Roman law, 252, 253, 317, 318.
Ruth, 198.

SALT, 176–178.
Satan's counterfeits, 262–264.
„ seed, 124, 125.
„ work, 124, 129, 147.
Service, 274–279.
Seven churches, 255–259, 342–344.
Sheaves and shining, 193, 194.
Sheep, The lost, in Old Testament, 188–191, 210.
Shepherds in Old Testament, 204, 206, 207.
Shunamite, The, 198.
Soldiers, 249, 250.
Solomon's kingdom, 98, 105, 120.
„ parables, 211–216.
„ proverbs, 216–221.
Son, The, 55–61.
„ and the Spirit, 62, 63.
Sowing and reaping, in Epistles, 239–243.
„ „ „ in Proverbs, 220–221.
Spirit, The, 7, 62, 63.
„ typified by oil, The, 134, 174–177.
„ The work of the, 194, 200, 202.
„ The fruit of the, 58, 240–242.
„ Temples of the, 245.
Syrophœnician woman, The, 162, 226.

TEMPLES of the Holy Spirit, 245.
Thief in the night, A, 83, 84.
Thorns, 11, 281, 282, 290.
Thought answered by a parable, 25, 48.
Travellers in difficulties, 312.
Tribulation, The Great, 81, 94, 138, 159, 161, 243, 261.
Trinity, The, 55–63.
Types, 2, 170, etc.
„ and miracles, 230.
Typical teaching of Israel's history, 14, 18, 19, 167, 168, 235, 236.
Two classes of hearers, 3, 4.

Two classes represented, 32.
„ individuals represented, 33.

UNCLEAN animals, 141, 142, 180–183.
Unleavened bread, The feast of, 131, 179, 234, 235.

VINEYARD, The, in Old Testament, 171–173.

WATCHING, 17, 73, 211, 219, 246.
Water turned into wine, 230, 231, 305.

Wedding garment, 32, 56, 316.
Weights and measures, 188.
Widows in Old Testament, 198.
Wine, 173, 176.
Wisdom compared to gold, &c., 244.
Wisdom's feast, 217, 218.
Withered hand healed, 225, 226.
Woman's earnestness, A, 320, 321.
          household work, A, 313.
Word of God, The, 279–289.

ZACCHÆUS, 227, 228.
Zechariah's visions, 203, 204, 205, 264, 265.

THE END